SHAKESPEARE AND THE CLASSICS

by J. A. K. THOMSON

GREEKS AND BARBARIANS

THE GREEK TRADITION

IRONY

THE ART OF THE LOGOS

THE CLASSICAL BACKGROUND
OF ENGLISH LITERATURE

CLASSICAL INFLUENCES ON
ENGLISH POETRY

J. A. K. THOMSON

Shakespeare and the Classics

'gentle, never school'd, and yet learned'
AS YOU LIKE IT
I. i. I *ad. fin.*

London
GEORGE ALLEN & UNWIN LTD
RUSKIN HOUSE MUSEUM STREET

First published in 1952

PRINTED IN GREAT BRITAIN BY
J. W. ARROWSMITH LTD., QUAY STREET AND SMALL STREET, BRISTOL

PREFACE

IT is certain that too many books are written about Shakespeare, and it will be for readers to decide whether the existence of another has been justified. The sole object of this Preface is to explain, not excuse, the book's deficiencies. These arise from the circumstance that it is the work of a classical student, not an expert in Elizabethan literature. All I have done, as it was all I am qualified to do, was to reconsider those classical elements in Shakespeare on which I might suppose without presumption that I had something to say.

I have used the text of the *Globe* edition as being on the whole that which is most familiar to readers and most nearly approaches a vulgate. In general I have not been punctilious about quoting Elizabethan authors in the form in which their words originally appeared. In a book which raises no textual problems the convenience of the general reader is to be consulted. The Latin quotations I have translated as closely as I could without exaggeration or understatement or that subtle colouring of the true sense which the earnest advocate half unconsciously gives to the evidence. Not to translate at all I could not think right where so much depends on whether the reader agrees with me on the meaning of the Latin.

I have said enough for a Preface, and perhaps too much. Yet one thing I must add. In estimating the extent of Shakespeare's classical learning I have sought to establish what he certainly did know rather than to discuss what he may have known. He may have known a good deal more than I credit him with. I am very willing to believe that. But in scholarship it is fatal to let the wish to believe induce belief without sufficient evidence; and surmises and speculations, however plausible, are not evidence. Let us have the evidence first and let speculation—which of course may be very valuable and even necessary—be founded upon that.

J. A. K. THOMSON

CONTENTS

Prestige of the Classics in Shakespeare's youth (9–17) —
Shakespeare's Education (17–19) — Low standard of
classical scholarship in Elizabethan England (19–21) —
External evidence for Shakespeare's classical attainments:
Jonson, Beaumont, Digges, Fuller, Milton, Dryden,
Beeston (21–29) — Farmer's *Essay* (29–31) — Internal
Evidence: Criteria (31). Illustrations (32–35) — Sources
of Shakespeare's classical knowledge (36–39) — Internal
evidence continued: Poems: *Venus and Adonis* (40–42),
Lucrece (42–44), Sonnets (44–46), *Phoenix and Turtle*
(46–47), *Passionate Pilgrim* (47), *Lover's Complaint* (47).
Plays: *Comedy of Errors* (48–51), *Titus Andronicus* (51–58),
Two Gentlemen of Verona (58–60), *Taming of the Shrew*
(60–66), *Love's Labour's Lost* (66–77), *Midsummer Night's
Dream* (77–81), *Romeo and Juliet* (81–83), *Henry VI* (83–96),
Richard III (96–98), *Richard II* (98), *King John* (99), *Henry IV*
(100–104), *Henry V* (104–107), *Henry VIII* (107–108),
Much Ado (108–110), *Merry Wives* (110–112), *As You Like It*
(112–116), *Hamlet* (116–119), *Macbeth* (119–124), *Lear*
(124–125), *Othello* (126–127), *Twelfth Night* (127–129),
Measure for Measure (129), *All's Well* (129–130), *Winter's
Tale* (130–133), *Cymbeline* (133–135), *Tempest* (135–139),
Pericles (139–140), *Troilus and Cressida* (141–145), *Julius
Caesar* (145–148), *Antony and Cleopatra* (148–150), *Timon*
(151–152).

Danger of over-estimating Shakespeare's direct obliga-
tions to classical authors in the original (152–153) — Shakespeare comes first before the world as a writer on classical
subjects (154–156) — Greene's attack (156–160) — Nashe's
criticism (161–162) — Chapman and Shakespeare (163–
176) — Jonson and Shakespeare (177–179) — Reaction of
Shakespeare to criticism (179–191) — He gives up classical
models (191–192) — Begins again under Plutarch's influence
with *Julius Caesar* (192–193) — Structure and significance
of *Julius Caesar* (194–204) — Character of Cicero in *Julius
Caesar* (205–209) — Chapman's *Seven Books of the Iliad*
(210–211) — *Troilus and Cressida* (211–215) — *Antony and
Cleopatra* (216–221) — *Coriolanus* (221–222) — *Timon*
(222–224).

Shakespeare and Greek Tragedy (224–227) — Ancient
poetic style (227–231) — Shakespearian style (232–236) —
Shakespeare develops dramatic elements in Plutarch
(236–237) — Shakespeare's treatment of classical mythology
(238–242) — His debt to Plutarch (242–254).

Shakespeare and the Classics

IF, about the time when Shakespeare began to write, you had visited the universities, or consulted educated people anywhere, inquiring where you should look for the leading figure in contemporary literature, whom must we suppose that most of them would have named? Calderon or Cervantes or Tasso or Montaigne or Spenser? None of these, but Joseph Scaliger, whom men called *princeps literarum*. To what did he owe this eminence? To his classical scholarship. If you had asked Scaliger himself (who was not ignorant of England and English writers) whom he considered the head of English literature, he might have replied in the words of Henri Estienne that George Buchanan was *poetarum nostri saeculi facile princeps*, 'easily the first poet of our time'. This judgment was formed entirely on the basis of Buchanan's Latin verses. Or take Isaac Casaubon. He was an almost exact contemporary of Shakespeare, and he was living in England, chiefly in London, during the very years when Shakespeare was writing his great tragedies. Who except a handful of scholars now remembers Isaac Casaubon? He was a man of vast and accurate learning, which he applied with discretion, and he had the rare virtue among Renaissance scholars of personal modesty. Alas and it is not possible to discern any element of greatness in him.[1] Yet on no other ground than his classical, especially his Greek, learning the possession of this amiable little gentleman, sick and bent double with unremitting study, becomes an object of contention between France and England. He is the personal friend of Henri Quatre, and of James I, who could never have enough of his conversation.

Such an estimate of relative values in literature is so far from any that could now be made that even historians, although they

---

[1] This could not be said of Joseph Scaliger, who was a man of genius and in his own field a very great critic.

know the facts, hardly grasp their implications. Yet a little reflection will show how important they must have been. We are for the most part what our education has made us. Let us see then what education was like when Shakespeare was young. It is roughly true to say that nothing was studied at the universities that was not studied in Latin. Of the grammar schools it might be said that their primary function was to teach the rudiments of Latin. To know Latin was the same thing as to be educated. Both at his school and at his university (if he got so far) the boy had the importance of the Latin language and the supremacy of the ancient authors inculcated day after day by his schoolmaster and his tutor. And of course, although no doubt among themselves they made fun of their preceptors, the pupils believed what they were told. It is natural to assume that what you have studied to the exclusion of almost everything else must have an altogether exceptional value. In the schools and universities—I do not say outside them, for the master spirits of the age, the great creative minds who were destined to prevail with posterity, had long asserted their independence—in the centres of learning the prestige of the ancient classics was not only unshaken, it was unchallenged. Even to say that is not to say enough. In their adoration of antiquity the scholars were prepared to throw away nearly the whole of medieval literature as childish or worthless or inartistic. Even in the literature of their own age they doubted the value and permanence of anything written in the vernacular. If immortal fame was what you desired—and Renaissance men desired it very much—you must write in Latin, and classical Latin at that; not the language of the medieval cloisters, but that of Virgil and Ovid, of Caesar and Cicero. Even if one takes an enlightened schoolmaster like Ascham, one finds him maintaining that, while a literature may and should be produced in English which shall be capable of holding its own in comparison with the Latin or the Greek, the way to produce such a literature is by the sedulous imitation of classical models. Ascham was before Shakespeare's time, but Sir Philip Sidney was not, or not much; and in this matter Sidney agrees with Ascham. To please these critics—of whom Sidney at least had great influence—the English poet must deeply imbue his mind in classical books and almost slavishly follow classical rules and methods of composition. So far from deprecating the study of Latin, they think it the only way of learning to write well in English.

This view, which now seems merely paradoxical, did not strike Elizabethan readers like that, for it had a long tradition behind it. The Middle Ages never claimed for their own vernacular authors anything like the dignity, one might almost say the reverence, accorded almost without question or criticism to the Latin poets and moralists. The Renaissance, that product of the Middle Ages, continued in this devotion, merely restricting it to those ancient writers whom we now, accepting the Renaissance verdict, regard as 'classical'. This feeling was no doubt strongest in the academies, but it permeated all classes, even the illiterate, in whose minds, when England became Protestant, there probably still lingered some vague reverence for the language of the old Church. One has also to take into consideration the international character with which the course of time had endowed the Latin tongue and which gave it a special authority. For it was not only scholars who addressed each other in it, but diplomatists, historians, philosophers, theologians, scientists. As late as 1687 Newton found it necessary to compose his *Principia* in Latin. When Shakespeare was born it is improbable that foreign readers would have considered anything written in English as properly literature at all. English to them was a semi-barbarous dialect. The only Englishmen who had a reputation in Europe for literature were such as had expressed themselves in the learned language: the great medieval logicians and theologians; Roger Bacon perhaps, certainly Sir Thomas More; in Shakespeare's own day Buchanan, Camden for his *Britannia*, Francis Bacon for his *Instauratio Magna*, John Barclay for his *Euphormionis Satyricon*, Owen for his *Epigrammata*, and some others. That, and not Spenser and Shakespeare, was what 'English Literature' meant to Europe. And this of course could not but have some repercussion on the English mind. It is true, and should not be forgotten, that even then the English were beginning to perceive that they had produced, or were on the way to producing, a notable literature of their own.

But there was not as yet a great deal of it, at least upon their reckoning, which left out most of what had been written in English before their own time. In these circumstances it was difficult for even the sturdiest patriot to maintain, against the whole voice of educated Europe, that English literature had already earned the right to be placed on an equality with the masterpieces of Greece and Rome. Even from his fellow-countrymen the claim, if he made it, would have been heard at best with an indulgent smile.

Nevertheless the Elizabethans took up the challenge. But it was felt to be hard and heavy. The burden of it was increased by a difference between England and the Latin countries which could not be overcome, for it lay in the very nature of language. France and Spain and Italy could feel that their literatures were a development, if not a continuation, of Latin literature; the English with their Teutonic speech could not do that. They resolved, since they could not be the heirs of Rome, to conquer and annex her. They could do this, they thought, by assimilating Latin literature, in such a way that the Latin masterpieces became English masterpieces by the power of style. This is the aim, sometimes professed, of all the best Tudor and Elizabethan translators. They rarely thought of making what is called a literal translation, but rendered their author's meaning so far as they understood it, which was often incompletely, in their own manner, however much that might be at variance in quality and tone from the original. Take North, the translator of Plutarch. If he knew a word or two of Greek, it was as much as he knew. But then he did not translate Plutarch from the Greek but from the French version of the *Parallel Lives* by Jacques Amyot. Even that he sometimes mistook. Amyot, whom the French have always recognized as a notable figure in their literature, is a true scholar and a master of prose style, whose version, though full of the colour and sentiment of his age, is reasonably accurate. North takes it and expands, variegates, elaborates it in the idiom of Tudor England. The result has an independent life of its own. In North's version Plutarch becomes, so far as that was possible, an Englishman and his book a masterpiece of *English* literature.

Although North had more native literary genius than any other of the translators, he is sufficiently typical of the rest, though some of them, and eminently Philemon Holland, were better able to combine accuracy with style.

Of course not all the translators had this high aim. Some made no attempt to rival the ancients in style, but were content to supply the unlearned public with the means of knowing what was in the works they chose or were commissioned to translate. The rapidly increasing number of people who could read, but had never been able to master, Latin were no doubt grateful. But learned pates were shaken. Many thought that the classics should not be translated at all. This no doubt was taking a very high line, yet some even of the 'University Wits'—though not Marlowe— appear to have taken it; at least they are prone to sneer at a dramatist who cannot read his Seneca, his Plautus and Terence, in the original. The suggestion was that he could not but fail as a dramatic artist. How much of this they sincerely believed, it is no longer possible to say; but they professed to believe it, and perhaps, as happens to many people, they convinced themselves by the repetition of their own professions. Yet there is not the least reason why we should question their sincerity in doubting if an elaborate art-form like the drama, as they tried to write it on the somewhat rare occasions when circumstances were propitious to them—composed in ordered acts and scenes, and in a style largely based on ancient rhetoric—could be produced by an un-educated man, that is, a man ignorant of Latin. In truth their own function, whether or not they realized it, was not very different from that of the good translators. It was to make an English drama that might fairly be matched against the Latin, while taking from the Latin all that could serve its purpose. To assist them in this work they had, intermediaries between them and the Roman playwrights, the many academic authors who had written tragedies and comedies in what is called modern Latin.[1] The University Wits carried on this practice, but in English; adding however a great deal of their own that was not Latin at all either in origin or in character. We shall never be

[1] Really classical Latin, written by modern authors.

able to discover how far they recognized the essential Englishness
of these additions. For they had no glimmer of the historic sense.
Seneca and Terence to them were exactly like Elizabethans writing in Latin. It was therefore easy for them to imagine that, when
they wrote themselves, they were writing the sort of plays that
Seneca and Terence would have written, if these poets had written
in English. From this they drew the conclusion that every
English dramatist must make himself familiar with Seneca and
Terence in the original. It was not a sound conclusion, and it was
refuted by the event. Yet the event might have been foreseen.
Elizabethan drama, however strongly affected by classical influences, was not classical at heart or in origin; it was a popular
entertainment. Therefore any play which required for its appreciation anything like a real knowledge of Latin could not long
maintain itself against a vernacular theatre, as soon as that had
acquired an adequate technique of its own. Yet the struggle of
opposing tendencies, though brief, was sharp while it lasted, and
represented, at least at first, not so much an attempt to break
away from classical drama as an attempt to assimilate it.

Non-dramatic poetry is, for the study of Shakespeare, very
much less important; yet here also scholarship was felt to be
necessary. Why this should be so, is too large a question to be
answered in one or many pages. The reasons are historical and
well enough known, at least to all who have felt an interest in the
Renaissance. The fact itself is certain. It may be expressed in this
way: Elizabethan poetic style is formed on the basis of a 'rhetoric'
or 'art of poetry' which has been elaborated out of classical
practice. Thus the purpose of *The Arte of English Poesie*, which
was evidently composed a good many years before its publication
in 1589, is described as being 'That there may be an art of English
Poesie, as there is of the Latin and the Greeke'. What this means,
as we discover in reading the treatise, is that English poetic style
should model itself upon Latin. That was the critical orthodoxy
of the time. This is not to say that all the poets were orthodox;
Donne, for one, was not. By 'Elizabethan poetic style' is not
meant the style of every Elizabethan poet, but that which may be
said to underlie the sonnets of Sidney, of Spenser, of Shakespeare;

to underlie *Hero and Leander* and *Venus and Adonis*. Everyone who has a feeling for style at all is sensible of this common factor and will not require a detailed analysis of its elements. It is enough if one recognizes that Elizabethan poetic style has intimate affinities with Renaissance poetic style in general, as one sees it in sixteenth-century French and Italian writers. It is essentially Latin in origin, its chief original being unquestionably Ovid. Now it is true that English poets almost from the first showed marked independence both in the choice of their subjects and in their treatment of them. Spenser alone would suffice to prove that. But Spenser would have been both surprised and offended by the suggestion that his work implied a repudiation of the classics. On them he looked as his masters, on them no less than on Chaucer, and for style a great deal more. So with Sidney and Marlowe. The web of their style, with whatever embroideries of their own inwrought, is wholly woven on the loom of the traditional *ars poetica*.

In this way we may form for ourselves some conception of the prestige of Latin in literature Shakespeare could not—how could he?—fail to be strongly influenced by it. But in addition to this literary prestige we have to consider the social advantage conferred by a classical education. A man might fall, like Robert Greene, into poverty or disgrace; but if he had studied Latin at a university, it was something remembered in his favour. If he had made no such studies, it counted against him socially. A youth of good family would of course in normal circumstances be educated as a gentleman, that is to say in a competent knowledge of Latin literature. It is a question if these circumstances existed in the case of Shakespeare; the probability is great that they did not. How he would feel about it we may guess from the complaint of Orlando to his brother in *As You Like It*. 'My father charged you in his will to give me good education: you have trained me like a peasant, obscuring and hiding from me all gentleman-like qualities.'[1] Orlando is no doubt thinking of certain accomplishments thought necessary in a gentleman, but he knew that these

[1] Act I, scene I.

were acquired as part of a process which involved the study of Latin. The *Cortegiano* of Castiglione, which had been translated into English by Sir Thomas Hoby in 1561, and might be regarded as the manual of the Renaissance gentleman, commends and describes a culture in which the study of Latin is an essential element. The courtiers of Elizabeth and James were imbued, some deeply, with this culture. The ordinary private gentleman had at least a tincture of it. If it was a young nobleman whose education was to begin, it was generally undertaken by one or more tutors teaching different subjects useful to a young nobleman. But, whatever else he learned, he learned Latin. So it may fairly be said that a knowledge of Latin was the mark, if not the proof, of a gentleman. In the present age, when to be a gentleman, by birth or education, gives a man no special advantage—when the very word in its old-fashioned sense has become obsolete—the situation which confronted Shakespeare would not arise. But the structure of Elizabethan society was still largely feudal. It was graded from top to bottom in a series of definite *strata*, which it was important not to confuse.

> Take but degree away, untune that string,
> And, hark, what discord follows! each thing meets
> In mere oppugnancy.

You had your rank, your 'degree', in society, and if you forgot this, you were sharply reminded of it. Even the professions were graded, and of these the profession of actor ranked lowest. Shakespeare had some justification for counting himself, as he evidently did, by birth a gentleman; and he had been driven, perhaps by poverty, to become an actor. He hated it.

> Alas, 'tis true I have gone here and there,
> And made myself a motley to the view,
> Gored mine own thoughts, sold cheap what is most dear,
> Made old offences of affections new.

This is in sonnet cx, and again in sonnet cxi he cries:

> O, for my sake do you with Fortune chide,
> The guilty goddess of my harmful deeds,
> That did not better for my life provide
> Than public means which public manners breeds.

16

It is probable enough that Shakespeare's success as a dramatist more or less reconciled him to the stage; but that was later. When he wrote the Sonnets he was not reconciled.

Of Shakespeare's education we know, from external evidence, hardly anything, perhaps nothing at all, for the evidence is hearsay. It is comprised in a single sentence of that Life which Rowe contributed to his edition of *The Works of Shakespeare* in 1709. 'He'—that is Shakespeare's father—'had bred him, 'tis true, for some time at a Free-School, where 'tis probable he acquir'd that little *Latin* he was Master of.' This Life was avowedly based largely on tradition, and traditions, even when they rest on a basis of truth, are never exact in their details. But this particular statement about the school is very likely to be true. Yet it does not help us much. The 'Free-School' would, one naturally supposes and perhaps most people (including some scholars) have assumed, be Stratford Grammar School. Rowe in his investigations about Stratford must have learned, if he did not know before, about its ancient grammar school. Yet he does not identify his 'Free-School' with it. Where he hesitated perhaps we also should hesitate. Whatever the school, it is not clear how long Shakespeare remained there. For Rowe proceeds: 'But the narrowness of his Circumstances, and the want of his assistance at Home, forc'd his Father to withdraw him from thence, and unhappily prevented his further Proficiency in that Language', namely Latin. This can only mean that Shakespeare did not even learn all the Latin which the school provided. This early break in his education reduces the question to a very hypothetical condition. Nevertheless, as Rowe implies, some Latin he must have learned. The grammar he used is likely to have been Lily's, which had come to be generally accepted, although it was originally composed for the special use of the 'children' of St. Paul's. The likelihood is increased when we find Shakespeare quoting from Lily, as he does more than once. He is also aware of Priscian, though perhaps only as a name frequently on the lips of schoolmasters, or in some abbreviated form, since Priscian's *Institutiones*

Grammaticae consist of eighteen books. It would be more interesting to know what Latin authors he read. But on this point we are reduced to guessing, though our guess may have a certain degree of probability. Only let us be clear about what we mean. When we say that a schoolboy has 'read' Virgil, it probably means that he has, with the help of his teacher, struggled through a single book of the *Aeneid*. Or if one finds it written that Queen Elizabeth or Lady Jane Grey knew Greek, it is impossible to take that very seriously. Some Greek they certainly knew, but it cannot have been much, for their very preceptors did not know much. We must consider this point and not expect Shakespeare or anyone else to know Latin as one knows the multiplication table. One can only know Latin more or less.

Although we cannot be certain in what Latin authors Shakespeare did his reading, we can tell what authors were usually read by schoolboys when he was young. On this matter nothing is more instructive than some lines written by Michael Drayton, a Warwickshire man like Shakespeare, and of much the same age and station. They come in a verse Epistle to Henry Reynolds.

> For from my cradle you must know that I
> Was still inclin'd to noble Poesy,
> And when that once *Pueriles* I had read,
> And merely had my *Cato* construed,
> In my small self I greatly marvell'd then,
> Amongst all other, what strange kind of men
> These Poets were; and pleased with the name,
> To my mild Tutor merrily I came. . . .
> Who me thus answered smiling, 'Boy,' quoth he,
> 'If you'll not play the wag, but I may see
> You ply your learning, I will shortly read
> Some poets to you.' Phœbus be my speed,
> To it hard went I, when shortly he began,
> And first read to me honest *Mantuan*,
> Then Virgil's *Eclogues*.

By *Pueriles* Drayton means *Pueriles Sententiae* or 'Thoughts for Boys', a collection of copy-book maxims in easy Latin much used in schools for the instruction of beginners in that language.

By 'Cato' is meant the so-called *Distichs of Cato*, a body of moral precepts or prudential sentiments, each of them expressed in a couple of hexameter lines. They had a great repute in the Middle Ages—Chaucer has several references to 'Catoun'—and it is a little surprising that Elizabethan children should be kept to them. But they had great advantages for the old-fashioned schoolmaster, being brief, prudential and easily memorized. That Shakespeare read the Distichs can be only a surmise; there is no proof or even evidence of it. For the same reason we cannot tell if he read the *Colloquies* of Corderius or the *Pueriles Sententiae* or a similar collection (for there were others) of easy sentences. The case is rather different with Mantuan, whom Shakespeare names and quotes. Mantuanus was the pen-name of Johannes Baptista Spagnuoli, a Carmelite monk, who composed in Latin hexameters a number of pastoral poems called after the example of Virgil Eclogues or *Bucolica*. We find them dull reading now, but they had for more than a century a prodigious vogue, due less to their not inconsiderable accomplishment in Latin versification than to the infusion in them of a moralizing and even satirical element into the refined rusticity of the Virgilian type of pastoral. This pleased the temper of sixteenth-century Protestantism and attracted the schoolmasters, always on the look-out for moral reading for their lads. Mantuan had considerable influence upon Spenser, evidently not so much for his poetry as for his denunciation of ecclesiastical abuses, a subject that never interested Shakespeare, who, if he read Mantuan at all, probably thought him a bore. He certainly knew about him, and was able to quote the first line of his eclogues. But scholars ought not to say that this proves that Shakespeare had 'read' Mantuan, at most it creates a presumption that he had. As for Virgil's *Eclogues*, which come next in Drayton's list, all we can say is that it is not impossible that Shakespeare procured some acquaintance with them. And other possibilities will suggest themselves as we proceed.

It will be observed that of these Drayton books only the Virgil is strictly 'classical', although Mantuan had formed his style upon classical models. It suggests, what is probably true, that classical studies had not yet reached in England that degree of nicety which enables one to distinguish the latinity of Virgil from that of 'Cato' or even Mantuan. This reflection must occur to anyone who reads the undiscriminating language that is sometimes used about the scholarly attainments of certain Elizabethan authors, including the University Wits. It is for instance absurd to think of Lyly or Marlowe, or even of Jonson or Chapman, as classical scholars in the sense that Milton or Gray was such. They merely had, in greater or less degree, the scholarship of their time, which was markedly below that of contemporary France or Holland. (I am not speaking of learning, but of scholarship.) The reasons for this are somewhat obscure, but there is no doubt of the fact. Consider John Lyly, who of the University Wits was evidently the most deeply read in ancient literature. In his *Campaspe*[1] he brings upon the stage a number of famous Greek philosophers, namely Plato, Aristotle, Diogenes and Chrysippus. Here[2] are their dates: Plato 427–348 B.C., Aristotle 364–322 B.C., Diogenes died in 323 B.C. and Chrysippus in 207 B.C. It is as if a modern dramatist were to give us a debate on the nature of poetry between Doctor Johnson, Coleridge and Matthew Arnold without representing one of them as older than the other. Moreover the views expressed by Lyly's philosophers are not so much what they actually held as what medieval tradition had assigned to them. If it be said that all this occurs in a comedy and therefore does not matter, the answer is that to a scholar it would matter; a scholar does not think his *own* ignorance funny. Then there is Marlowe. He translated a good deal, even if we do not count *Hero and Leander*, which is only nominally a translation. He produced, evidently when very young, a version of Ovid's *Amores*, by him or his publisher called *Elegies*, which is just as apt a title as the other, though it is not found in any manuscript of the *Amores*.[3] This translation is full of spirit and colour, and shows a fine metrical sense; but it is grossly inaccurate, almost as inaccurate as Ezra Pound. This inaccuracy is entirely excusable

[1] The full title is: *A most excellent Comedie of Alexander, Campaspe and Diogenes.*

[2] From Ritter and Preller.

[3] A Roman 'elegy' was usually a love-poem.

on the ground of its author's youth, the pravity of the text he had before him, and the state of scholarship at the time. But there it is. He also translated, no doubt at a later period, the first book of Lucan's *Pharsalia*. In this version, which is in blank verse, the Latin is rendered line by line—one English line for each Latin— in an attempt to follow the original. That was an error of judg- ment, because a line of blank verse is shorter than a dactylic hexameter, so that the struggle to pack all Lucan's meaning into an equivalent number of English verses could not always be successful. This we may deplore, for no one was better fitted than Marlowe to reproduce in English the grandiloquent style of the Roman. Yet it is clear that he had the makings and some of the tastes of a scholar; moreover he had the *unum necessarium*—a deep delight in ancient poetry for its own sake.

From this and much more[1] it will appear that Shakespeare's ignorance of Latin was only comparative.

Since we cannot tell for certain what school Shakespeare attended, how long he stayed there, or what he learned, our only safe course is to leave surmises and examine what evidence exists in virtue of which we may reach some reasonable conclusion about his scholarship. The evidence may be divided into external and internal, the external being the testimony of others, and the internal being derived from the poems and plays of Shakespeare himself. It is convenient to begin with the external evidence. It is slight enough, being confined to the scanty references to Shakespeare that are made by his contemporaries and by others, not his contemporaries, who were nevertheless in a position to know by credible tradition something about the matter.

Jonson must lead the way.

> And though thou hadst small *Latin* and less *Greek*,
> From thence to honour thee, I would not seek
> For names; but call forth thund'ring *Aeschylus*,

---

[1] Compare Bush on Peele's *Tale of Troy* in *Mythology and the Renaissance Tradition*, p. 51 f.

Euripides and *Sophocles* to us,
Pacuvius, Accius, him of *Cordova* dead,
To life again, to hear thy Buskin tread,
And shake a Stage: or, when thy Socks were on,
Leave thee alone for the comparison
Of all that insolent *Greece* or haughty *Rome*
Sent forth, or since did from their ashes come. . . .
For a good *Poet's* made as well as born.
And such wert thou. Look how the father's face
Lives in his issue, even so the race
Of *Shakespeare's* mind and manners brightly shines
In his well-turnéd and true-filéd lines:
In each of which he seems to shake a Lance,
As brandish'd at the eyes of Ignorance.

These lines, it is well known, occur in a set of commendatory verses contributed by Jonson to the First Folio (1623).[1] However familiar they may be, they are not always fairly interpreted. They have the character of an *éloge*, and in an *éloge* we are not to expect a balanced criticism. We know from other sources that Jonson was ready enough to find fault with Shakespeare's work; only in a set panegyric one does not mention faults. This does not mean that the commendation was insincere. It has the ring of sincerity. One feels that in the very title of the verses: *To the memory of my beloved, the Author Mr. William Shakespeare: and what he hath left us.* And yet I do not think that Ben really believed that, as he puts it later,

> Neat *Terence*, witty *Plautus*, now not please;
> But antiquated and deserted lie.

His own Comedy of Humours is very much a reversion to Latin Comedy, nor had insolent Greece and haughty Rome any more determined champion than Ben. Yet there is nothing in Jonson's verses so hyperbolical as Donne's *Second Anniversary*. To us indeed they do not sound hyperbolical at all, though Jonson himself probably considered that he had done Shakespeare more

[1] They may be conveniently found, printed according to the original spelling and punctuation, in Appendix B of Sir Edmund Chambers's *William Shakespeare*, vol. II, p. 207 f.

than justice. He has at any rate given him something better than mere adulation, for there is good criticism in the verses, particularly on the quality of Shakespeare's art, which he understood better perhaps than any critic till we come to Coleridge. On the other hand nobody in the days of Elizabeth or James took commendatory verses *aù pied de la lettre*; nor must we; that would be too naïve. We must therefore bear this in mind when we ask what Jonson truly meant by saying that Shakespeare had small Latin and less Greek.

Well then, it is not a claim, it is an apology; and there can be only one explanation. It is this. The deficiencies of Shakespeare in classical learning were, even in 1623, too much a matter of common knowledge for Jonson to say nothing about them, especially when Jonson was considered, and considered himself, the great authority on just that point. Accordingly he very wisely prefers admitting the fact to denying it, arguing that it did not prevent his friend from surpassing all other dramatists, ancient and modern. That indeed is just the theme of his verses. To turn his admission into a claim, or, as some do, into a boast, is a perfectly illegitimate proceeding. Let us not deceive ourselves by the supposition that Jonson meant that Shakespeare was a considerable Latin, and even something of a Greek, scholar. 'Small Latin and less Greek' is a *façon de parler*.

The truth of this is clear from other evidence. Here is an anecdote in Rowe's *Life*. 'In a Conversation between Sir *John Suckling*, Sir *William D'Avenant*, *Endymion Porter*, Mr. *Hales of Eaton*, and *Ben Jonson*; Sir *John Suckling*, who was a profess'd admirer of *Shakespeare*, had undertaken his Defence against *Ben Johnson* with some warmth; Mr. *Hales*, who had sat still for some time hearing *Ben* frequently reproaching him with the want of Learning, and Ignorance of the Ancients, told him at last, That if Mr. *Shakespear* had not read the Ancients, he had likewise not stollen anything from 'em; (A Fault the other made no Conscience of) and that if he would produce any one Topick finely treated by any of them, he would undertake to shew something upon the same Subject at least as well written by *Shakespear*.'

The authenticity of this anecdote, in essence if not in its

details, seems unquestionable; nor do I know that it has been questioned. We see from it what Jonson's settled opinion of Shakespeare's scholarship was, and in fact Ben's 'envy' of his friend is elsewhere alluded to as a thing generally known. It was not really 'envy'—that is, jealousy—at least in a conscious form, but a genuine conviction that Shakespeare would have been a better poet, if he had been a better scholar. That was the true point at issue, not whether Shakespeare was a scholar or not; that he was not, is tacitly admitted by all the company. What Mr. Hales of Eton resented was Jonson's assumption that Shakespeare's comparative ignorance of Latin detracted from his merits as a poet. 'If Mr. Shakespeare had not read the ancients' is not hypothetical, for 'if' here is equivalent to 'although'. Now the authority of this company is quite decisive. Not to mention Jonson himself, who had been intimate with Shakespeare for years, Davenant was actually Shakespeare's godson, and Hales was at least old enough to have known him. What people who had none of these means of ascertaining the truth may have said in later generations cannot have any weight against this testimony.

Another witness who was in a position to know is Francis Beaumont. In a verse-letter to Mr. B.J. (that is, Ben Jonson), which must have been written about 1615, while Shakespeare was still alive, he has these words:

> Here I would let slip
> (If I had any in me) scholarship,
> And from all Learning keep these lines as clear
> As *Shakespeare's* best are, which our heirs shall hear,
> Preachers apt to their auditors to show
> How far sometimes a mortal man may go
> By the dim light of Nature . . .

Beaumont, writing to so erudite a correspondent, feels disposed to be apologetic about his own scholarship. Looking round for some other author to keep him in countenance, he naturally turns to Shakespeare. For there, thinks Beaumont, you have the most striking instance of a great contemporary poet, who is in no sense a classical scholar. These lines ought by themselves to decide the issue, for both Jonson and Beaumont were on terms of intimacy with Shakespeare.

Then see what is said by Leonard Digges, who was about twenty-eight years old when Shakespeare died. He may not have known Shakespeare, who was not much in London in the last years of his life, but he certainly knew people who had been well acquainted with him. Here is part of what Digges says in some 'commendary verses' prefixed to an edition of Shakespeare's Poems which appeared in 1640.

> Next, Nature only helped him, for look thorough
> This whole Book, thou shalt find he doth not borrow
> One phrase from *Greeks*, nor *Latins* imitate,
> Nor once from *vulgar Languages* translate . . .
> So have I seen when *Caesar* would appear,
> And on the stage at half-sword parley were
> *Brutus* and *Cassius*, oh how the Audience
> Were ravish'd, with what wonder they went thence,
> When some new day they would not brook a line
> Of tedious (though well-laboured) *Catiline*;
> *Sejanus* too was irksome; they priz'd more
> Honest *Iago*, or the jealous *Moor*.

Only 'Nature'—native genius—helped him, he got nothing from the Greeks, nor did he imitate the Latins. He was no scholar, like Jonson, but a greater poet, at least a more successful dramatist. That is the testimony of Digges. And he is not giving his personal opinion, he is proclaiming what everybody knows.

The evidence of Fuller and Milton does not carry the same weight, because it is not grounded upon personal acquaintance, they being only children when Shakespeare died. But they lived in a time when the poet was well remembered by many people. (Jonson for example did not die till 1637.) Their testimony then, even if it be at second hand, is of very great value. In his *Worthies of England* (published in 1662), in the division *Warwickshire*, Fuller compares Shakespeare to Ovid and Plautus, 'who was an exact Comaedian, yet never any Scholar, as our Shake-speare (if alive) would confess himself.' And he proceeds: 'He was an eminent instance of the truth of that Rule, *Poeta non fit, sed*

25

nascitur, one is not *made* but *born* a Poet. Indeed his Learning was very little.' Everyone remembers the allusion in *L'Allegro* (about 1632):

> Then to the well-trod stage anon,
> If *Jonsons* learned Sock be on,
> Or sweetest *Shakespear* fancies childe,
> Warble his native Wood-notes wilde. (131–4)

The contrast between the learning of Jonson and the untutored genius of Shakespeare is not the less marked because it is only implied.

Finally we get Dryden, writing at a time when the tradition was by no means dead. In his *Of Dramaticke Poesie: An Essay* (1688) he has written these celebrated words. 'Those who accuse him'—Shakespeare—'to have wanted learning, give him the greater commendation; he was naturally learned; he needed not the spectacles of books to read Nature; he looked inwards, and found her there.' That is Dryden's reply to Jonson. And then Rowe, assembling what was left of the tradition for his *Life*, is led to surmise that it was at some free-school that Shakespeare acquired 'that little Latin he was master of'.

What evidence could be more decisive? The jury might well be forgiven if it rose at this point and said it wished to hear no more. But it must not do that until it has considered another statement which points, although perhaps it does no more than point, in an opposite direction. It is an entry among the memoranda kept by John Aubrey (1626–97) and contributed to Wood's *Athenae Oxonienses*. It is necessary to quote it.

> 'Though, as Ben Jonson says of him, that he had but little Latine and lesse Greek, he understood Latine pretty well, for he had been in his younger yeares a schoolmaster in the countrey—from Mr. Beeston.'

Since the good faith of Aubrey is above suspicion, the only question is how much value we can fairly attach to the testimony of Mr. Beeston, Aubrey's authority. This was William Beeston, a son of Christopher Beeston, who had been an actor in the same company with Shakespeare himself. William had spent his own working life in the theatrical profession, and was living in retirement, apparently in London, when Aubrey questioned him. Dr. Smart says[1]—and what he says we can accept—William Beeston in his old age 'was visited by the younger men of letters, who listened to his tales of past times. Dryden himself took pleasure in his conversation, and was accustomed to call him "the chronicle of the stage".'

Ever since Dr. Smart's book was published the very greatest importance has been attached to Beeston's reminiscence, in favour of which some scholars, so far as I can judge, are prepared to set aside the authority of Jonson and others who knew Shakespeare personally. I do not know what a judge, accustomed to weigh evidence, would say to that; it is certain that he would require a great deal of convincing. What an old gentleman, full of green-room stories, may say in conversation to young inquirers, cannot of course always be taken very seriously. But William Beeston's statement is hardly that kind of story. It would be not only unkind but uncritical to suggest that he invented it to please his auditors. But it is necessary to point out that it is entirely unsupported by any external evidence. And there are many reflections to make one hesitate. It must be regarded as a little odd that Dryden, who was strongly interested in what might be called the Jonson versus Shakespeare question, and who took pleasure in Beeston's company, was apparently never undeceived by Beeston in the matter of Shakespeare's Latin. Again, while it is true that Rowe's *Life* is an unsatisfactory production, one would have expected him to mention the schoolmaster tradition, if it had any real life in it. One may also wonder a little why, if Shakespeare had been a schoolmaster, his sympathy throughout the plays is always with the schoolboy against the master. Above all why did not somebody, when Jonson was running down Shakespeare's scholarship, retort like Beeston, 'He must have known more Latin than you say, for he was a schoolmaster'? It is also to be considered that what Beeston reported was not a matter within his personal knowledge. Presumably he got it from his father, who of course would be a most weighty authority. But we

---

[1] *Shakespeare—Truth and Tradition*, p. 86.

cannot be sure, and the plain truth of the matter is that what William Beeston said is hearsay evidence. Now if posthumous hearsay evidence conflicts with contemporary first-hand evidence, it must be ruled out of court. But I find to my dismay that some of our best Shakespearian scholars prefer it to the first-hand evidence.

Assuming, as I am prepared to do for the sake of argument, that Beeston's statement is true, we have still to ask what it means. Since Shakespeare must have been very young when he became 'a schoolmaster in the country', it will not be suggested that he had been appointed the headmaster of a grammar school. Consequently, if the school in which he taught was a grammar school, he could only have been an assistant master or usher. How much Latin would such a teacher be expected to know? It is quite easy for an intelligent young man to drill a junior class in the rudiments of Latin without his having read much Latin literature himself. Is anyone so innocent of the facts as not to be aware that this is, and always has been, true? I ask the question because I find scholars who, after accepting Beeston's tradition, proceed to argue as if this proves that Shakespeare must have had a good knowledge of Latin literature. It is a large assumption, which could never be made by anyone who has much experience of the teaching in schools, now or at any time. If it be said that Shakespeare did not necessarily teach in a grammar school, that it is more likely that he was a 'petty' or parish schoolmaster—well, one knows from Love's Labour's Lost and The Merry Wives of Windsor what the Latin teaching of such a functionary was like. 'A caricature'? Yes, but a caricature of something that existed. It is just conceivable that Shakespeare, though one would have thought him too young for such responsibility, might have been a tutor in some great country house. But that would not necessarily mean his teaching Latin at all.

On the whole the great probability is that any Latin teaching that Shakespeare may have undertaken in his young days would be confined to instruction in the rudiments of the language and perhaps some elementary book like Corderius. That Shakespeare was fully capable of teaching Latin up to that point, no reader of the plays is at all likely to deny. We must, I think, confess that Beeston's reminiscence helps us less than we could have hoped. Perhaps it does not help at all. We are thrown back upon the evidence of the plays and poems, for that at least is certain, in fact the only quite certain evidence we have. For clearly it would be useless to say that Shakespeare's Latin scholarship must have reached a fairly high standard, if his own words prove that it did not. Thus there is nothing for it but to reconsider the internal evidence.

An opinion that the internal evidence did in fact prove that Jonson's estimate of the scholarship of Shakespeare was unduly low began to find expression about the beginning of the eighteenth century. It was apparently entertained by Pope. At first it was modestly asserted, but gradually its champions became more and more confident. They seem to have been impressed by the show of classical learning in Shakespeare without inquiring too strictly how he came by it. At all events they dealt largely in general assertions without committing themselves to specific instances. When they did condescend to particulars they rarely helped their case. There was a Mr. Langhorne who about the middle of the century published a translation of Plutarch's *Lives*. In his *Preface* he gives it as his conviction that Shakespeare was a good classical scholar, observing (by way of proof) that Hamlet's most famous soliloquy is an exact translation of a passage in Plato. He does not say what passage, so that Platonic scholars can only surmise that he is thinking of certain words used by Socrates in the *Apology* (40), which imply that death may conceivably be a dreamless sleep. As if nobody had ever entertained that notion except Socrates! In any case to describe Hamlet's soliloquy as 'an exact translation' of the Greek is so false that there is no point even in calling it a lie. At last, in the second half of the eighteenth century, a true scholar intervened. In an *Essay on the Learning of Shakespeare*, first published in 1767, Richard Farmer proved in the most convincing way, namely by parallel quotations, that when Shakespeare seems to be following the ancients, he is, in instance after instance, merely following their translators. It was singularly difficult to find conclusive evidence that he went to the originals at all. That Farmer should overstate his case was in the circumstances perhaps inevitable; how far he overstated it has still to be decided. It must be remembered that his essay (which is not long) did not attempt to cover all the possible or conjectural allusions and imitations; it dealt only with admitted cases. This left the field open to the hunter of *possible* allusions. The temptation to seek for these is almost irresistible to a man of any reading. It is all the more important to recognize that, with the rarest exceptions, we are merely guessing, although of course one guess may be better than another.

Farmer convinced most of the scholars, his contemporaries, including Johnson, a critic with whom, on a point of common sense, it has always been found dangerous to disagree. Yet there remained an undercurrent of feeling that anyone who used ancient mythology so exquisitely must have read more of it in the original than Shakespeare was now supposed to have done. This feeling found expression in a rather casually constructed book called *A Consideration of Farmer's Essay on the Learning of Shakespeare* by the once famous journalist Maginn. But, although the author gives proof of considerable reading in classical literature, he cannot be said to do more than, here and there, score a debating point against Farmer. A more serious antagonist was Churton Collins, whose *Studies in Shakespeare* accumulated a mass of parallels, or what he took to be parallels, between Shakespeare and the ancients. The difficulty lay in proving that these were not accidental or what we might expect in any case. That difficulty Collins, in spite of his learning and fairness in argument, was not able to overcome. It was reserved for a scholar of modern times to pursue a line of argument which has done more than anything else to weaken the strength of Farmer's position. This was J. S. Smart, who argued in a manner convincing to most minds (including mine) that the local anecdotes, in Rowe and elsewhere, implying Shakespeare's illiteracy were quite untrustworthy. It is not certain how far these anecdotes were accepted as true by Farmer; but the general tone of his essay is undoubtedly that of a man who considers that Shakespeare's learning amounts to little or nothing. It is difficult to believe that any contemporary scholar would adopt that tone now.

But, it will be observed, none of this destroys the evidence produced by Farmer. It only affects the conclusion he drew from it.

Since it is impossible to discuss any problem except on the basis of some general agreement, I will assume the assent of readers to the following proposition. An apparent parallel in Shakespeare to some passage in an ancient author must, if we are to be convinced of borrowing, fulfil two conditions. First, the *thought* must have something uncommon in it; that is to say, it must be a thought which was not likely to occur to Shakespeare independently. Second, the *wording* of the thought must exhibit a turn which indicates that he had the original in his mind, since otherwise he might be using a translation, which we know to have been a common practice with him. When one applies these tests to the suggested allusions and imitations, it cannot but surprise the investigator to observe how few survive the ordeal. No doubt much depends on his judgment. Mine may be too strict, though I hope not. At all events any judgment must be worthless which permits the judge to believe what he would like to believe. He must ask for proof. Shakespeare wrote so much, and there is in him such a play of mind and power of expression, that he could not but seem very frequently to be echoing the words or thoughts of other men. But is this on the face of it probable? It is not as if he were a poet like Milton or Gray, who were not only deeply read in Greek and Latin, but whose work often looks like a mosaic of classical reminiscences. Shakespeare could never be described as a bookish poet. The treasury of his own mind was always adequate to his demands upon it. If then he ever appears to be echoing the words of a Latin or Greek author, the probability must always be that it is a coincidence, unless fairly clear evidence can be produced to the contrary.

Nevertheless each allusion or supposed allusion is entitled to be weighed on its merits. Those which I myself accept as probable or certain will be recorded in due course. Some are too fanciful to be worth arguing about. A good many lie on the margin of doubt. It may be interesting to mention one or two. In the *Merchant of Venice*, II. v. 29 f. Shylock says to Jessica:

> When you hear the drum
> And the vile squeaking of the wry-neck'd fife,
> Clamber not you up to the casements then,
> Nor thrust your head into the public street.

In *Carm.* III. 7. 29, 30 Horace says to a girl:

> prima nocte domum claude neque in vias
> sub cantu querulae despice tibiae.[1]

Is the parallel a coincidence? On the whole, yes, because the advice is such as might occur to any parent or jealous lover as suitable for a young woman left alone at night in a city house. If Shakespeare needed any suggestion, it is more likely to have come from *The Jew of Malta*, where the situation of Abigail the daughter of Barabas is not dissimilar from that of Jessica. Moreover my translation of *querula tibia*, 'complaining flute', rather exaggerates the closeness of the parallel.

In *A Midsummer Night's Dream*, I. i. 234 f., Helena says:

> Love looks not with the eyes, but with the mind;
> And therefore is wing'd Cupid painted blind:
> Nor hath Love's mind of any judgement taste;
> Wings and no eyes figure unheedy haste:
> And therefore is Love said to be a child,
> Because in choice he is so oft beguiled.

Propertius says (II. 12. 1 f.):

> Quicumque ille fuit puerum qui pinxit Amorem,
> nonne putas miras hunc habuisse manus?
> Hic primum vidit sine sensu vivere amantes
> et levibus curis magna perire bona.

---

[1] 'At nightfall shut up the house, and do not look down into the streets at the tune of the squeaking fife.'

idem non frustra ventosas addidit alas,
   fecit et humano corde volare deum;
scilicet alterna quoniam iactamur in unda,
   nostraque non ullis permanet aura locis.[1]

If Shakespeare ever read this passage, which is in itself unlikely, we could say that he had it at the back of his mind when he wrote the speech of Helena. But Renaissance poetry is full of conceits about the blind archer-boy, and Shakespeare is writing in that vein. The parallel with Propertius (which after all is not a true one) is accidental.

Laertes says of Ophelia in *Hamlet* (v. i. 261 f.),

> Lay her i' th' earth:
> And from her fair and unpolluted flesh
> May violets spring!

It has been suggested that when he wrote these words Shakespeare was imitating or remembering some words of the Roman satirist Persius, who says (I. 38, 39):

> nunc non e tumulo fortunataque favilla
> nascentur violae?[2]

Few scholars are likely to believe that Shakespeare ever mastered Persius, that very difficult author. But, says Professor Baldwin,[3] he had read Mantuan, for he quotes a line of his in *Love's Labour's Lost*; and if he read Mantuan, he would naturally make use of the commentary which was generally printed with the text; and in this commentary he would find the line and a half of Persius quoted and be struck by them. It will be observed that all this is very hypothetical. I confess that my own scepticism here is

---

[1] 'Whoe'er he was that painted Love as a boy, thinkest thou not that he had a wondrous hand? First he saw that lovers lived in blindness, wasting great blessings on a trifling fancy. Not idly too he added the waving wings and drew the god flying over the human heart; since, in sooth, we toss on waves that rise and fall, and in no place does the breeze stay with us steadfast.' (This very Victorian translation is by Postgate; it has at least the merit of accuracy.)

[2] 'Now from your tomb and lucky ashes will not violets be born?'

[3] *Shakspere's Small Latine and Less Greeke*, II. 543; I. 649.

almost total. The parallel does not meet the requirement that there should be something not too obvious in the thought expressed. For what could be more natural, especially for a brother, than the fancy that violets might spring from the grave of an unmarried girl? Such fancies have almost the character of folklore; at any rate they are literary commonplaces, above all in the poetry of the Renaissance. The reader may think of Herrick:

> In this little urn is laid
> Prewdence Baldwin, once my maid,
> From whose happy spark[1] here let
> Spring the purple violet.

Herrick may have been thinking of Persius, but why should Shakespeare?

The French King in *Henry V*, III. v. 50 f. bids his nobility

> Rush on his[2] host, as doth the melted snow
> Upon the valleys, whose low vassal seat
> The Alps doth spit and void his rheum upon.

Anyone who has read the Satires of Horace cannot but be reminded of the line,

> Furius hibernas cana nive conspuit Alpes[3] (II. v. 41)

According to an ancient scholiast, annotating this line, Furius was a poet who had introduced in an epic of his the hexameter:

> Iuppiter hibernas cana nive conspuit Alpes,

where the offending word for Horace was *conspuit*, 'voided his rheum'. It is quite within the range of possibility that Shakespeare had read, or had read in, the Satires of Horace, for they were much admired at the time, Jonson for example knowing them pretty much by heart. What then are we to think? It would seem that here at least both conditions are satisfied: the thought is not obvious, and the expression is distinctly unusual. Yet we are bound to observe that the tone is very different. What is felt by

---

[1] fortunata favilla!
[2] King Harry's.
[3] 'Furius has bespitten the wintry Alps with white snow.'

Horace to be ludicrous and disgusting, Shakespeare, apparently without satire[1], thinks entirely suitable on the lips of the speaker. And—what is still more to the point—it seems very probable that Elizabethan taste did not find either the thought or the expression of it in any way remarkable. It seemed (apparently) a perfectly natural thing to imagine and to say. If this be true—and I leave the decision to those who know the period better than I—our two conditions are not met after all.

Clearly, if we are to prove that Shakespeare was something of a scholar, it must be on more certain grounds than we have discovered hitherto. We must pursue our inquiries farther, having it always in mind that what we are looking for is not classical influence on Shakespeare—there is abundant evidence of that— but traces of a direct or first-hand acquaintance with Latin books. It will be useful to define the limits of such an inquiry. Thus it would be idle to discuss Shakespeare's debt to Plutarch in the plays derived from the *Parallel Lives*, for he never gets any nearer to Plutarch than the translation of a translation. Even in the case of Ovid, whom if any ancient poet he might have been expected to read in the original, it is certain that he made use of Golding's version of the *Metamorphoses*, a work from which he is constantly drawing allusions and illustrations. Plutarch's *Lives*, Ovid's *Metamorphoses*—these were his great source-books; and for both, although in the case of the *Metamorphoses* evidently not always, he depends on other men's translations. That narrows our inquiry very much. Still, when we have excluded those passages where Shakespeare is dependent on the translators, and passages where he may be dependent on them, we do find a residue of places which call for some further examination. There are, besides, one or two actual quotations. The claim of Shakespeare to the possession of some classical scholarship must rest largely on these places and these quotations.

But before examining them we ought to have some notion of

___

[1] Dover Wilson, *New Shakespeare, Henry V, ad loc.*, thinks that Shakespeare may have wished to make the French King ridiculous.

the sources of Shakespeare's knowledge. They were not all literary, but I shall begin with those that were. In the first place no one will need to be reminded that Elizabethan literature, prose as well as poetry, is full of classical names, allusions, quotations. It is evident that Shakespeare was not a bookish man, but he could not have read the books of his contemporaries at all without acquiring, were it only unconsciously, a stock of classical lore. One need not press so obvious a point, although it is only too easy for us now to forget it, since contemporary literature does not contain many classical allusions, and what people read most of all, novels and newspapers, have none or next to none. If however we remember that they were the rage in Shakespeare's youth, we shall not be in the least surprised at the number of them in him; we may rather be surprised at their comparative infrequency. On the other hand if we forget this, we shall get a very false impression from them of the extent of his first-hand classical knowledge. The truth is, he has little in the way of classical knowledge that could not have been picked up in the course of his reading in English authors, were it only Lyly and Spenser. When we think of this we should also consider that by no means all the poetry, in particular not all the plays, that got written came into the printer's hands. Shakespeare's own sonnets existed in manuscript for some years, and when they were published it was apparently without his sanction and perhaps against his wishes. Many of his plays were not printed until after his death. Where such conditions prevailed, he must have read a good many unpublished verses circulating among his friends, and assuredly he would read a good many manuscript plays offered to his company. The verses, if they conformed to fashion, would be full of classical allusions. A large proportion of the plays would be on classical subjects. Then there were the translations. Of these it is demonstrable that Shakespeare read North's *Plutarch* and Golding's *Metamorphoses*—a storehouse of ancient mythology. After Chapman began publishing his version of the *Iliad*, it is next to certain that he read that. It looks as if he had read the *Aethiopica* of Heliodorus in Underdowne's translation. He could have read, and very possibly did read, B.R.'s version of the first two books of Herodotus, and R.B.'s version of Terence. Then there was Newton's *Seneca*, and the renderings of Virgil by Phaer and Stanyhurst. All these were available to Shakespeare in the earlier part of his career as a dramatist. In 1601 appeared Philemon Holland's admirable rendering of Pliny's *Natural History*, crammed with facts and fancies about the ancient world. In 1603 appeared Florio's *Montaigne*, which Shakespeare undoubtedly read and which is replete with quotations from Latin, and references to Greek, authors. The man who read these books, however rapidly and superficially, could not help amassing a fund of classical information.

Add to this that as an actor during the reign of the University Wits he must have studied several parts of a classical character.

There was much to be learned in conversation. Shakespeare would be constantly meeting university men who liked (as they did in those days) to air their Latin. There were fellow-dramatists of a studious bent, like George Chapman and Ben Jonson, whose conversation was larded with quotations from the classics, and who were not displeased to communicate their learning. His dramas prove that Shakespeare was a good listener. It is possible that Chapman was not on speaking terms with him, but certainly Ben was, and as certainly it was Ben who did most of the speaking. Jonson really had read his Horace and his Sallust, his Seneca and Quintilian, his Juvenal and his Tacitus; and he was not a man who kept his treasure under a bushel. The friends did not always agree. There was for example a controversy between them about the right way of making a classical drama. But this would only increase Jonson's volubility on the subject of the ancients. From him alone Shakespeare could have picked up a modicum of Latin learning.

But there were other ways in which some knowledge of Greece and Rome was impressed upon the most illiterate Elizabethan. There was an almost continuous succession of masques, shows, revels, processions, royal progresses and the like, in each of which there was sure to be one or more characters drawn from ancient history or mythology. You would see Hercules with his club, Atlas sustaining his globe, Fortune with her wheel, Mercury with

37

his caduceus, Jove upon his eagle, Juno with her peacock, Arion riding his dolphin. There would be nymphs and satyrs, 'Greeks' and 'Trojans', and so on. Every Londoner was able to recognize these characters from their attributes. Elaborate accounts of many such 'revels' have been preserved, so that we know very well what they were like. The classical element figured very largely in many, perhaps most, of them. Anyone who has read *Kenilworth* will have a fair general idea of their nature. Now all that has gone, or survives only in the Lord Mayor's Show, and even in that one would be surprised to see any Roman, except perhaps Julius Caesar or Agricola. But whoever in reading Shakespeare finds allusions to Jove with his thunderbolt or Ceres with her sheaves or Venus with her doves should not conclude from this that the poet was remembering what he had read in books. It is rather more likely that he was remembering what he had seen in London streets or noblemen's gardens.

We must also weigh the probable influence on Shakespeare's mind of certain works of art, which he would have the opportunity of seeing in churches, ancient civic buildings, and on occasion in the houses of his patrons. He was evidently interested in pictures, although the only painter he mentions is Giulio Romano, whom we will hope he did not admire too much. Since the Middle Ages the English had forgotten how to paint, and most pictures of any quality in English houses were by Italian or Spanish masters—the Dutch influence just beginning. When the subjects were not people, they were often allegorical and classical. Besides the pictures there was a great deal of tapestry, arras, frescoes, 'painted cloths'. The subjects of these were even more apt to be allegorical and classical, although of course many were Biblical. The 'painted cloth' was hung on walls, where it took the place, no doubt at less expense, of arras or wall-painting. On such a cloth it was possible to depict a whole 'history', like that of the Siege of Troy in the painting viewed by Lucrece (1366 f.). Or one might have an elaborate tapestry, like that which is (or was) hung on a staircase in the Victoria and Albert Museum, recording the life of Cyrus the Great. Both of these, it will be noted, are classical subjects. There was also a good deal of carving and painted glass, representing such scenes as the death of Priam—'So like a painted tyrant Pyrrhus stood'—the Sibyl with a scroll of prophecy issuing from her mouth, a Siren combing her hair, and so on. Would not Shakespeare have eyes for all this?

His first acknowledged poem, *Venus and Adonis*, appeared in 1593. In the Dedication to Lord Southampton the author, as we all know, describes it as 'the first heir of my invention'. It is probable that he already had some reputation as a dramatist; but he may have thought that dramatic work was not exactly what he meant by 'invention'. It is a point I am not qualified to discuss. But what seems quite clear is that to *Venus and Adonis* the author attached real importance. A high claim is asserted for it in the Latin motto:

> Vilia miretur vulgus; mihi flavus Apollo
> Pocula Castalia plena ministret aqua.[1]

The words come from Ovid's *Amores*, I. 15. 35, 36, and are taken from a passage in which Ovid claims to be ranked among the great poets of the past. The lines were very well known, and Shakespeare need not have gone to Ovid for them.[2] Moreover it is far from certain that Shakespeare himself prefixed the motto to *Venus*; it may have been the publisher. And the slight arrogance, though natural enough in a young poet, is not characteristic of Shakespeare at any time of his life.[3] These considerations must induce caution. On the other hand, since *Venus* is carefully written, and the author would naturally be anxious to have it carefully printed, we may reasonably incline to suppose either that he chose the motto himself or that he gave it his approval. And on the whole it seems, at least to me, more likely than not that he looked it out for himself in the *Amores*. For people knew

---

[1] 'Let common things be admired by the vulgar; to me may fair-haired Apollo minister cups full of the Castalian water'—the water of inspiration.

[2] Gabriel Harvey in the note on Speght's *Chaucer* has this: '*Vilia* etc.: quoth Sir Edward Dier, betwene iest & earnest.'

[3] The sonnets which promise immortality are different.

SHAKESPEARE AND THE CLASSICS

their Ovid in those days, and Shakespeare was writing an Ovidian poem.

The story of Venus and Adonis is told (by Orpheus) in the tenth book of the *Metamorphoses*, 524-738. It contains however a story within the story, namely the fate of Atalanta, 560-704, which, it will be observed, occupies about two-thirds of the whole narration. Shakespeare's long poem then is an expansion of seventy verses in Ovid on the lines, though not in the spirit, of the *Faerie Queene*, III. i. xxxiv–xxxviii. The expansion is effected in the main by stylistic elaboration, but other parts of the *Metamorphoses* have been used, in particular the story of Salmacis, which is related in iv 285-388. Salmacis was a naiad who wooed the youthful son of Hermes and Aphrodite with such ardour that their embraces became indissoluble, and the two persons changed into one, Hermaphroditus. The behaviour of Venus in Shakespeare, although the description of it is not verbally modelled on that of Salmacis, is far more like it than it is like the wooing of the Ovidian Venus. It is well known that the description of the boar in Shakespeare, 619-630:

> On his bow-back he hath a battle set
> Of bristly pikes, that ever threat his foes . . .

is markedly influenced by Golding's language in translating the passage in the *Metamorphoses*[1] which describes the Boar of Calydon. He has also read the story of Narcissus, whom he names, and it is possible that the wooing of Narcissus by Echo had some influence upon him as he wrote. But what is most remarkable is the freedom with which he has treated his source. If he kept a Latin Ovid open before him, he troubled very little to consult it. Thus in the original story Adonis upon his death changes into a red flower, 'all one colour with the blood', says Golding. But what Shakespeare says is:

> A purple flower sprung up, chequer'd with white,
> Resembling well his pale cheeks and the blood
> Which in round drops upon their whiteness stood (1168-70)

[1] VIII. 273 f.

Compare Golding's description of the end of Narcissus.

A ruddie colour where he smote rose on his stomach sheere,
Lyke Apples which doe partly white and striped red appeare ...
His lively hue of white and red ...
But as for bodie none remaind: In stead thereof they found
A yellow floure with milke white leaves new sprong upon the ground.

It looks as if Shakespeare had got mixed in his recollection—at least he could not have been looking at the Latin here. Nor could he, when he says at the end that Venus

>   yokes her silver doves: by whose swift aid
> Their mistress mounted through the empty skies
> In her light chariot quickly is convey'd;

for in Ovid the chariot is drawn not by doves but by swans.[1] He was trusting to his memory, which told him that the sacred bird of Venus was the dove. And in fact her chariot is drawn by doves in *Metamorphoses*, XIV. 597.[2]

One may detect other signs of acquaintance with the *Metamorphoses* as a whole. For instance, in Shakespeare Venus runs to the cry of the hounds.

> And as she runs, the bushes in the way
> Some catch her by the neck, some kiss her face,
> Some twine about her thigh to make her stay:
> She wildly breaketh from their strict embrace (871–4)

There is nothing of this in Ovid's account of Venus. But hear him (in Golding's version) on the flight of Daphne, *Metamorphoses*, I. 507 f.

>   alas alas how would it grieve my heart,
> To see thee fall among the briers, and that the blood should start
> Out of thy tender legges, I wretch the causer of thy smart,
> The place is rough to which thou runst.

If this passage was in Shakespeare's mind, it would be another indication that he was writing without much reference to the

---

[1] x. 708. 9. 'iunctisque per aera *cygnis* carpit iter.'
[2] 'perque leves auras iunctis invecta *columbis.*' Cf. *Amores*, I. 2.

Latin text. He may in fact not have possessed the text, for a Latin *Metamorphoses* would be a large and expensive volume. We may suppose that, when he began to write *Venus and Adonis*, he shut his Golding and his Ovid (however come by) and wrote out of his own mind. That was the right way to go to work.

There are in the general body of *Venus and Adonis* a number, but, considering the subject and the conventional way of treating such a subject, a surprisingly small number, of allusions to classical tales and persons. All these allusions are of a perfunctory character and such as could be plucked in Elizabethan times from every hedgerow. There is a reference to Mars and Venus (97–114), to Narcissus (161–2):

> Narcissus so himself forsook
> And died to kiss his shadow in the brook,

for which see *Metamorphoses*, III. 346–510; to Titan, meaning the Sun, as often in Spenser and the Latin poets; to Tantalus (599–600):

> That worse than Tantalus' is her annoy,
> To clip Elysium and to lose her joy.

One may, if it seems worth while, compare Ovid, *Amores*, II. 2. 43:

> quaerit aquas in aquis et poma fugacia captat.[1]

In 725 there is a reference to 'modest Dian', in 728 to Cynthia as the Moon, in 745 to the Destinies. Such things prove nothing.[2]

Of *The Rape of Lucrece* the general character is the same as that of *Venus and Adonis*. There are casual references to Narcissus, to Orpheus before Pluto, to Philomel—the commonplaces of Renaissance poetry, and all, as it happens, to be found in the *Metamorphoses*, whence comes nine-tenths of Shakespeare's classical mythology. Of classical *learning* there is no trace, unless one were to count as such some thirty stanzas beginning at line

---

[1] 'He', Tantalus, 'seeks water in water and catches at the elusive fruit.'
[2] A great many such are quoted by E. I. Fripp in *Shakespeare Studies*, 1930.

1366. The passage is too long for quotation, nor need it be quoted, being so accessible. One must allow that it does reveal considerable knowledge of the Trojan matter. But it is such a knowledge as Lydgate's *Troy Booke* or Caxton's *Recuyell of the Historyes of Troye* could give without the necessity of reading any Latin at all. So far from proving that Shakespeare went to Virgil or Ovid for the materials of the picture he describes, it goes to prove the contrary, for what he gives is the medieval rather than the classical form of the story. In the medieval mind the Greeks, and especially Sinon, who in the *Aeneid* induces the Trojans to admit the Trojan Horse, tend to be monsters of cruelty and treachery. That view largely prevailed until scholars could read Homer and see the Greek side of the quarrel, and it so far coloured Shakespeare's thoughts that he reproduced it, with qualifications, in *Troilus and Cressida*. But I get the impression that in this passage he is describing some actual 'painted cloth' or cartoon for tapestry, which he had seen, having for its subject the Trojan War.[1]

Lucrece is based on Ovid's *Fasti*, II. 563–694, which again is evidently based in part on Livy, v. 37, 38. It often follows the original rather closely, at least far more closely than the story of Adonis in the *Metamorphoses* has been followed in the earlier poem. If, as I find it stated, there was no English translation of the *Fasti* then existing or available, the inference would seem to be that Shakespeare made direct use of the Latin original. And, in fact, here and there in *Lucrece* there are touches which can hardly have been suggested by Painter or taken from any other English source that is known to us. For example:

> Her breasts...
> A pair of maiden worlds unconquered,
> Save of their lord no bearing yoke they know (407–9)

is surely a development of line 746 of the *Fasti*:

> nunc primum externa pectora tacta manu.[2]

---

[1] I find that I have been anticipated in this suggestion by Sir Sidney Colvin. See 'The Sack of Troy in Shakespeare's "Lucrece" and in some Fifteenth Century Drawings and Tapestries' in *A Book of Homage to Shakespeare*, 1916.

[2] 'Breasts now for the first time touched by a stranger's hand.'

A captive victor that hath lost in gain (730)

That is clearly suggested by Ovid's

quid, victor, gaudes? haec te victoria perdet.[1]

Here is another clear instance. Shakespeare says (1604, 5):

Three times with sighs she gives her sorrow fire,
Ere once she can discharge one word of woe.

Ovid says (*Fasti*, II. 823):

ter conata loqui, ter destitit.[2]

This is fairly conclusive evidence that Shakespeare had read the Latin *Fasti* or that part of it which told the story of Lucrece. But it does not prove that he was a Latin scholar. He persists in calling Collatia—*Collatium*. If a Frenchman quoted 'O *Caledonium* stern and wild!' more than once, we should hardly describe him as having a scholarly acquaintance with *The Lay of the Last Minstrel*. That however is a trifling objection, worth mentioning perhaps but not worth pressing. What strikes the candid reader, comparing *Lucrece* with the passage in the *Fasti*, is the absence rather than the presence of evidence for a direct use of the Latin. In a poem dealing in such elaboration of detail with so singular an incident as the Rape the astonishing thing would be if the Latin original were not echoed over and over again. And it is the astonishing thing that happens. Apart from one or two echoes or imitations Shakespeare might as well not have read the *Fasti* at all. We may suppose that he did read it in a cursory way, lay it down and write *Lucrece*, as he had written *Venus*, entirely from his own resources.

It is natural to expect in poems which, like *Venus* and *Lucrece*, have a classical subject, a certain amount of classical knowledge. We are not entitled to expect this in the Sonnets of Shakespeare, and certainly we do not find it. There are, as there could not fail to be in poetry of that age and tradition, classical names and allusions of the sort that had become common form. Without

[1] 'Why, victor, dost thou triumph? This victory will destroy thee.'
[2] 'Three times she strove to speak, three times she failed.'

them Elizabethan poetic style loses its character and denies its origin. So there is an allusion to the phoenix in XIV, to the beauty of Adonis and Helen in LI, to 'Mars his sword' in LV, to Saturn in XCVIII, to Philomel in CII, to the Sirens in CXIX. Time, personified with a sickle and an hour-glass, is often mentioned, and Love—that is, the god Love—more than once. There is much too about Fortune, who plays so great a part in Latin literature. But these references are tralaticious and prove nothing.

There are however some points which require a fuller discussion. One is too vague and general to be worth pursuing, but it may be mentioned. The early Sonnets are variations (in part) upon the theme *forma bonum fragile est*,[1] on which Ovid descants in the famous passage of his *Art of Love* (II. 113 f.) which begins with these words. But the theme had been played upon over and over again before Shakespeare took it up; you might say that all the sonneteers from Petrarch downwards have their variations on it. So a poet writing towards the end of the seventeenth century need not have taken his cue directly from Ovid—who himself took it from his predecessors. Not many will think it likely that Shakespeare was under the immediate influence here of Ovid.

But in LX there is a definite reminiscence.

> Like as the waves make towards the pebbled shore,
> So do our minutes hasten to their end;
> Each changing place with that which goes before,
> In sequent toil all forwards do contend.

This ultimately comes from a passage in *Metamorphoses* (XV.181 f.):

> ut unda impellitur unda
> urgeturque prior veniente urgetque priorem,
> tempora sic fugiunt pariter pariterque sequuntur
> et nova sunt semper.

Ultimately, but, it would seem, not immediately. Shakespeare has not gone behind Golding, whose version runs:

> But looke
> As every wave dryves other fourth, and that that commes behynd
> Bothe thrusteth and is thrust itself: Even so the tymes by kind

---

[1] 'Beauty is a fragile boon.'

Doo fly and follow bothe at once, and evermore renew.
For that that was before is left, and streyght there dooth ensew
Another that was never erst. Ech twincling of an eye
Dooth chaunge.

One need not exclude the possibility that Shakespeare had read the Latin. But, if he had, his memory of it was coloured by the language of Golding.

I may add that the last two Sonnets (CLIII and CLIV) are thought to be free renderings of a poem by a certain Marianus which are to be found in the Erotic section of the Greek Anthology. It may be so; but the authenticity of these two sonnets is so doubtful, that it would be quite unsafe to use them in evidence. If they are allowed to be Shakespeare's, it will not follow that he read the epigram of Marianus in its original Greek; he would be content with the Latin translation. Yet anyone who knows the fertility of the Renaissance in the invention of conceits about Cupid will, I think, hesitate before deciding that the fancy, not after all a very recondite fancy, expressed in the two final sonnets could not have occurred to an Elizabethan poet independently of any Marianus.

The Phoenix and The Turtle might be made the subject of a commentary as extensive and multifarious as The Golden Bough, so full is it of esoteric classical and post-classical lore. But it is not in the least necessary to suppose that its author knew much or anything of this lore in its original sources. The phoenix had always been a mystical, indeed a mythical, bird; but its fame in the Middle Ages was started by a short poem, attributed to Lactantius, called De Ave Phoenice, 'Concerning the Bird Phoenix'. The Bird was there allegorized into a figure of Christ. The Renaissance, finding it described in earlier, pagan authors, including Ovid,[1] preferred to regard it, on the evidence of these authors, as a symbol of immortality or of the immortal soul. But what chiefly impressed the men of the Renaissance, as indeed the ancients themselves, was its uniqueness. It is the sole Arabian bird.

---

[1] Metamorphoses, xv. 392 f.

Every Elizabethan was bound to know that. He would also know that the turtle-dove embodied and symbolized perfect conjugal love, as the phoenix symbolized its eternity. The 'death-divining swan' and the 'treble-dated crow' are both classical, and can be traced, the former as far back as Aeschylus, the latter as far back as Hesiod, although it was not from these poets but from Latin authors that the Renaissance first learned about them. The couplet:

> That thy sable gender makest
> With the breath thou givest and takest

embodies a strange belief of popular zoology which can be traced at least as far back as Aristotle.[1] I think we may take it that Shakespeare did not consult the *De Generatione Animalium*.

No safe conclusion can be drawn from *The Passionate Pilgrim* and *A Lover's Complaint*. The *Complaint* hardly anyone now attributes to Shakespeare, while the *Pilgrim* cannot be all from his hand. It is perhaps worth observing that sonnets IV, VI, IX and XI (the 'Adonis sonnets') in the *Pilgrim*, if they are not by Shakespeare, are based on *Venus and Adonis* and not on Ovid, for they contain the Shakespearian divergences from the Latin. We may return to this point when we have reached *The Taming of the Shrew*. Meanwhile there does not appear to be much else to be said on the classical learning discoverable in the poems.

We come now to the plays. The simplest and fairest method of dealing with them is to go through them in their chronological order, noting the classical allusions. But difficulties obtrude themselves. One arises from the fact that many allusions appear, no doubt in slightly different form, in more than one play. When such an allusion has once been explained, it would be intolerable to repeat the explanation. But the effect of omitting an increasing number of explanations is to make the later plays seem much

---

[1] *de generat. anim.* III. 6. 756 f.

emptier of classical matter, compared with the earlier, than in fact they are. I can only hope that the reader will bear this in mind. A more formidable difficulty lies in the chronology itself. It does not affect the question, how much Latin Shakespeare knew. Yet it cannot be satisfactory to anyone who would like to trace the development (if there was any) of Shakespeare's classical learning, to begin like the Folio with *The Tempest*. We must therefore, as I said, take the plays in their chronological order. But then we are very far from knowing, with any precision, what that order is. On the other hand, in a general way, we do know. There are plays which are demonstrably early, others which are demonstrably late; and between these lie a number which belong to Shakespeare's middle period. Fortunately no conclusion reached here will be found to depend on the correct dating of a particular play. In view of this I can hope that the reader will allow me a little freedom in arranging my material with a view to greater clarity in the result. For example, it is very probable that Shakespeare's first surviving work is to be found in *Henry VI*. It seems best, however, and can do no perceptible harm, to reserve our treatment of that until we come to the Historical Plays, and to begin with three dramas which are generally accepted as the earliest or among the earliest: *The Comedy of Errors*, *Titus Andronicus*, *The Two Gentlemen of Verona*.

The plot of *The Comedy of Errors* is interwoven, according to a process used by Terence—but not by Plautus—, of two originally distinct plots, that of the *Amphitruo* and that of the *Menaechmi*, plays freely translated from the Greek by the Roman comic dramatist Plautus. Whether Shakespeare was responsible for the combination of plots in our *Comedy* or found it already made in a play which he re-wrote or worked over, is a question which may never be decided. The combination is effected with great skill, though it seems wasted ingenuity or worse. The *Amphitruo* by itself and the *Menaechmi* by itself are far better comedy than the Shakespearian play, because in each of them the confusion of persons is credible or at least plausible, whereas the conditions involved in *Errors*—that identical twins with identical names should have, by accident, servants who are also identical twins with identical names—reduce it to the level of a farce. Nor is it saved from being a farce by those flashes of poetry and touches of nature, even of pathos, which Shakespeare could not help introducing. What immediately concerns us however is this. The man who designed the plot of *Errors* must have known his Plautus, and to all appearance known him in the original, since the *Amphitruo* had not, so far as we know, been translated into English, although of the *Menaechmi* a version by Warner came out in 1595. Was this man Shakespeare? Sir Edmund Chambers is prepared to believe so, saying that he 'has no reason to doubt that Shakespeare could have read Plautus in the original'.[1] I can see no limit to what Shakespeare could have done, if he tried. But in reading the *Errors* the fact that thrusts itself on one's attention is that, while the structure of the play is Plautine, the superstructure is the work of a man who appears never to have looked at the *Latin* of Plautus at all. Anachronisms, which in this play are numerous, may be discounted. In a farce, especially an Elizabethan farce, such things, though they may tell us a good deal about the author's scholarship, are permitted and even enjoyed. But throughout *Errors* there is not, so far as I can discover, one reminiscence, one echo of the language of Plautus. Now, if Shakespeare came to the writing of the play with the words of the *Amphitruo* and the *Menaechmi* fresh in his mind, is it really credible that no trace at all of his reading would appear in the diction of the *Comedy*? Was the mind of Shakespeare so unimpressible? In view of this I am disposed to accept the view that he worked on a pre-existing plot, though in such a manner as to make the play in effect his own. At any rate there is nothing in it which *proves* that he had read the Latin *Menaechmi*. The plot of the *Amphitruo*—the impersonation of the absent husband—was common property.

There are, as there could not fail to be in a play set in (supposedly) classical times, fractions of classical knowledge revealing themselves here and there. But they do not come from Plautus.

[1] *William Shakespeare*, I. p. 312.

Nor do they prove any knowledge of Latin. When Aegeon begins a narrative with the words,

> A heavier task could not have been imposed
> Than I to speak my griefs unspeakable,[1]

he is echoing the third line of the second book of the *Aeneid*:

> infandum, regina, iubes renovare dolorem.

But this line was so well known and so often quoted and imitated—as for instance in *Dido Queen of Carthage*—that familiarity with it would not of itself prove acquaintance with the *Aeneid*. That Shakespeare had this acquaintance, need not be denied; at least it will not be denied by me. But we are looking for positive proof, and that is not supplied by the reminiscence of a tag. Besides, there was always Phaer's translation. . . . There is reference to a Centaur and a Phoenix. But they turn out to be public houses. . . . The author knows of the Sirens, though he is wrong about the colour of their hair; and of Tartarus, though he confuses it with the medieval limbo. . . . He has heard of Circe. . . . But all this comes from the public stock of knowledge.

We hear of 'the plain bald pate of father Time himself' (II.ii.71). This comes ultimately from Phaedrus, the eighth fable of his fifth book, the moral of which is that one should 'take Time by the forelock'. It looks like the invention of some allegorizing 'sophist', but it captured the popular imagination. There is a line in 'Cato':

> fronte capillata post est Occasio calva.[2]

By Shakespeare's time the image was familiar even to the illiterate, who would have every chance of seeing Time presented in masques and public shows as an elderly bald man with a tuft of hair in front.

In v. i. 332 f. occur these words:

> One of these men is Genius to the other;
> And so of these. Which is the natural man,
> And which the spirit:

---

[1] I. i. 32 f.

[2] 'Opportunity has her forehead covered with hair, but is bald behind.'

Here is an allusion to the Greek belief in a *daemon* (to which the Romans gave the name of *genius*), a spiritual being which accompanied a man through his life, accomplishing his destiny. In Shakespeare's time it was a received opinion that the genius of a man resembled him exactly in appearance and might be mistaken for him, though that is not implied in the classical conception. The word *genius* is found once in the *Menaechmi*, but in a different sense; it does not appear at all in the *Amphitruo*. So the author of the lines did not get the suggestion from Plautus. He had not so far to go. He might have read in Spenser:

> that celestiall powre, to whom the care
> Of life and generation of all
> That lives, pertaines in charge particulare,
> Who wondrous things concerning our welfare,
> And straunge phantomes doth lett us ofte foresee,
> And ofte of secret ills bids us beware:
> That is our Selfe, whom though we do not see,
> Yet each doth in him selfe it well perceive to be.[1]

One did not need to read Latin to know about the genius.

In IV. iv. 47 *respice finem*[2] is quoted. It is the Latin version of a Greek proverbial saying, the origin of which was attributed to Solon in conversation with Croesus. It is a phrase that anybody might pick up in Elizabethan times, like *status quo* or *ne plus ultra* in ours. It tells us nothing about the scholarship of the user.

There are many readers, familiar with *Romeo and Juliet* and *A Midsummer Night's Dream*—to mention only youthful plays— who would like to deny the Shakespearian authorship of *Titus Andronicus*. It is not so much perhaps the style that troubles them as a kind of moral insensitiveness, not pervasive but frequent, which is at least uncharacteristic. Nevertheless, if Shakespeare chose for once to write in the vein of English Seneca, its dissimilarity from the normal tone of his writing would be no argument against the authenticity of the play. And the evidence, both

[1] *Faerie Queene*, Book II. XII. xlvii.
[2] 'Look to the end.'

internal and external, that it is, at least for the most part, authentic is almost irresistible. My proper course in such a case is, I think, to assume that *Titus* is wholly the work of Shakespeare; and then to see what comes of that assumption.

The plot is said to be founded on a medieval story; and this I have not read. As developed in *Titus* it involves two myths, which must have been woven into the story by men of some scholarship or reading. One is the myth of Tereus and Philomela, the other is the myth of the Feast of Thyestes. Lavinia suffers all that Philomela suffered, as the story is told in Ovid; and Tamora, like Thyestes in Seneca, unwittingly eats the flesh of her own children.

There is some Latin quoted in *Titus*, and of these quotations two, in a modified form, are taken from Seneca. In II. i. 135 we have:

Per Styga, per manes vehor.[1]

It is apparently a confused memory of *Phaedra* 1177,

Per Styga, per amnes igneos amens sequor.[2]

Amnes might very easily become *manes*, though a scholar would observe that it ruined the metre. In IV. i. 81 f. we have something more remarkable:

Magni Dominator poli,
Tam lentus audis scelera? tam lentus vides?[3]

Seneca has (*Phaedra* 668):

Magne regnator deum,
Tam lentus audis scelera? tam lentus vides?

How did this difference arise? Well, Magni Dominator poli is not a *varia lectio* for Magne regnator deum. It comes from another part of Seneca—his translation of the famous hymn of the Greek Stoic philosopher Cleanthes. I need quote only the relevant words:

duc, O parens celsique dominator poli,
quocumque placuit.[4] (*Epistle* 107)

[1] 'I am swept through Styx and the dead.'
[2] 'I follow through Styx and rivers of fire in my frenzy.'
[3] 'Lord of the great firmament, art thou so unmoved in hearing these crimes, so unmoved in seeing them?'
[4] 'Lead me, O Father and Lord of the lofty sky, whither it pleaseth thee.'

The English poet has got the two passages mixed. True, but it is a mistake which could have been made only by a man who knew his Seneca well enough, or so he thought, not to bother about verifying his quotation. Indeed his familiarity with Seneca is indicated by many echoes and turns of phrase. In the first scene of the play, line 150 f., Titus utters a valediction over the bodies of his newly interred sons.

> In peace and honour rest you here, my sons;
> Rome's readiest champions, repose you here in rest,
> Secure from wordly chances and mishaps!
> Here lurks no treason, here no envy swells,
> Here grow no damned grudges; here are no storms,
> No noise, but silence and eternal sleep:
> In peace and honour rest you here, my sons!

Mr. Cunliffe, I think, was the first to point out that this rather fine passage is modelled on some lines in Seneca's *Troades*:[1]

> Felix Priamus
> dicimus omnes: secum excedens
> sua regna tulit: nunc Elysii
> nemoris tutis errat in umbris
> interque pias felix animas
> Hectora quaerit. felix Priamus![2]

Seneca is not the only Latin author known to *Titus*. In IV. ii. 20 Horace is quoted:

> Integer vitae scelerisque purus,
> Non eget Mauris jaculis nec arcu (*Carm.*, I. 22. 3)[3]

And this interesting comment is added by the quoter:

> O 'tis a verse in Horace; I know it well:
> I read it in the grammar long ago.

---

[1] 152 f.

[2] ' "Happy Priam", all we say: dying, he has taken his royalty with him: now in the secure shades of the Elysian grove he roams and, happy among the souls of the good, he looks for Hector. Happy Priam!'

[3] 'The man who is innocent in his life and unspotted of sin does not need the darts of the Mauritanian nor a bow.' I give the Latin as it is given in the *Globe* edition, not as it appears in a modern text of Horace.

In the Latin grammar, forming part of the boys' lesson for the day.[1] Then Ovid is quoted in IV. iii. 4: Terras Astraea reliquit, 'Justice has left the earth'. So common a quotation might be picked up from others. But there are some references which prove familiarity with at least the *Metamorphoses* of Ovid. For example,

> The emperor's court is like the house of Fame (II. i. 126).

The house of Fame is described in a brilliant passage of the *Metamorphoses* XII. 39 f. and it is to this, and not to Chaucer's poem or any other, that the allusion is here made. In II. iii. 61 f. we read:

> Had I the power that some say Dian had,
> Thy temples should be planted presently
> With horns, as was Actaeon's; and the hounds
> Should drive upon thy new-transformed limbs,
> Unmannerly intruder as thou art!

The story of Actaeon is related at length in the third book of the *Metamorphoses*, 138–252. No doubt it was well known to people who had never read Ovid, and was a favourite subject with painters and tapestry-weavers. In I. i. 325–6, we read:

> tapers burn so bright and everything
> In readiness for Hymenaeus stand.

Hymenaeus, or rather Hymen, was a great figure in wedding masques, so that the line does not by itself imply any knowledge of Ovid. Yet it may, for it was chiefly from Ovid, as at the end of the ninth and the beginning of the tenth book of the *Metamorphoses*, that the Renaissance learned about Hymenaeus. Again,

> I have read that Hecuba of Troy
> Ran mad for sorrow (IV. i. 20)

is an allusion to *Metamorphoses* XIII. 538 f. Indeed it is hardly open to doubt that we are dealing with a poet who is familiar with the Latin book, since a copy of it is actually a stage-property. See IV. i. 41 f.:

> TIT. Lucius, what book is that she tosseth so?
> YOUNG LUC. Grandsire, 'tis Ovid's Metamorphoses.

[1] Lily, twice.

There he would find the story of Pyramus and Thisbe.[1]

> So pale did shine the moon on Pyramus
> When he by night lay bathed in maiden blood. (II. iii. 231 f.)

There also he would find a long and highly sensational account of the fighting between the Lapiths and the Centaurs at the marriage-feast of Hippodamia (XII. 210 f.), which explains the line (v. ii. 204):

> More stern and bloody than the Centaurs' feast.

But the great proof of the poet's use of Ovid is the interweaving in the plot of the myth of Tereus, Progne (Procne) and Philomela according to the version of it given in the sixth book of the *Metamorphoses* (412–674).

Titus reveals some acquaintance with other Latin writers than Seneca and Horace and Ovid. There are allusions to Virgil. It is true that the words

> like the stately Phoebe 'mongst her nymphs (I. i. 316),

which echo *Aeneid*, I. 498–501, are influenced by the translation of Phaer. But this may be no more than a transient indebtedness such as even a scholar might acknowledge. A university man would read Virgil as a matter of course, at least books II, IV and VI of the *Aeneid*. The following lines allude to a famous passage in IV:[2]

> conflict such as was supposed
> The wandering prince and Dido once enjoy'd,
> When with a happy storm they were surprised
> And curtain'd with a counsel-keeping cave (II. iii. 21 f.)

The opening of *Aeneid* II has suggested the lines

> To bid A neas tell the tale twice o'er,
> How Troy was burnt and he made miserable (III. ii. 27, 28)

Book VI. 74 f. has suggested

> Will blow these sands, like Sibyl's leaves, abroad (IV. i. 105),

and Book III. 577 f. perhaps

[1] IV. 55 f.
[2] 160 f.

not Enceladus
With all his threatening band of Typhon's brood (IV. ii. 93)

And of course Book II has supplied the matter of lines v. iii. 80 f.

> as erst our ancestor,
> When with his solemn tongue he did discourse
> To love-sick Dido's sad attending ear
> The story of that baleful burning night
> When subtle Greeks surprised King Priam's Troy,
> Tell us what Sinon hath bewitch'd our ears,
> Or who hath brought the fatal engine in . . .

The 'fatal engine' is of course the Trojan Horse (*fatalis machina*).

There is a curious passage, IV. i. 12 f.:

> Ah, boy, Cornelia never with more care
> Read to her sons than she hath read to thee
> Sweet poetry and Tully's Orator.

Cornelia was 'the mother of the Gracchi', and her sons of course Tiberius and Gaius. It was chiefly from Plutarch, who loves all virtuous ladies, that the Renaissance knew of her. The 'sweet poetry' would probably be Ovid; 'Tully's Orator' is the *Orator ad M. Brutum*, Cicero's sketch—for it is no more—of the ideal orator. Young women of good family were educated, at the height of the Renaissance, in the knowledge of Latin and in some cases even Greek. Accordingly Lavinia was capable of taking young Lucius through the *Orator*, where he could study the structure of the Ciceronian period. Ovid and Cicero—these were the two instructors of the Renaissance.

There are a good many other passages drawn, directly or indirectly, from other classical authors, such as Herodotus and Livy. How much of it is first-hand knowledge it is impossible now to say—probably very little. Herodotus and Livy began even in classical times to be digested into synopses, while their best stories were retold by the poets, as Ovid retells the story of Lucretia. There was a whole class of literary men who collected the myths and legends out of the old poets. In particular Hyginus, the librarian of the great Palatine library founded by Augustus, busied himself in this way, having such opportunities. A collection of myths, passing under his name but evidently a later abridgment of his work, was exceedingly popular in Renaissance times. And there was the encyclopaedic Pliny. When therefore we read a passage like this (I. i. 177 f.),

> this funeral pomp,
> That hath aspired to Solon's happiness
> And triumphs over chance in honour's bed,

we cannot be sure that the author has read Herodotus, Book One, even in B.R.'s translation. For the saying of Solon to Croesus, 'Count no man happy before his death', appears in a score of later authors, borrowing from Herodotus or from one another.[1] And when we read v. iii. 36 f.

> Was it well done of rash Virginius
> To slay his daughter with his own right hand,
> Because she was enforced, stain'd and deflower'd?

we are not bound to suppose that the author of these lines had read Livy v, for the tale of Virginia was in all the story-books. I will therefore say no more about these passages than just this, that, taken with the passages that show a knowledge of Seneca and Ovid, Horace and Virgil, they suggest a considerably wider range of classical reading than is discoverable in the plays which are certainly Shakespeare's own.

This conclusion would be strongly reinforced if it could be proved that *Titus* reveals a knowledge of Greek. In I. i. 136 f. we read:

> The self-same gods that arm'd the Queen of Troy
> With opportunity of sharp revenge
> Upon the Thracian tyrant in his tent . . .

The reference is to a scene in the *Hecuba* of Euripides in which the eyes of Polymestor, a Thracian tyrant, are destroyed by Hecuba the Trojan queen. The story is related by Ovid (*Metamorphoses*, XIII. 551 f.), and one would have little hesitation in saying that the source of the English poet here is Ovid, were it not for the addition of the words 'in his tent'. Ovid says nothing about a tent,

---

[1] We have already met it in the form *respice finem*.

but it is in his tent that Polymestor is blinded in Euripides. Again, in I. i. 378 f. we read:

> Thou are a Roman; be not barbarous:
> The Greeks upon advice did bury Ajax
> That slew himself; and wise Laertes' son,
> Did graciously plead for his funerals.

The source of the last three of these four lines is the *Ajax* of Sophocles, which even gives the English poet his 'Laertes' son'. It cannot be the thirteenth book of the *Metamorphoses*, for there Ulysses is the villain of the piece, not, as in Sophocles, the chivalrous foe. It would seem that the author of *Titus*, or this part of it, had read the *Ajax*, though no doubt in a Latin version or with its aid.[1] The fact that both passages, the one implying some knowledge of Euripides, the other of Sophocles, occur in almost immediate succession must mean something. What it means I must leave to the experts to decide, contenting myself with this general observation that the classical allusions which occur most frequently in Shakespeare's other plays are most evident in the second act of *Titus*.

The Two Gentlemen of Verona looks both cut-down and confused; but that it is substantially the work of Shakespeare is doubted only by critics who are inclined to doubt everything. That we may keep on the safe side, it will be assumed here to be authentic throughout. The classical allusions are few and such as may be called 'Shakespearian', for Shakespeare has, as I have indicated, a stock or repertoire of them which is made to serve most of his purposes. It may well be argued that a man who had read a good deal of Latin would have cast his net wider.

One of the Shakespearian allusions, one of which he never seems to be weary, is to Hero and Leander. It occurs in *The Two Gentlemen*; in fact it occurs twice.

> some shallow story of deep love:
> How young Leander cross'd the Hellespont (I. i. 21)

[1] An *Ajax Flagellifer*, which from its title must have been translated from or based upon the play of Sophocles, was performed before King James at Oxford.

And again, III. i. 119, 120:

> Would serve to scale another Hero's tower,
> So bold Leander would adventure it.

It is possible, though scarcely likely, that these allusions were the result of reading Marlowe's *Hero and Leander*, which was published in 1593. The story was exceedingly well known before Marlowe touched it, not only from its original telling in Ovid's *Heroides* (18 and 19), but from later accounts, including that of 'Musaeus', from which Marlowe drew the materials for his own poem. There was a translation, in case Shakespeare needed it, of the *Heroides* by Turbervile (1567). Ovid again, either in Latin or in Golding, is the inspiration of III. i. 153 f.:

> Why, Phaethon—for thou art Merops' son—
> Wilt thou aspire to guide the heavenly car
> And with thy daring folly burn the world?

For this see the *Metamorphoses*, II. 1–240. There is an allusion to Orpheus in III. ii. 78 f.:

> For Orpheus' lute was strung with poets' sinews,
> Whose golden touch could soften steel and stones,
> Make tigers tame and huge leviathans
> Forsake unsounded deeps to dance on sands.

The enchanting force of Orpheus' harp was of course known to everyone, but, since it is certain that Shakespeare read Golding, we may suppose that most of what he knew about Orpheus was derived from the *Metamorphoses*, in which he has a very prominent part. In particular his power of enchantment is described at the end of Book X and the beginning of Book XI. The passage IV. iv. 172 f.

> 'twas Ariadne passioning
> For Theseus' perjury and unjust flight

is also inspired by Ovid.[1] All these allusions—to Leander, to Phaethon, to Orpheus, to Ariadne—are Shakespearian. This supplies an argument for the authenticity of the *Gentlemen*.

---

[1] *Heroides*, x. But Ovid is fond of the story and repeats it elsewhere, as in the *Ars Amatoria* and the *Fasti*.

We need not dwell on the mention of Elysium (II. vii. 38) or of the chameleon that lives on air (II. i. 172 and iv. 22, 23). Elysium is depicted in the sixth book of the *Aeneid*, the chameleon is described by Pliny in several places and by Aulus Gellius, x. 12. 1 f. Isidore and others. Both had passed into the common fund of knowledge in Shakespeare's time.

We may next consider a group of plays, early but in the main not so early as those we have examined. They are *The Taming of the Shrew, Love's Labour's Lost, A Midsummer Night's Dream* and *Romeo and Juliet*.

The Taming of the Shrew. Critics are not agreed upon the extent of Shakespeare's contribution to the comedy as we now have it. In particular the scenes in which Bianca appears have been thought not to be his. I shall however follow my usual method and assume, for the moment, that the whole play is the undivided work of Shakespeare.

Nobody is likely to question the authorship of the Induction and it provides us with some interesting matter. There is no point in lingering over such phrases as 'Apollo plays' (ii. 38) or 'the lustful bed On purpose trimm'd up for Semiramis' (ii. 40), because these were public property.[1] But I may be permitted to enlarge a little on ii. 52 f.:

> Adonis painted by a running brook,
> And Cytherea all in sedges hid,
> Which seem to move and wanton with her breath,
> Even as the waving sedges play with wind.

Now this is a picture not of any scene in Ovid's story of Venus and Adonis, but of a scene in his story of Salmacis and Hermaphroditus. The story of Salmacis is related in the fourth book of the *Metamorphoses* (285 f.), and of course had been read by Shakespeare, if not in the original, at least in Golding. We have already made this observation in dealing with *Venus and Adonis*.

---

[1] Semiramis is a Renaissance favourite. Her legend had already begun by the time of Augustus (Diodorus Siculus), but continued to grow through later centuries.

The whole narrative must be read in Ovid; here perhaps it will be enough to say that the nymph Salmacis watched Hermaphroditus bathing in a pool.

> fruticumque recondita silva
> dilituit, flexuque genu summisit, at ille,
> scilicet ut vacuis et inobservatus in herbis,
> huc it et hinc illuc, et in alludentibus undis
> summa pedum taloque tenus vestigia tinguit (339–43)[1]

If the reader is not convinced by this parallel on the ground that it is too general, let me quote *The Passionate Pilgrim*, VI.

> Scarce had the sun dried up the dewy morn,
> And scarce the herd gone to the hedge for shade,
> When Cytherea, all in love forlorn,
> A longing tarriance for Adonis made.
> Under an osier growing by a brook,
> A brook where Adon used to cool his spleen:
> Hot was the day; she hotter that did look
> For his approach, that often there had been.
> Anon he comes, and throws his mantle by,
> And stood stark naked on the brook's green brim:
> The sun look'd on the world with glorious eye,
> Yet not so wistly as this queen on him.
> He, spying her, bounced in, whereas he stood:
> 'O Jove', quoth she, 'why was not I a flood?'

In this sonnet the parallel is quite unmistakable, as will appear when I continue a little farther the passage in Ovid which I had begun to quote. After 'vestigia tinguit' he proceeds:

> nec mora, temperie blandarum captus aquarum
> mollia de tenero velamina corpore ponit.
> tum vero stupuit, nudaeque cupidine formae
> Salmacis exarsit.[2]

---

[1] 'And, hidden in shrubby bushes, she lurked and knelt. But he, as if the sward was empty and he unmarked in it, paces back and forth, and dips the soles of his feet and as high as the ancle in the plashing ripples.'

[2] 'Presently, charmed by the feel of the tepid water, he laid aside the soft garments from his young body. Then was Salmacis amazed and inflamed by desire of his naked loveliness.'

No one is likely to deny that this sonnet is influenced by the Ovidian passage. Yet here, and in the picture described in *The Shrew*, we have the same confusion between Venus and Adonis on the one hand, and Salmacis and Hermaphroditus on the other. Again, in both Ovid's *stagnum*, which means a pool or lake, is called a 'brook'. Since it is a canon of textual criticism that community of error normally implies community of origin, I believe that the sonnet (which has a juvenile appearance to me) was in fact written by Shakespeare.

The Adonis picture is to be followed by another.

> We'll show thee Io as she was a maid,
> And how she was beguiled and surprised,
> As lively painted as the deed was done (55–7)

This comes from *Metamorphoses* I. 568 f., especially 597 f.:

> iam pascua Lernae
> consitaque arboribus Lyrcea reliquerat arva,
> cum deus inducta latas caligine terras
> occuluit tenuitque fugam rapuitque pudorem.[1]

And this picture is to be succeeded by one of Daphne (58–60):

> Or Daphne roaming through a thorny wood,
> Scratching her legs that one shall swear she bleeds,
> And at that sight shall sad Apollo weep.

This is an allusion to the Daphne episode narrated in the first book of *Metamorphoses* (I. 452 f.), especially to the words of Apollo to Daphne 508 f.:

> me miserum! ne prona cadas, indignave laedi
> crura notent sentes, et sim tibi causa doloris.[2]

We have seen that this passage must have been in Shakespeare's

---

[1] 'By now she had left the pastures of Lerna and the Lyrcean fields overgrown with trees, when the god drew a mist over the broad lands, concealing them, and stayed her flight and reft her maidenhead.'

[2] 'Woe is me, take heed that you do not fall upon your face or the brambles scratch your legs that are too beautiful to be hurt, and I be the cause of your pain!'

mind when he wrote of the search of Venus for her dead love in
Venus and Adonis. And here it is again.

> while we do admire
> This virtue and this moral discipline,
> Let's be no stoics nor no stocks, I pray;
> Or so devote to Aristotle's checks
> As Ovid be an outcast quite abjured (I. i. 29 f.)

These lines for the most part explain themselves. Such ethical
instruction as was given in Renaissance schools and colleges was
drawn rather from the classical moralists than from the Bible
and its expositors. If we leave out Publilius Syrus, ' Cato ' and
such later authors, we should probably find that the most influential pagan moralists were Cicero and Seneca. But behind them of
course were the Greeks, whose disciples they were. Roman moral
philosophy is, nine-tenths of it, Stoic. But Aristotle's *Ethics*[1] was
always a famous book. What exactly are meant by his 'checks' is
not very clear, but all ancient ethics insist greatly on the importance of self-control. One doubts if the speaker had really read
Aristotle; and if he did, it would be of course in a Latin translation.
Very few Englishmen at that time could read the difficult Greek.
It is interesting to note that Ovid is taken as the advocate of a less
tight-laced morality. Ovid, like Macchiavelli, has been made
responsible for the sins of many.

> thou may'st hear Minerva speak (I. i. 84)

The goddess of wisdom.

> to me as secret and as dear
> As Anna to the queen of Carthage was (I. i. 158)

Anna, the sister of Dido, appears as her confidante in the fourth
Aeneid. But she appears also in the *Fasti* of Ovid, under the name
of Anna Perenna.

> Redime te captum quam queas minimo. (I. i. 167)

---

[1] The Nicomachean Ethics, though the Eudemian Ethics was also known
and even the Magna Moralia.

From Lily, abbreviated from Terence, *Eunuch.* I. i. 29, 'quid agas ? nisi ut te redimas captum quam queas | minimo.'[1]

> I saw sweet beauty in her face,
> Such as the daughter of Agenor had,
> That made great Jove to humble him to her hand,
> When with his knees he kissed the Cretan strand (I. i. 172 f.)

The daughter of Agenor is Europa, *Agenore nata*, see *Metamorphoses*, II. 858, with the context, which tells her story.

> Be she as foul as was Florentius' love,
> As old as Sibyl and as curst and shrewd
> As Socrates' Xanthippe (I. ii. 69 f.)

The story of Florentius may be found in the first book of Gower's *Confessio Amantis*, where he is called Florent. It resembles the Wife of Bath's Tale in Chaucer. But, so far as I know, it has not a classical origin.—It is not so much the Sibyl of Virgil (*Aeneid* VI) that is in the speaker's mind as the Sibyl of legend. He would know the story of the boys finding her at Cumae, hung up in a basket, shrunk with age to the bulk of a grasshopper and wishing only to die.—The shrewish character of Xanthippe is noted first, not by Plato, but by Xenophon in his *Memorabilia*, a favourite book throughout the Renaissance. After Xenophon she became a legend and anecdotes about her multiply.

> Fair Leda's daughter had a thousand wooers (I. ii. 244)

Helen. The 'thousand wooers' (mille proci in Latin) are not in Homer and are merely a round number.

> Though Paris came in hope to speed alone (I. ii. 248)

What is in the speaker's mind, here and in the previous quotation, is the Epistle of Paris to Helen and the Epistle of Helen to Paris in the *Heroides* of Ovid (XVI and XVII).

> My hangings all of Tyrian tapestry (II. i. 351)

Tyrian dye was red ('purple'), but the reference is pretty certainly

---

[1] 'What are you to do ? What but redeem yourself from captivity at as low a price as you can ?'

not to the colour of the hangings. The speaker is thinking of the famous passage in *Aeneid*, I. 455 f. where Aeneas wonders at the workmanship of the artists who depicted the siege of Troy in the temple at Carthage, for the Carthaginians are called Tyrians by Virgil. Tyrian tapestry would thus mean the finest kind.

> Preposterous ass, that never read so far
> To know the cause why music was ordain'd!
> Was it not to refresh the mind of man
> After his studies or his usual pain? (III. i. 9-12)

'Preposterous' here means 'putting the cart before the horse', since (according to Lucentio) music should come after study. This comes from Aristotle (*Politics* v.[1] 5). The passage is too long to quote. It is part of Aristotle's discussion whether music should have a place in education. He thinks it should (a) as a form of discipline—the ancients were strongly impressed by the influence of music on the feelings, and so on the character—(b) for recreation or pastime (παιδιά), (c) for the rational use of our leisure. It is the second reason of which Lucentio is thinking.[2] Aristotle of course had long been translated into Latin.

> Hic ibat Simois; hic est Sigeia tellus;
> Hic steterat Priami regia celsa senis. (III. i. 27)

Heroides, I. 33, 34.

> Aeacides
> Was Ajax, call'd so from his grandfather (III. i. 52)

Aeacides strictly means 'son of Aeacus', but the meaning was often extended to imply a grandson or even a remoter descendant. The epithet—for it is that rather than a name—is Homeric.

> I read that I profess, the Art to Love. (IV. ii. 8)

The *Ars Amatoria* or *Ars Amandi* of Ovid.

---

[1] VIII.

[2] ἥ τε γὰρ παιδιὰ χάριν ἀναπαύσεως ἐστί, τὴν δ' ἀνάπαυσιν ἀναγκαῖον ἡδεῖαν εἶναι· τῆς γὰρ διὰ τῶν πόνων λύπης ἰατρεία τίς ἐστιν.
'Amusement has for its end recreation, and recreation is necessarily pleasant, for it is a kind of healing of the pain that comes through toil.'

c

Did ever Dian so become a grove
As Kate this chamber with her princely gait? (II. ii. 260, 1)

This reflects a passage in the first book of the *Aeneid*, where in a wood Aeneas meets Venus disguised in hunting garb, and wonders if she can be Diana (328-9):

O dea certe,
an Phoebi soror?[1]

When she reveals her divinity it is by her gait:

vera incessu patuit dea (405)

This is one of those quotations that everybody knew, and it is in Shakespeare's head more than once.

Love's Labour's Lost contains what is, for Shakespeare, an unusually large number of classical quotations and allusions. Indeed, a good deal of the play would have been pointless to a spectator who had not something of a classical education or was unfamiliar with the kind of society in which such an 'academe' as that described there was conceivable. [The inference is that the play was intended, at least originally, for presentation before a select audience capable of seizing the points] Clearly much depended on that and, as we cannot hope now to seize them all, we are often left to grope in the dark, and no doubt miss some of the fun. There is little doubt, I suppose, that Armado and Moth and Holofernes, these three at least, are satirical portraits of living contemporaries. But the portraits of a great artist are never mere caricatures, and for this reason, that a mere caricature is not a living man or woman. What the great creators do is to invent a living character, and then endow him with the more striking idiosyncrasies of the person satirized. Such a character has a life of his own, as for example Mr. Skimpole has a life independent of Leigh Hunt, some of whose qualities Mr. Skimpole has and some not.[2] It very often happens also that more than one original suggests traits in the invented character, as in the Antiquary and a

---

[1] 'O thou—goddess at least—perhaps the sister of Phoebus?'
[2] Cf. F. A. Yates: *A Study of Love's Labour's Lost*, Introduction, pp. 18, 19.

good many others among Scott's people. If then we say, as I am disposed to say, after others, that Holofernes is a caricature of George Chapman, the translator of Homer, we must not identify him with Chapman or suppose him incapable of saying some, or even many, things that Chapman himself would never have said. The circumstance that some have seen in Holofernes a caricature of Florio rather than of Chapman should put us on our guard. Sometimes he looks like Florio, at most times (I think) like Chapman. We must be content with indications.

As Holofernes is so important for us in his character of 'pedant' or schoolmaster, I will begin with him instead of running through the play in order of acts and scenes, which is the method hitherto employed. He first appears in Act IV, Scene ii accompanied by Sir (dominus, *dominie*) Nathaniel, a 'curate', and Dull, a constable, whose name does him some injustice. It must be remembered that curates and parsons generally were regarded as competent to teach Latin, and often did so, like Sir Hugh Evans in *The Merry Wives of Windsor*. It is part of the fun of *Love's Labour's Lost* that Nathaniel is a humble admirer of Holofernes and submits to have his Latin corrected by that humbug. The first words of Holofernes are these (IV. ii. 3 f.):

'The deer was, as you know, sanguis, in blood; ripe as a pomewater, who now hangeth like a jewel in the ear of caelo the sky, the welkin, the heaven; and anon falleth like a crab on the face of terra, the soil, the land, the earth.'

An audience of young gentlemen would laugh at this, remembering these dictionary synonyms.[1] Of course sanguis does not mean '*in* blood'. Holofernes however might say that he was content to give the nominative of the appropriate word. On the other hand caelo is in the ablative, which is the wrong case. Shakespeare's knowledge of Latin was at any rate sufficient to tell him that these were errors. He must therefore mean that Holofernes did not know his own subject.

[1] A popular dictionary was Elyot's, enlarged by Cooper. For this see Prof. Baldwin's *Shakspere's Small Latine*, vol. I.

Nathaniel replies:

'Truly, Master Holofernes, the epithets are sweetly varied, like a scholar at the least: but, sir, I assure ye, it was a buck of the first head.'

By 'epithets' he means synonyms—the synonyms that Holofernes has been using, which are not sweetly varied at all, Nathaniel's speech being part of Shakespeare's satire against such 'scholars'. To him Holofernes (who like a good many schoolmasters cannot bear being contradicted) replies:

Sir Nathaniel, haud credo.

Then Dull, not understanding Latin, interrupts:

'Twas not a haud credo; 'twas a pricket.

This gives Holofernes an opportunity to air his learning.

'Most barbarous intimation! yet a kind of insinuation, as it were, in via, in way, of explication; facere, as it were, replication, or rather, ostentare, to show, as it were, his inclination, after his undressed, unpolished, uneducated, unpruned, untrained, or rather unlettered, or ratherest, unconfirmed fashion, to insert again my haud credo for a deer.'

One cannot, nor is one meant to, make complete sense out of this balderdash. But the general drift of the passage is a complaint by Holofernes that he has been interrupted by a repetition of his own words on the lips of an ignoramus. The complaint however is made obscure by the pedantry of its expression. Pedants have always been fond of using words in their original sense, partly to display their erudition, partly from a genuine distress at the debasing of the currency in speech. Now 'intimation' is derived from *intimus*, which means 'innermost', and so may be taken in the sense of 'thrusting inwards'. In the same way 'insinuation' literally means 'insertion'. Dull is accused of breaking into the conversation of two learned men with an 'explication', which means much the same as 'explanation', or a 'replication', which means much the same as a 'reply'. If this interpretation is accepted —and it is borne out by 'to insert again my haud credo'—it implies a knowledge of the Latin words involved. They are no doubt common words, like those actually quoted in Latin—*facere*, *ostentare*—but they ought to have some weight with us in considering the amount of Latin known to the author. We may put it in this way. Shakespeare knows enough Latin to parody the talk of a Latin teacher, including his perpetual 'as it were's and 'or rather's, which translate *quasi* and *vel potius*, indispensable words to the scholar.

After this specimen of Holofernes' conversation we need only pick from the rest of it anything that looks significant. In IV. ii. 23 he uses the expression *bis coctus*, which he translates well enough by 'twice-sod'. In line 32 Nathaniel exclaims 'omne bene, I say', meaning perhaps 'may everything turn out well'. This also may pass. Such phrases were in the grammars . . . Dictynna as a title of the Moon—'a title to Phoebe, to Luna, to the moon' (38)—Shakespeare could have got from Ovid.[1] Presently Holofernes volunteers an extempore 'epitaph' on the death of the deer, encouraged in this by Nathaniel, who says 'Perge, good master Holofernes, perge.' It is the ordinary Latin word for 'proceed' and must have been excessively familiar to Elizabethan school-boys.[2] At this point Jacquenetta appears, interrupting some ambiguous remarks of Holofernes, who recommends caution in speech: 'vir sapit qui pauca loquitur', 'he who says little is wise', a maxim which is found in Lily's grammar. Latin adages of this kind were exceedingly popular both in the Middle Ages and later, as late even as the eighteenth century. Erasmus assembled a great number of them in his *Adagia*, a work which everybody read and plundered. Their profitableness for the teacher of Latin is obvious. It is possible that Shakespeare learned *vir sapit* at school. At school too he may—though this is perhaps less likely—have learned the first line of Mantuanus,

> Fauste, precor gelida quando pecus omne sub umbra
> ruminat . . .[3]

---

[1] *Metamorphoses*, II. 441, V. 619; *Fasti*, VI. 755.

[2] The teacher must be imagined as teaching in Latin, which would necessitate his saying *Perge* to the pupil, struggling to construe, as often as the modern master has to say 'Go on'.

[3] 'Faustus, I pray, now that the flock is ruminating in the shade.'—The quarto has *Facile* for *Fauste*, leaving it open to doubt how many (if any) of these errors are attributable to Holofernes himself. If he really said *Facile*, it shows that he could not scan, as well as that his memory failed him. No *scholar* could have said *Facile* here; but then Holofernes is no scholar.

Presently Holofernes makes as if to quote Horace, but does not, being perhaps interrupted by Nathaniel, who shows him the verses of Berowne. Holofernes bids him read them: 'Lege, domine'[1]—another of those school formulas. Similar scraps of Latin are dropped by Holofernes as the scene proceeds. Here is his criticism of Berowne's poetry.

'For the elegancy, facility, and golden cadence of poesy, caret: Ovidius Naso was the man. And why, indeed, Naso, but for smelling out the odoriferous flowers of fancy . . .'

It is characteristic of Holofernes to spoil the rather charming description of the Ovidian style by discoursing on the etymology of Naso, which is apparently derived from *nasus*, a nose. This derivation, a source of amusement to schoolboys, is taken seriously by the pedagogue. . . . I leave out some other scraps of school Latin.

Holofernes reappears in the first scene of what Rowe treated as the fifth act. His first words are in Latin—'satis quod sufficit', 'Enough is enough', an adage. Nathaniel then mentions Armado, and of him Holofernes says, 'Novi hominem tamquam te'.[2] The phrase is taken from Lily's Grammar, where it appears under the heading of *quasi*. As Terence supplied many of Lily's examples, sometimes abbreviated or simplified from the original, it is not improbable that Terence supplied this one, for he has 'Chremem nosti? . . . tamquam te'.[3] Erasmus, whose *Colloquies* were not unfamiliar to Shakespeare, has *novi tamquam te*.[4] After some animadversions on Armado's manner of speaking, Holofernes proceeds:

'This is abhominable—which he would call abbominable. It insinuateth me of insanie: anne[5] intelligis, domine? to make frantic, lunatic.'

[1] 'Read, master.'
[2] 'I know the man as well as I know you.'
[3] *Phormio*, 63–5.
[4] In *Proci et Puellae*.
[5] Folio *ne*.

Holofernes says 'abhominable' because he derives the word from *ab* and *homo*, as if it meant originally 'inhuman'. This etymology was not peculiar to him, for it seems to have been rather commonly entertained by old scholars. Then 'insinuateth me of insanie', which is marked in texts as corrupt, means 'inserts insanity into me'—that is, 'makes me frantic, lunatic'—*insinuate* being used again in its original meaning. As for *anne*, that is a conjecture, to heal the Folio reading of *ne*. Neither *anne* nor *nonne* carries any conviction. All that is wrong with *ne* is its position and, if it were put after *intelligis* instead of before it, we should get what is by far the most probable form of the question in Latin, namely *intelligisne, domine?* As for the Latin of Nathaniel which follows, the text is too uncertain for useful comment. But, if he said *bone* instead of *bene*, Holofernes would be more than justified in his remark that Priscian had been 'a little scratched'.[1]

At this point Armado, Moth and Costard appear, causing Nathaniel to remark 'Videsne quis venit?' and Holofernes to reply 'Video, et gaudeo'.[2] *Venit* would be *veniat* according to the rules of Ciceronian syntax. But very likely Shakespeare did not know that or intend to make Nathaniel commit another solecism. Besides it is not exactly a solecism and would pass in Plautus or Terence. As Armado approaches, he greets Holofernes with the single vocable 'Chirrah!' What he really means is χαῖρε, the regular Greek form of salutation, which in Latin is transliterated *chaere*.[3] 'Chirrah!' is Armado's attempt to pronounce this word, for of course he is a mere pretender to learning. But where did he find the word? The answer is not difficult; it is one of the 'forms of salutation' given in the *Colloquies* of Erasmus, the earlier and more elementary part of which was intended for, and used by, schoolboys. Holofernes—and small blame to him—can make nothing of 'Chirrah!' and supposes it to be some new or fashionable way of pronouncing 'Sirrah', although Armado was far too polite a man to address a stranger so unceremoniously. The

---

[1] The Folio has *bone*, emended by the *Globe* editors to *bene*.
[2] 'Do you see who is coming?' 'I see and rejoice.'
[3] See the Prologue to Persius' *Satires*, quis expedivit psittaco suum *chaere*? 'Who taught the parrot to say his "good morning"?'

comment of the sardonic Moth, 'They have been at a great feast of languages, and stolen the scraps', is designed to draw the attention of young gentlemen, brought up on the *Colloquies*, to the pretentious ignorance of both Armado and Holofernes.

The whole scene is full of hidden meanings and suggestions which have baffled commentators. Perhaps they have been too quick-despairing. There are possible explanations which may be offered, though these are not, and could not in the circumstances be, more than possible. I will mention two more.

(*a*) HOL. Thou disputest like an infant: go, whip thy gig.

MOTH. Lend me your horn to make one, and I will whip about your infamy circum circa,—a gig of a cuckold's horn. (v. i. 70)

This is the *Globe* reading. But circum circa is an emendation (by Theobald) of the Quarto reading unum cita, which has been regarded as nonsense. The art of textual emendation has surely progressed far enough by this time to make us reject such guessing, especially when it renders the syntax so unlike what is characteristic of Shakespeare, and after all adds so little to the sense. In fact *unum cita* is perfectly good Latin so far as it goes; we have only to take *cita* as the imperative of *citare*, to 'summon' or 'cite'. 'Summon (or cite) one' witness or example. The phrase is very natural in the mouth of Latin disputants, whether in the law-courts or the schools. It seems a possible solution then to keep the reading of the Quarto 'unum cita', putting a full stop after 'infamy', and to suppose that Moth intends to say 'Produce a single specimen of a (cuckold's) horn from which to make a whipping-top'. I leave it to others to decide whether this is pressing the Latin too hard.

(*b*) Almost at the beginning of the *Colloquies* of Erasmus,[1] and one of the first things a schoolboy would be taught to read in it, is a short dialogue between Georgius and Livinus. After exclaiming upon the emaciated appearance of Livinus, Georgius proceeds:

'Unde prodis?' LI. 'E collegio Montis Acuti.' GE. 'Ergo ades nobis onustus literis.' LI. 'Immo pediculis.'[2]

[1] *Colloquia Familiaria*. I quote from the Tauchnitz edition of 1829.
[2] 'Where do you come from?' 'From the college of the pointed Mountain.' 'Then you come to us laden with learning.' 'No, with lice.'

What lad but would remember and laugh at that passage about the 'college' on the hill which had so considerable a draw-back? Erasmus had suffered during his student days at Paris in that school, which is of course the Collège de Montaigu, and in this dialogue he takes his revenge upon it. Now observe what Armado says to Holofernes.

'Do you not educate youth at the charge-house on the top of the mountain?'

To which Holofernes answers, 'Or mons, the hill'.

> ARMADO. At your sweet pleasure, for the mountain.
> HOLOFERNES. I do, sans question. (v. i. 87 f.)

All this insistence on *mons*, the hill or mountain, is not just tiresome trifling. It is designed to enforce the recollection of that passage in the *Colloquies*. And the sting in the allusion is the suggestion that the 'college' or 'charge-house' kept by Holofernes is no better than a sort of Dotheboys Hall.

There is little else in the scene to detain us, and nothing of importance. There are some schoolboy Latin jokes, which the commentators explain. Apparently Shakespeare's audience was young enough to enjoy them.

In the long second scene of the fifth act Holofernes with Costard, Sir Nathaniel, Moth and Armado present a kind of masque, in which—as it is finally arranged—Costard takes the part of Pompey, Nathaniel of Alexander, Holofernes of Judas Maccabeus, Moth of Hercules, Armado of Hector. The characters and achievements of these heroes were known to Elizabethan audiences in the barest outline only and mixed with many inaccuracies and misconceptions, but they were known—known, I think, hardly at all from books, at least much less from them than from the shows, masques and mummeries in which they were presented to the populace. How much more exact and extensive Shakespeare's own knowledge in the matter was, we have no means of judging; but he is obviously making fun of the popular notions about these worthies which are embodied in Holofernes' entertainment. Since he does make fun of them, there is no point in describing them, for they are no evidence for the extent of his own classical knowledge.

Having now finished with Holofernes, we are free to consider the other scenes of *Love's Labour's Lost*. We may pass over as common form the lines about devouring Time (*tempus edax rerum*) and his scythe, with which the King begins the play. We may also pass over as scarcely germane to our subject his description of the 'little academe' which he proposes to institute. It is to be 'still and contemplative in living art', a phrase traced by the late Professor J. S. Reid, the Ciceronian scholar, to a classical source in the Stoic philosophy, although the 'contemplative life'[1] can be traced even farther back, through Aristotle and Plato to the Pythagoreans. But, since it seems impossible that Shakespeare could have known this, we need not go more deeply into the matter. . . . In the prose passages which follow there is a good deal of equivocal talk, with some mention of Hercules and Cupid, which we can neglect. And so we come to Act Three.

In the first scene a conversation begins which calls for some explanation, if that be possible.

MOTH. . . . here's a costard broken in a shin.[2]

ARMADO. Some enigma, some riddle: come, thy l'envoy; begin.

COSTARD. No egma, no riddle, no l'envoy; no salve in the mail. . . .

ARMADO. . . . Doth the inconsiderate take salve for l'envoy, and the word l'envoy for a salve?'

MOTH. Do the wise think them other? Is not l'envoy a salve?

One joke in this passage is obvious enough—a confusion about the word 'salve'. Costard supposes that, in calling for a 'l'envoy', Armado is offering him some kind of salve to heal his broken shin. When Armado laughs at this, Moth argues that Costard is quite right, for the best authorities consider that 'l'envoy' is a kind of *salve*, that is a form of salutation like those listed by Erasmus in his *Colloquies*. In fact an *envoi* (as we now call it) does take the form of an address to someone, and this would seem to justify Moth. If this be how the passage is to be explained, it is another indication of how much these 'forms of salutation' had been impressed on the schoolboy mind.

[1] θεωρητικὸς βίος
[2] Costard has just barked his shin.

There would seem to be nothing else in the Act that calls for notice, for the line

Though Argus were her eunuch and her guard (198)

involves no more than the knowledge of Argus, the hundred-eyed monster, that kept watch upon Io. Everybody knew his story, which is related in the first book of the *Metamorphoses*, 625–723.

In Scene One of Act Four we find (in Armado's letter) a quotation which Shakespeare is quite fond of making, for it appears in other plays. It is the famous 'veni, vidi, vici' of Julius Caesar. This apophthegm (which is not in any book of Caesar but is reported by Suetonius as occurring in a dispatch, *div. Iul.* 37) was thrice celebrated in Renaissance times and helped greatly to confirm the prevalent notion of Caesar as the arrogant superman. . . . In the third scene Berowne exclaims:

By the Lord, this love is as mad as Ajax; it kills sheep.

The killing of the sheep by Ajax is related in Sophocles' play, from which Horace got the story.[1] It was from the Latin poets that the Elizabethans learned most about Ajax, to whom they often allude, not always for nice reasons. . . . Beginning at line 101 come the pretty verses 'On a day—alack the day!' etc., which were afterwards printed in *The Passionate Pilgrim*. They are very anacreontic in character, but verses of this character had already been written by Spenser and were not a novelty. We must not assume any knowledge of Anacreon even in the Latin versions of that poet. . . . Later, there are some classical allusions:

To see great Hercules whipping a gig (167)

And Nestor playing push-pin with the boys,
And critic Timon laugh at idle toys. (169, 170)

'Great' Hercules means Hercules the big and strong; there is no allusion to his moral or intellectual qualities. Nestor had come to typify the wisdom and gravity of old age. Shakespeare is constantly alluding to these two. This cannot be said about Timon,

---

[1] '(Aiax) mille ovium insanus morti dedit,' 'Ajax in his frenzy put a thousand sheep to death.' *Serm.* II. 3. 197. Cf. Ovid, *Amores*, I. 7. 7, 8.

though he wrote a play about him. Observe that the 'critic' Timon is the Timon of Lucian, not of Plutarch.[1] Later, in Berowne's wonderful speech, we find another cluster of classical allusions (IV. iii. 339 f.).

> Love's tongue proves dainty Bacchus gross in taste:
> For valour, is not Love a Hercules,
> Still climbing trees in the Hesperides?
> Subtle as Sphinx; as sweet and musical
> As bright Apollo's lute, strung with his hair.

Bacchus everybody knew, and Hercules, although he did not *climb* the trees like a schoolboy after apples. The Sphinx here is not of course the Egyptian statue, but the Sphinx of Thebes, whose riddle was solved by Oedipus. The notion of Apollo's lute as strung with his hair is not, so far as I can remember, classical, and may be a fancy of Shakespeare's own.

It is scarcely worth while considering the doggerel spoken by the masquers in Act Five. It contains a number of very common Latin words—*canis, manus, quoniam, ergo*—the very commonness of which betrays the poverty of Holofernes' latinity. The last sentence (if it be indeed part of the play) has hitherto baffled all interpreters. It is this:

> The words of Mercury are harsh after the songs of Apollo.

I cannot explain them any more than another. But I admit to having sometimes entertained the thought that—since *Love's Labour's Lost* is so enigmatical—the fact that Mercury (Hermes) was the god of interpretation ('hermeneutics'), especially the interpretation of oracular utterances, like those of the Delphic Apollo, may have some significance.

In this play therefore we can say that, while there is a great deal of classical quotation and allusion, it is all of the kind that could be picked up by any intelligent person in Shakespeare's age. It is the odds and ends of classical scholarship, very brilliantly

---

[1] Lucian's dialogue was called 'Timon or the Misanthrope', and was a favourite piece with Renaissance readers.

used, mostly for a satirical purpose. The only definite result we have got from our examination is the practical certainty that Shakespeare had read Lily's Grammar and part at least of the *Colloquia Familiaria* of Erasmus.

A Midsummer Night's Dream has, like *Love's Labour's Lost*, the appearance of having been written for a special occasion, namely the marriage of two persons of great distinction. It is a medley, though a very happy one, of ancient and modern, natural and supernatural; the scene throughout being Athens and its vicinity. It is not the Athens of history but of pre-history or rather mythology, though probably Shakespeare, like Plutarch himself, regarded Theseus as a historical king of Athens, which indeed he may have been, even if all we are told about him should be proved to be myth. It was in Plutarch, that is in North, that Shakespeare evidently read about Theseus, who is the subject of the first biography in the Greek writer's *Parallel Lives*. There is no evidence that he used the Knight's Tale in Chaucer or the last book of Statius' *Thebais*. It was perhaps a memory of Golding's *Metamorphoses* (VIII. 537) that led him to call Theseus a 'duke'. As regards the other *dramatis personae*, the Greek names are according to custom latinized, with the exception of Philostrate, which in Latin is Philostratus. Helena is not a likely name for a mortal girl in the Greece of Theseus, for whom there could be only one Helen. Hermia, I suspect, is suggested by Hermes, whom Shakespeare knows, rather than by Hermos, casually mentioned by Plutarch as a distinguished Athenian. Better scholars than Shakespeare ever pretended to be were equally careless about classical nomenclature. He might perhaps have been more careful than to make Aegeus (whom he calls Egeus and pronounces trisyllabically) the father of Hermia, when in fact he was the father of Theseus, as Plutarch keeps on telling him. Titania is really an adjective, applied to more than one goddess in the *Metamorphoses*, where Shakespeare must have found it.

There are, as one would expect in a play set in ancient Athens, classical allusions. Yet they are not numerous, and they are in no sense recondite. Diana as goddess of chastity, Phoebe as the moon-goddess, 'the simplicity of Venus' doves'—references of that sort are not worth recording. We have already discussed the picture of Love as winged, blind, a child, perjured (i. i. 234 f.). Hiems or Winter was a common enough figure in Elizabethan masques —he appears in the final scene of *Love's Labour's Lost*—so that a reference to 'old Hiems' thin and icy crown' would not puzzle Shakespeare's audience at all.[1] Also even the groundlings knew about Dido.

> by that fire which burn'd the Carthage queen,
> When the false Troyan under sail was seen (i. i. 173, 174).

The tale of Pyramus and Thisbe was hardly so familiar, although it had long been popular among authors. It first appears in literature in the fourth book of the *Metamorphoses* (45–166), where Shakespeare found it. It is followed with remarkable fidelity in Peter Quince's production; the lion, the wall, the tomb of Ninus—everything is there except the mulberry tree, which is important only for Ovid.

In ii. i. 70, 71 there is a reference to

> the bouncing Amazon,
> Your buskin'd mistress and your warrior love.

The Amazons are often described in the Latin poets, although the buskin is not so characteristic of them as the half-moon shield. Perhaps in Shakespeare's mind some memory was stirring of the huntress Diana or the Carthaginian girls who had the custom when hunting 'to bind their legs high up with a buskin'.[2] But he is not very safe on the Amazons. In iv. i. 116 f. we read:

> I was with Hercules and Cadmus once,
> When in a wood of Crete they bay'd the bear
> With hounds of Sparta . . .

[1] For the actual phrasing Shakespeare may have been indebted to the *Metamorphoses*, ii. 30: 'glacialis Hiems canos hirsuta capillos', 'Frozen Hiems with shaggy white hair.' When Hiems came to be represented as an old man, I do not know; the word is feminine in Latin.

[2] Alte suras vincire cothurno, *Aeneid*, i. 337—a passage Shakespeare appears to have known.

The description of the hounds which follows is clearly influenced by the description of Actaeon's hunting-dogs in Golding's version of *Metamorphoses*, III. 206–225. Shakespeare's lines are very delightful and only a pedant would find fault with them. But a pedant would say that the bear was not 'bayed' in early Greece, but merely destroyed when found. Besides, no Amazon ever was in Crete, hunting or not. And the chronology is wrong. Hercules was more or less a contemporary of Hippolyta, but Cadmus had become a snake long before she was born. It is another anachronism when Dido is mentioned in I. i. 173, for she belongs to a later generation than Theseus. These slips are rather amusing than otherwise, but the pedant might say that a better scholar would have avoided them.

In II. i. 77 f. comes a list of the loves of Theseus which seems to be taken from North's Plutarch (*Theseus*):

> Didst thou not lead him through the glimmering night
> From Perigenia, whom he ravished?
> And make him with fair Aegle break his faith,
> With Ariadne and Antiopa?

Though Theseus is represented in the play as sufficiently devoted to Hippolyta—since to represent him differently would be altogether *mal à propos* at a marriage festivity—he was, particularly in the Middle Ages, coupled with Aeneas as a false lover because of his desertion of Ariadne.

A number of classical allusions in the body of the play may be passed over as inconsiderable. But some interest attaches to the lines:

> For night's swift dragons cut the clouds full fast,
> And yonder shines Aurora's harbinger. (III. ii. 379, 380)

The dragon-borne car is probably taken from Ovid, *Metamorphoses*, VII. 218, 219.[1] But in Ovid the car belongs not to Night but to Medea. The transference is natural, for Medea is a witch-queen (almost like Hecate), who gathers her simples under the moon. The association of witchcraft with the night produces an

---

[1] 'Nec frustra volucrum tractus cervice draconum | currus adest', 'Not fruitlessly the chariot arrives, drawn by the necks of winged dragons.'

association of ideas. Night's dragons recur in 2 *Henry VI*, IV.
i. 4 f., *Cymbeline* II. ii. 48. The Moon-goddess had a chariot,[1]
which according to Milton was drawn by dragons. *Il Penseroso*,
59, 'Cynthia checks her dragon yoke.'

The list of 'sports' supplied to Theseus in v. 1. 44 f. has some
matter for us:

> 'The battle with the Centaurs, to be sung
> By an Athenian eunuch to the harp.'
> We'll none of that: that have I told my love,
> In glory of my kinsman Hercules.
> 'The riot of the tipsy Bacchanals,
> Tearing the Thracian singer in their rage.'
> That is an old device; and it was play'd
> When I from Thebes came back a conqueror.
> 'The thrice three Muses mourning for the death
> Of Learning, late deceased in beggary.'

The battle (of the Lapiths and their friends) with the Centaurs at
the marriage of Hippodamia to Pirithous is described at great
length by Ovid in the twelfth book of the *Metamorphoses*, 210–400
or thereabouts. It might very well have been sung 'to a harp' by
a minstrel of the Homeric type but not, in the heroic age, by a
eunuch. This is in fact an anachronism on the part of Shakespeare
put into his head by what he knew, which was evidently a good
deal, about music. Viola says in *Twelfth Night*, I. ii. 56 f.:

> Thou shalt present me as an eunuch to him:
> It may be worth thy pains; for I can sing
> And speak to him in many sorts of music.[2]

The words

> that have I told my love
> In glory of my kinsman Hercules

were probably suggested by something in Ovid's narrative.
After Nestor, who tells the story, has ended his account of the
battle, Tlepolemus, a son of Hercules, who has been listening,
breaks out into a complaint that Nestor has said nothing of the

---

[1] Theocritus, *Pharmac.*, 166.
[2] Consult Richard Noble, *Shakespeare's Use of Song*, pp. 133–5.

part played in the combat by Hercules. Nestor admits the charge, explaining that he cannot bear to praise Hercules because of the calamities brought by that hero upon his family (536 f.). Shakespeare, who had noted this in Ovid or Golding, evidently thought it a good touch—which it is—to make Theseus, the 'kinsman', if not the son, of Hercules, give honour where honour was due, Shakespeare being fond of Hercules anyway and always mentioning him when he can. As for the kinship, Theseus was, according to some, a son of Poseidon, who of course was the brother of Zeus, the father of Hercules. ... 'The Thracian singer' is Orpheus, whose lynching by infuriated women is related at the beginning of the eleventh book of the *Metamorphoses*. The phrase was suggested to Shakespeare by the Threicius vates of line 2. ... 'When I from Thebes came last a conqueror' recalls the incident at the end of the *Thebais* of Statius which was the germ of that poem of Boccaccio, which in turn suggested the Knight's Tale in Chaucer. Shakespeare however is not referring either to Chaucer or Boccaccio, nor directly to Statius.

I do not claim that I have exhausted the classical references in the *Midsummer Night's Dream*, a play in which it is natural that they should be found. Thus in an essay contributed to a volume called *A Tribute to Walter de la Mare* (Faber, 1948) Dover Wilson sees traces of the influence upon *The Dream* of Apuleius, whose 'Golden Asse' was translated by Adlington in 1566. This is very probable. It does not however tell us anything about Shakespeare's classical *scholarship*, which is my proper subject.

Romeo and Juliet is not founded on a classical story, and the leading characters have not much time for classical allusions, which tend to be the fruit of meditation. The drama has indeed a classical feature in the form of a versified Prologue, but it is not otherwise classical either in form or substance.

To take the allusions as they come:

Aurora's bed (1. i. 142)

This recalls the Virgilian 'Tithoni croceum linquens Aurora

cubile' (*Aeneid* IV. 585 and elsewhere).[1]   But Shakespeare is more likely to have got the hint of it from a classicizing English poet, not improbably Spenser, than from Virgil.

> at lovers' perjuries,
> They say, Jove laughs   (II. ii. 92)

This is from Ovid's *Art of Love*, I. 633.

> Iuppiter ex alto periuria ridet amantum.[2]

The line was almost proverbial, so that Shakespeare did not have to search through Ovid for it, nor need Juliet have read the *Ars*.

> Else would I tear the cave where Echo lies,
> And make her airy tongue more hoarse than mine,
> With repetition of my Romeo's name.[3]

These lines imply knowledge of the tale of Echo and Narcissus in *Metamorphoses*, III. 439 f.[4] 'Airy tongues that syllable men's names', says Milton, echoing Shakespeare in turn.

In II. iv. 40 f. Mercutio rattles out:

'Dido a dowdy; Cleopatra a gipsy; Helen and Hero hildings and harlots; Thisbe a grey eye or so, but not to the purpose.'

These were familiar names in Elizabethan ears. With them therefore we need not concern ourselves, nor with 'Titan's fiery wheels' (II. iii. 4), Titan meaning the sun;[5] nor with 'the blind bow-boy' (II. iv. 14); nor with 'the pale reflex of Cynthia's brow' (III. v. 20). When Juliet cries (III. ii. 1 f.):

> Gallop apace, ye fiery-footed steeds,
> Toward Phoebus' lodging: such a waggoner
> As Phaethon would whip you to the west,

---

[1] 'Aurora leaving the saffron bed of Tithonus.'

[2] 'Jupiter on high laughs at lovers' perjuries.'

[3] II. ii. 162 f.

[4] For Echo's cave see 394, 'solis ex illo vivit in antris', 'thereafter she lives in lonely caves', that is (by transferred epithet) 'alone in caves'.

[5] Compare 'Phoebus . . . harnessed his fyrie-footed teeme', *Faerie Queene*, I. XII. ii.

she is thinking of the first part of the second book of the *Metamorphoses*, which brilliantly relates the story of Phaethon, who took over the car, ablaze with gems, of his father Phoebus and drove them too furiously towards the west, which is 'Phoebus' lodging', since he sets there. Do not think the allusion out of character, for Juliet would be educated like the daughters of Baptista in the *Shrew* and know her Ovid, at least the *Metamorphoses*.

In I. i. 134 f. the lines,

> I, measuring his affection by my own,
> That most are busied when they're most alone,

are influenced by the first sentence of the third book of Cicero's *de Officiis*: 'Publium Scipionem . . . dicere solitum scripsit Cato . . . *numquam se minus otiosum esse quam cum otiosus, nec minus solum quam cum solus esset.*'[1] This is one of the most frequently quoted of ancient sentences and has been absorbed into modern literature. Shakespeare therefore need not have read it in Cicero. But it is not at all impossible that he did, for Tully's *Offices*, and especially the third 'book' of that work, was in the hands of every student, if not of every schoolboy. No doubt he could have read it in the translation of Nicolas Grimalde (1580). But most probably he knew it as a current saying. That it was familiar to him is suggested by the words of the Duke in *Twelfth Night*, I. iv. 40, 'I myself am best when least in company'. May not then his familiarity with the Ciceronian epigram explain the disputed words in the *Tempest*, III. i. 15: 'Most busy lest, when I do it'? I suggest 'Most busy, when lest [that is, *least*] I do it.'

We may now consider an early group of Shakespeare's historical or chronicle plays, of which *Henry VI* very probably contains the earliest of all his surviving work. The group I shall review consists of the three Parts of *Henry VI*, *Richard III*, *Richard II*, and *King John*.

King Henry VI presents a complication of difficult problems of text and authorship. These, if they can be solved, must be solved

[1] 'Cato has written that Publius Scipio was in the habit of saying that he was never less idle than when he was idle, nor less alone than when he was alone.'

by experts. But we too must follow some method in our investigation. The fairest, or at least the most impartial, is, I think, to go through the three Parts of the play on the assumption that Shakespeare was the sole author. If the evidence of classical quotations and allusions helps us to decide the question whether Shakespeare was in fact the sole author, so much the better.

As usual, I will follow the simple plan of taking the references in the order in which they come, beginning with Part One.

> Like captives bound to a triumphant car. (I. i. 22)

This must be an allusion to the Roman triumphs. It is not however accurate. In a Roman triumph the captives were not bound to the victor's car but preceded it.[1] The error did not originate with Shakespeare. It looks as if it might spring from a confusion with the so famous act of Achilles in dragging the body of Hector 'at his chariot wheels'.

> A far more glorious star thy soul will make
> Than Julius Caesar (I. i. 55)

This is another allusion to Roman history. It was popularly believed that, after the burning of Caesar's body in the forum, his soul ascended into the sky as a star. The most interesting evidence on this point is that quoted by Pliny, *Nat. Hist.*, I. §94, the interest consisting in the fact that he gives the very words of Octavius (later, Augustus) after the games in honour of Venus Genetrix instituted by him. 'Iis ipsis ludorum meorum diebus sidus crinitum per septem dies in regione caeli quae sub septentrionibus est conspectum. id oriebatur circa undecimam horam diei clarumque et omnibus e terris conspicuum fuit. eo sidere significari volgus credidit Caesaris animam inter deorum immortalium numina receptam, quo nomine id insigne simulacro capitis eius, quod mox in foro consecravimus, adiectum est.'[2] In confirmation of

---

[1] Mantegna has got it right in his *Triumph of Caesar*.

[2] 'During those very days of my games a long-haired star'—that is a comet—'was observed for seven days in the northern quarter of the sky. It arose about the eleventh hour of the day and was brilliant and clearly visible from all lands. It was popularly believed that the star was a sign that the soul of Caesar had been received among the immortal gods, on which account that blazon was added to the image of his head which shortly afterwards we consecrated in the forum.'

this the 'Julian star' (Iulium sidus) appears on the imperial coinage. The prodigies at Caesar's death are recorded in Virgil's *Georgics*, I. 416–486, Ovid's *Metamorphoses*, xv. 789 f., and Plutarch's *Caesar*. The star is specially mentioned by Ovid and by Suetonius (*div. Iul. ad finem*). All these were favourite authors throughout the Renaissance, so that the story was well known.

> The spirit of deep prophecy she hath,
> Exceeding the nine sibyls of old Rome   (I. ii. 55, 56)

The sibyls, of whom there may have been originally one, the Erythraean, gradually increased in number as time went on. They belonged to different places, the most celebrated being She of Cumae, who instructed Aeneas. But there was never, strictly speaking, a Roman Sibyl. The nine Sibyls of our passage are suggested by the nine Sibylline books offered, according to the story, by an old woman to Tarquinius.[1] These are not the same as the 'Sibylline Oracles', which have come down to us in twelve books of Greek hexameters. However the confusion arose, the Sibyls are often nine in Renaissance literature and art.

> Now am I like that proud insulting ship,
> Which Caesar and his fortunes bare at once   (I. ii. 139, 140)

This comes from Plutarch, who in his *Life of Caesar* tells us that Caesar, attempting to cross the Adriatic in a storm, bade the captain not fear, because he was 'carrying Caesar and his fortune'. Before Plutarch the incident had been narrated and developed with grandiose rhetoric by Lucan,[2] and Lucan was a favourite author with the Elizabethans. But it is in Plutarch that we find the actual phrase about bearing Caesar and his fortune. It is perhaps worth adding as an indication of scholarship that 'insulting' here means *insultans*, 'bounding', 'joyfully leaping'.

> like thee, Nero,
> Play on the lute, beholding the towns burn   (I. iv. 95 f.)

This too famous anecdote is told for the first time, very briefly, by

---

[1] Priscus or Superbus.
[2] *Pharsalia*, v. 476-677.

Suetonius in his *Life of Nero*. Our author at least knows that it was a lute on which Nero played, and not a 'fiddle'.

A witch . . . like Hannibal (I. v. 21)

The Romans were apt to ascribe Hannibal's victories to various unsoldierly devices. In Livy he is 'perfidious'; in the *Punicum Bellum* of Silius Italicus, more read in the sixteenth century than now, he actually has recourse to necromancy.

Divinest creature, Astraea's daughter (I. vi. 4)

Astraea was Justice in one of her embodiments or according to one of her epithets. She left the earth on the coming of the Iron Age. I do not know about the daughter, Astraea being *virgo* according to Virgil's fourth eclogue.

Thy promises are like Adonis' gardens
That one day bloom'd and fruitful were the next (I. vi. 6, 7)

The 'gardens of Adonis' are described by Pliny XXI. 10. 34 §60. They were hardly gardens, but pots of quickly growing vegetation, cress or the like.

A statelier pyramis to her I'll rear
Than Rhodope's or Memphis' ever was (I. vi. 21, 22)

An Egyptian pyramid, called 'of Rhodope', is mentioned by Plutarch and Pliny. But there has been a confusion of names, and Rhodope ought to be Rhodopis, as in Herodotus II. In B.R.'s translation of Herodotus it is called the pyramid of Rhodope. Neither B.R. nor our poet can well be blamed for a blunder at least as old as Pliny.

an urn more precious
Than the rich jewel'd coffer of Darius (I. vi. 24, 25)

This is probably taken from a marginal note in North's Plutarch, *Alexander*: 'Some thinke that this place should be ment of the riche coffer, that was found among king Darius juells, in the which Alexander would have all Homer's works kept.' But this note in turn comes from Pliny, *Nat. Hist.*, VII. 108 (Detlefsen): Itaque Alexander . . . inter spolia Darii . . . unguentorum scrinio

capto, quod erat de auro margaritis gemmisque pretiosum . . .
HERCULE inquit LIBRORUM HOMERI CUSTODIAE DETUR. . .[1]

> I shall as famous be by this exploit
> As Scythian Tomyris by Cyrus' death (II. iii. 5, 6)

The story of Tomyris appears first in Herodotus (I *ad. fin.*), but
it got into Justin and the Latin epitomizers, from whom comes
her exclamation 'satia te sanguine', which she uttered as she
plunged the head of the defeated and slain Cyrus into a skin full
of (no doubt human) blood.

> Then follow thou thy desperate sire of Crete,
> Thou Icarus (IV. vi. 54 f. Cf. IV. vii. 17)

The tale of Daedalus and his son Icarus is related at length by Ovid
twice over, once in *Metamorphoses*, VIII. 183–259 and again in
Ars Amatoria, II. 23–96. It is one of the Shakespearian myths.

> As if with Circe she would change my shape! (v. iii. 35)

Circe as shape-changer comes from the *Odyssey*, but what our
author knows of her in this capacity almost certainly comes from
Ovid, especially from the fourteenth book of the *Metamorphoses*
(1–74, in particular 244–319).

> Thou may'st not wander in that labyrinth;
> There Minotaurs and ugly treasons lurk (v. iii. 188, 189)

The fullest account available to the poet of Theseus, Ariadne, the
labyrinth and the Minotaur is in the eighth letter of the *Heroides*
of Ovid ('Ariadne to Theseus').

> thus he goes,
> As did the youthful Paris once to Greece,
> With hope to find the like event in love,
> But prosper better than the Trojan did (v. v. 103 f.)

---

[1] 'So, when a casket of unguents, preciously constructed of gold, pearls and
gems, had been captured among the spoils of Darius, "By Hercules", said
Alexander, "let it be given for the guardianship of the books of Homer".'
This edition was known as 'the casket Homer'. The reader may like a reference to *Don Quixote*, I. VI.

The source is again the *Heroides*, XVI and XVII, 'Paris to Helen' and 'Helen to Paris'. The latter alone is now admitted to be Ovid's, but no one in Shakespeare's day questioned the authenticity of XVI.

This brings us to *Henry VI—Second Part*.

> the realms of England, France and Ireland
> Bear that proportion to my flesh and blood
> As did the fatal brand Althaea burn'd
> Unto the prince's heart of Calydon.   (I. i. 232 f.)

The story of Althaea and Meleager is told by Ovid, *Metamorphoses*, VIII. 451 f. It was known to Shakespeare, who refers to it more than once. It may be counted one of the Shakespearian myths.

> Aio te, Aeacida, Romanos vincere posse (I. iv. 65)

The line first appears in Cicero, *de Divinatione*, II. 56, where it is quoted, evidently from Ennius, as an example of oracular ambiguity.[1] The treatise on Divination was very well known both in medieval and Renaissance times, and this line was one of the best-known things in it. Cicero himself makes fun of it; not so the Middle Ages nor our poet.

> Tantaene animis caelestibus irae? (II. i. 24)[2]

Another very well-known line; the eleventh line of the *Aeneid*.[3]

> What did I then, but cursed the gentle gusts
> And he that loosed them from their brazen caves . . . ?
> Yet Aeolus would not be a murderer (III. ii. 88 f.)

Aeolus, king of the winds, and his cave, where the winds were kept when they were not let loose upon the world, are in the *Aeneid*, I. 52 f. But Aeolus was familiar from other poets as well as Virgil, for example Ovid. Neither calls his cave 'brazen', which

---

[1] It can mean either 'I say that thou canst conquer the Romans' or 'I say that the Romans can conquer thee'.

[2] 'Are heavenly minds capable of such rages?'

[3] I have seen it suggested that there is a joke intended—in the play, not by Virgil—as if *caelestibus* might be taken as 'clerical'. But that would be an American rather than an Elizabethan joke.

is an absurd name for a cave. Yet there may be some confused recollection of what Homer says (*Odyssey*, x. 3 f.), that the isle in which Aeolus lives is surrounded by a brazen or rather bronzen wall.

> How often have I tempted Suffolk's tongue . . .
> To sit and witch me, as Ascanius did
> When he to madding Dido would unfold
> His father's acts commenced in burning Troy. (III. ii. 114 f.)

The allusion is of course to the Dido episode in Virgil. But in the *Aeneid* it is Cupid in the form of Ascanius, not Ascanius himself, who 'witches' Dido; and it is Aeneas, not his son, who unfolds the tale of Troy. It is thought that this perversion of the *Aeneid* comes from the *Roman d' Éneas* (latter half of the twelfth century), in which it is Ascanius who excites Dido's love. *Dido, Queen of Carthage* follows Virgil, not the *Roman*; and this is an argument against supposing that Marlowe's hand has been at work in this scene. Marlowe was in any case too good a scholar to accept the false version of the story.

> O thou eternal Mover of the heavens (III. iii. 19)

In the cosmology of Aristotle, which was largely adopted by the medieval theologians, the earth was stationed in the centre of a number of concentric spheres set in motion by God; the outermost sphere being called the primum mobile, because it was the first to be moved.

> ambitious Sylla (IV. i. 84)

Sylla is the Renaissance spelling of Sulla. The phrase may be taken from Spenser, *Faerie Queene*, I. v. 49, 'Ambitious Sylla and sterne Marius.'

> Bargulus the strong Illyrian pirate (IV. i. 108)

'Bardulis Illyrius latro', 'Bardulis the Illyrian pirate', Cicero *de Offic.*, II. ii. 40. No doubt some Elizabethan edition read Bargulus. But our poet need not have gone beyond the translation of Robert Whyttington, 1533, *The Thre Bookes of Tullies Offices*, who has '*Bargulus* a Pirate from the See of Illiry' or the translation of Nicolas Grimalde, 1580, who has 'Bargulus the *Illyrian Robber*'.

gelidus timor occupat artus   (IV. i. 118)

Apparently suggested by Lucan, I. 246: 'gelidus pavor occupat artus'. But it is possible that our poet, like Lucan himself, had in mind certain phrases in Virgil, e.g. *Aeneid*, VI. 54: 'gelidus Teucris per dura cucurrit | ossa tremor', 'a cold shuddering ran through the hard bones of the Trojans'. Cf., *Aeneid*, II. 120. In *Aeneid*, VII. 446, we find 'subitus tremor occupat artus.' It needs a certain amount of scholarship to *misquote* in this way, for 'timor' is as good (or nearly) as 'pavor'.

> A Roman sworder and banditto slave
> Murder'd sweet Tully; Brutus' bastard hand
> Stabb'd Julius Caesar; savage islanders
> Pompey the Great   (IV. i. 135 f.)

Tully was actually killed by Herennius, a regular officer of high rank (*tribunus militum*) under orders from such government as Rome then had. He was betrayed to Herennius by Philologus, an ex-slave, in whose education Cicero had taken an interest.[1] It may be Philologus who is meant by the 'banditto slave'. But both 'sworder' and 'slave' are inaccurate. . . . Pompey was not killed by 'savage islanders' but by a Roman centurion in the Egyptian service, as related in the *Bellum Alexandrinum*, in Lucan, and in Plutarch's *Life of Pompey*. As for 'Brutus' bastard hand', that is an allusion to the story that Brutus the conspirator was an illegitimate son of Julius Caesar. It is interesting that Shakespeare, who must have known the scandal, since it is mentioned by Plutarch and was otherwise notorious, makes no use of it in his *Julius Caesar*. It is unlikely then that it is he who makes use of it here. There may have been a medieval source, unknown to me, of these errors. I am only concerned to draw fresh attention to them, adding the remark that a competent scholar towards the end of the sixteenth century would not be guilty of them.

> Kent, in the Commentaries Caesar writ,
> Is term'd the civil'st place of all this isle (IV. vii. 65 f.).

[1] See Plutarch, *Cicero*, ch. xlviii (Sintenis).

The reference is to Caesar's *Gallic War*, v. 14. 1: ex eis omnibus longe sunt humanissimi qui Cantium incolunt.[1] Caesar's accounts of his campaigns were by Renaissance scholars called his 'Commentaries' (or 'notes'), a name for them derived from Cicero, who, justly enough, did not regard them as full-dress histories.

> And now, like Ajax Telamonius,
> On sheep and oxen could I spend my fury (v. i. 25 f.)

Telamonius Ajax comes, through the Latin poets, from Homer, who uses the epithet to distinguish the more famous Ajax from another, the Locrian Ajax. It means 'the son of Telamon'. In a passage in *Antony and Cleopatra* Shakespeare evidently confuses Telamon with Telamonius, his son. But the author of these two lines is right, if that proves anything.

> Whose smile and frown, like to Achilles' spear,
> Is able with the change to kill and cure (v. i. 100 f.)

The allusion is to a story (not in Homer but ancient) that Telephus received from the spear of Achilles a wound which could be cured only by rust from the spear itself. The poet could have got this from Hyginus or from Ovid, who alludes to it more than once, e.g. *Amores*, II. 7, 8.

> quid? non Haemonius, quem cuspide perculit, heros
> confossum medica postmodo iuvit ope?[2]

> Meet I an infant of the house of York,
> Into as many gobbets will I cut it
> As wild Medea young Absyrtus did. (v. ii. 57 f.)

The story is alluded to, not related, by Ovid in Medea's Letter to Jason[3] and in *Tristia*, III. ix. 6. It is recounted by Hyginus and Valerius Flaccus, both drawing chiefly upon Apollonius Rhodius. Rather out of Shakespeare's reading, one guesses, though he

[1] 'Of all these'—i.e. Britanni—'those who inhabit Kent are by far the most highly civilized.'

[2] 'Again, did not the Thessalian hero'—Achilles—'with healing aid afterwards assist the sore-wounded man he had struck with his spear?'

[3] *Heroides*, XII. 113 f.

might easily have come across the story and remembered it. Somewhat surprisingly Seneca does not develop it in his *Medea*, for it is sufficiently 'tragic' in his sense.

There are two places where a knowledge of the Latin language is implied. ''tis bona terra, mala gens' (IV. vii. 61). This is elementary, but the other is more interesting.

Ah! sancta majestas, who would not buy thee dear? (v. i. 5)

Sancta majestas is evidently taken from the *Ars Amatoria*, III. 407, where it means the honour in which *poets* were anciently held.

La fin couronne les œuvres (v. ii. 28)

French for 'finis coronat opus', a semi-proverbial saying, 'the end crowns the work', often found at the end of old books. These scraps of trite latinity are of course no proof of scholarship. But we must remember that, even if a dramatist were a scholar, he had to consider his audience.

Henry VI—Third Part.

Di faciant laudis summa sit ista tuae![1] (I. iii. 49)

Ovid, *Heroides*, II. ('Phyllis to Demophoon'), line 66.

> Thou art as opposite to every good
> As the Antipodes are unto us,
> Or as the south to the septentrion. (I. iv. 134 f.)

The theory of the Antipodes (which originally meant 'people with their feet opposite to ours') was embodied in the Ptolemaic cosmology and is not modern. Septentrio or Septentriones was the usual Latin word for the North. Strictly it meant a group of seven stars near the pole-star.

> Environed he was with many foes,
> And stood against them, as the hope of Troy
> Against the Greeks that would have enter'd Troy (II. i. 50, 51)

The allusion is evidently to Hector, as is made clear by IV. viii. 25 'my Hector, and my Troy's true hope'. Also it was chiefly

---

[1] 'May the gods cause that to be the sum of your glory!'

Hector who kept the Greeks out of Troy. Otherwise Aeneas might be understood, since Virgil calls Ascanius 'spes altera Troiae', 'the *second* hope of Troy', that is, after his father Aeneas.

> And, if we thrive, promise them such rewards
> As victors wear at the Olympian games (II. iii. 52, 53)

All the reward that graced the victors at the Olympic games was a garland of wild olive. The author of this couplet can hardly mean that; he must be thinking of more substantial rewards. I fear he does not know the truth of the matter, but is just being vaguely classical, that being the poetical fashion of the time.

> And so obsequious will thy father be . . .
> As Priam was for all his valiant sons (II. v. 118 f.)

This also is verbiage, contradicted at least by Homer.[1] The only son that Priam cared much about was Hector.

> Nero will be tainted with remorse (III. i. 40)

Not for burning Christians, but for killing his mother.

> I'll slay more gazers than the basilisk;
> I'll play the orator as well as Nestor,
> Deceive more slyly than Ulysses could,
> And, like a Sinon, take another Troy. (III. ii. 187 f.)

The basilisk or 'royal' serpent was supposed (Pliny, VIII. §78; XXIV. §66) to have authority over the other kinds and to wear a crown. It is described among other serpents by Lucan in a passage of Book IV immensely celebrated in later times. The notion here implied that the basilisk could slay by a glance of its eye is later.[2] . . . Nestor's eloquence is noted in Homer, but it is later poets who dwell upon it.[3] Sinon we know from *Aeneid*, II. The 'eloquent' Nestor, the 'sly' Ulysses, the 'perfidious' Sinon (who is not in Homer at all) are stock characters of the medieval matter of Troy.

---

[1] *Iliad*, XXIV. 239 f.
[2] Cf. Isidore, *Etymol*, XII. iv. 6, 7.
[3] E.g., Ovid, *Metamorphoses*, XIII. 63, 'licet eloquio fidum quoque Nestora vincat', 'though he excels even loyal Nestor in eloquence'.

Our scouts have found the adventure very easy:
That as Ulysses and stout Diomede
With sleight and manhood stole to Rhesus' tents,
And brought from thence the fatal Thracian steeds ... (IV. ii. 17 f.)

The story of Rhesus is told in *Iliad*, X and the *Rhesus*, a tragedy attributed to Euripides. But these are Greek sources and there is nothing in the English lines which could not have been got from Ovid, with one exception. Ovid refers to the Rhesus story more than once, as for example in *Heroides*, I. 1 ('Penelope to Ulixes'). There we find the expressions *dolo*, 'with sleight' and *Ismariis equis*, 'Thracian steeds'. The first line was perhaps suggested by *Metamorphoses*, XIII. 247: 'omnia cognoram, nec, quod specularer, habebam', 'I learnt everything and I had nothing to spy out', words of Ulysses in describing his foray to capture the horses of Rhesus.[1] The exception is 'fatal steeds', where 'fatal' alludes to an oracle that the Greeks would be destroyed if the horses of Rhesus drank the water of Xanthus or Scamander. The poet, I think, got this from the Latin commentary (based on Servius) upon Virgil, *Aeneid*, I. 472. 3.

Thou art no Atlas for so great a weight (V. i. 37)

Atlas, who was originally perhaps a mountain in Arcadia, was imagined as a giant who bore the weight of the sky (supposed to be made of bronze) on his neck and shoulders. He is very often mentioned in ancient poetry, as by Virgil, *Aeneid*, IV. 481 'maximus Atlas | axem umero torquet stellis ardentibus aptum', 'giant Atlas spins on his shoulders the sky studded with burning stars'. Cf. Ovid, *Metamorphoses*, IV. 631–662, Seneca, *Hercules Furens*, I. 70 f., etc. At a later stage in the development of his myth Atlas was conceived as supporting not the sky but the globe of the earth; and this no doubt is the picture which is in our poet's mind. The modern 'atlas' (of maps) gets its name from having a picture of Atlas on the outside of it.

Jove's spreading tree (V. ii. 14)

[1] Cf. *Amores*, I. 10. 23, 24 and *A.A.*, I. 135–8.

The oak. The phrase is a translation of 'patula Iovis arbore' in Ovid.[1] It recurs in *As You Like It*.

> Let Aesop fable in a winter's night;
> His currish riddles sort not with this place (v. v. 25, 26)

As this is said to Crookback, an allusion is intended to the tradition, found in the ancient Lives of Aesop, that the fabulist was a hunchback. He was regularly so represented by artists and illustrators of his *Fables*, so that the audience could be expected to take the point. 'Currish' means 'bitterly satirical', like Thersites in *Troilus and Cressida*, the metaphor coming from the ancient comparison of the Cynic philosophers to dogs. Thus Apemantus in *Timon of Athens* is a 'dog'.[2]

> They that stabb'd Caesar shed no blood at all,
> Did not offend, nor were not worthy blame,
> If this foul deed were by to equal it. (v. v. 53 f.)

The Middle Ages and the Renaissance were, like the Romans themselves, divided on the question of Caesar's assassination, Roman philosophers and authors for the most part justifying or not disapproving of it, the imperial government naturally condemning it. This divergence between the official and the literary view of the matter persisted into medieval and modern times, Dante being an exception among the writers, for reasons that need not be repeated here. The implied condemnation of Brutus and his fellows in the lines quoted may partly be explained, I suppose, by the strength of monarchical sentiments among the players. But the point will be discussed on a better opportunity—that is, when we come to *Julius Caesar*.

> What scene of death has Roscius now to act? (v. vi. 10)

Roscius was an actor in *comedy* in the time of Cicero, who wrote a speech on his behalf, which still survives.[3] It was his contemporary

---

[1] *Metamorphoses*, I. 106.
[2] Cf. O.E.D., s.v., 'Cynic'.
[3] *Pro Roscio comoedo*.

and rival Aesopus that was the tragic actor. But Aesopus, having no Cicero to perpetuate his fame, dropped out of memory; while Roscius survived as a type of all actors, and rather particularly of tragic actors. It is perhaps not fanciful to suppose that the name Aesopus by suggesting the fabulist tended to create the impression that he must have been a comedian.

> Why, what a peevish fool was that of Crete,
> That taught his son the office of a fowl! . . . (v. vi. 18–25)

This passage is influenced by *Ars Amatoria*, II. 21–100, rather than by *Metamorphoses*. VIII. 183–235.

On the whole it must be said that throughout *Henry VI* the specially 'Shakespearian' myths make no great show, whatever that may imply.

King Richard III is for a large part of it a markedly 'Senecan' play, and, so far, classical. The ghosts in the last act—if indeed they are Shakespeare's—are altogether in the vein of Roman tragedy; so is the dream of Clarence in I: iv, although a 'romantic' imagination has been at work upon it. Richard himself has a good deal of the Senecan 'tyrant', made human and convincing by Shakespeare, who gives him a distinguishing quality of cynical humour. I assume that the play is wholly the work of Shakespeare, not because I am convinced of this, but to be on the safe side in collecting evidence. Not that there is much of this. The classical allusions are few and unimportant.

> Thou cacodemon! (I. iii. 143)

'Cacodaemon' is a latinization of the Greek κακοδαίμων, a 'devil'. We cannot infer from this any knowledge of Greek. The author may have got the word from Erasmus, who uses it in his *Colloquies*, a book known to Shakespeare. I give two references, the first from *Virgo Paenitens*, the second from *Exorcismus*. (1) *Catharina*. 'Apparuit mihi spectrum horribili specie. *Eubulus*. Is nimirum erat genius tuus malus, qui te eo instigabat. *Ca*. Prorsus opinor fuisse cacodaemonem.[1] (2) 'ibi Faunus narrat sibi conspectos duos teterrimos cacodaemones.'[2]

> the melancholy flood
> With that grim ferryman that poets write of (I. iv. 46)

The ferryman of course is Charon, but the melancholy flood may be either Styx, as in the usual account, or Acheron as in *Aeneid*, VI. 299. The influence of classical mythology on Christian ideas of Hell is very curious, and I do not know that it has been well studied. Renaissance poets are often content with a Virgilian 'Hell' without believing in it.

> Did Julius Caesar build that place, my lord? (III. i. 69)

The 'place' is the Tower of London. The mistaken belief that it was built by Caesar cannot apparently be traced farther back than an Anglo-Norman chronicle of the early fourteenth century. It is countenanced by Gray in *The Bard*, although so good a scholar must have known it was false. But, since it was credited in Elizabethan times, the line must be accounted a classical allusion.

> By a divine instinct men's minds mistrust
> Ensuing dangers; as, by proof, we see
> The waters swell before a boisterous storm. (II. iii. 42 f.)

It has been thought that these lines were suggested by some in the *Thyestes* of Seneca (957–961):

> mittit luctus signa futuri
> mens, ante sui praesaga mali.
> instat nautis fera tempestas,
> cum sine vento tranquilla tument.[3]

Some influence is very probable, but it is not direct, the English

---

[1] 'There appeared to me a spectre with a horrifying aspect.' 'No doubt it was your evil genius, who was persecuting you thereby.' 'I am wholly of the opinion that it was a cacodaemon.'

[2] 'There Faunus relates that there were seen by him two grisly cacodaemons.'

[3] 'The mind exhibits symptoms of sorrow to come, prescient of its ill beforehand. Swoops on the mariners the wild storm, when without wind the calm waters swell.'

lines being versified from a passage in More's *Historie of Richard III*: 'Before such great things men's hearts of a secret instinct of nature misgive them: as the sea without wind swelleth of himself some time before a tempest'. The passage is incorporated in Holinshed (*Chron.*, III. 721). 'Divine instinct' may have been suggested by Cicero, who uses it (*divino instinctu*) of the inspiration of oracles, *de divin*, I. 18. 34.

King Richard II has even less for us than *Richard III*.

Some of those branches by the Destinies cut (I. ii. 15)

The language of this line has surely been influenced by the final Chorus of *Doctor Faustus*, 'Cut is the branch that might have grown full straight'. But what the Destinies or Fates (*Parcae* or *Fata*), or rather one of them, Atropos, cuts is not a branch but a thread—the thread of life.

The frosty Caucasus (I. iii. 295)

This may not seem to be a classical allusion, but in fact it is, for the Caucasus was only known to Elizabethan poets out of books, where it is regularly described as cold or 'frosty'. It was long thought to be situated in the far north. Ovid says, *Metamorphoses*, VIII. 788–798,

> est locus extremis Scythiae glacialis in oris . . .
> devenit in Scythiam, rigidique cacumina montis,
> Caucason appellant.[1]

Seneca speaks of 'inhospitalem Caucasum' (*Medea*, 43).

The model where old Troy did stand (V. i. 11)

The medieval chroniclers, pursuing the Brut fable, said that London had been founded on the model of Troy, hence called Nova Troja or Troynovant.

---

[1] 'There is an icy region in the remotest borders of Scythia . . . [She] comes to Scythia and the peaks of the frozen range; they call it Caucasus.'

King John yields us very little that is new.

> It lies as sightly on the back of him
> As great Alcides' shows upon an ass. (II. i. 143, 144.)

Alcides is Hercules, about whom Shakespeare knows a great deal, including this alternative name of the hero. The skin worn by Hercules was that of a lion—the Nemean lion. As Hercules constantly appeared in shows and pageants clad in an imitation of this skin, the audience would not be puzzled by the allusion. There is however another allusion here, namely to the fable of the Ass in the Lion's skin. This too an audience familiar from school days with the chief fables in 'Aesop' and Avianus would have no difficulty in grasping.

> Be Mercury, set feathers to thy heels (IV. ii. 173)

Shakespeare has many references to Mercury, generally, as here, in his capacity of messenger for Jupiter. The 'feathers' were winged sandals, called by the Roman poets *talaria*.

> this pale faint swan,
> Who chants a doleful hymn to his own death. (V. vii. 21)

This is almost a translation of a line in *Metamorphoses*, XIV. 430: carmina iam moriens canit exequialia cygnus.[1] Yet, since the song of the dying swan was a common topic of Renaissance poetry, Shakespeare may have come near Ovid by chance.

> To set a form upon that indigest
> Which he hath left so shapeless and so rude . . . (V. vii. 26, 27)

Ovid, *Metamorphoses*, I. 7 (of Chaos) 'rudis indigestaque moles', 'a rude and undigested mass'.

It seems best to go on from this point through the rest of the plays that deal with English history, since, although *Henry IV* and *Henry V* belong to Shakespeare's middle period, while *Henry VIII* is late and only partially from his hand, they form a natural sequence.

[1] 'The swan when it is already dying sings funeral songs.'

King Henry IV: First Part. (I omit allusions to matters already discussed.)

honey of Hybla (i. ii. 47)

Shakespeare is rather fond of this allusion. 'Hyblaean' is almost a stereotyped epithet of honey in the Latin poets, as 'Hyrcanian' is of tigers. Hybla was a hilly district in Sicily which had the reputation of producing the finest honey, although it had a rival in Hymettus, a hill near Athens.

I will do it in King Cambyses' vein (ii. iv. 426)

We first hear of Cambyses (in literature) in Herodotus, who tells us that he became mad—in consequence, the Egyptians believed, of an act of sacrilege against Apis, the sacred bull—and a frantic tyrant. This endeared him to Senecan dramatists, such as Thomas Preston, whose *Cambises* was no doubt in the mind of Falstaff here.

on your eyelids crown the god of sleep (iii. i. 218)

The god of sleep in Latin is Somnus, described in a famous passage of the *Metamorphoses*, XI. 592 f. But it is possible that Shakespeare really means Morpheus, a minister of Somnus, who brings dreams to men; at least Morpheus, who is described in the *Metamorphoses* passage, 634 f., came to be thought of as the god of sleep ('in the arms of Morpheus'). So Spenser, *Faerie Queene* I. 1. xxxix f. where Morpheus is described in language strongly influenced by Ovid's description of Somnus.

To turn and wind a fiery Pegasus (iv. i. 109)

Pegasus was the winged horse that carried Bellerophon. Pegasus plays a great part in Renaissance poetry, and in heraldry, and was a familiar creature to Londoners. He sprang from the blood of Medusa, slain by Perseus, who was apt to be thought, erroneously, his rider.

> to the fire-eyed maid of smoky war
> All hot and bleeding will we offer them:
> The mailed Mars shall on his altar sit
> Up to the ears in blood. (iv. i. 114 f.)

The 'fire-eyed maid of smoky war' is Bellona, the sister of Mars, but an independent goddess with a temple of her own in Rome. The Latin poets represent her as bloodthirsty and inexorable, e.g., Virgil *Aeneid*, VIII. 703, 'cum sanguineo sequitur Bellona flagello', 'Bellona follows with bloody scourge'. Cf., Statius, *Thebais*, VII. 72, 73. These lines are unusually Senecan for a play like *Henry IV*, but Shakespeare was always capable of reverting, if only for a moment, to that style. It is worth observing that Seneca and the Latin epic poets, especially Lucan and Statius, gave the Elizabethan dramatists a false notion of the real character of Graeco-Roman civilization. Seneca and Statius were writing up legends of a prehistoric age when human sacrifice and other horrors were supposed to have happened. The Elizabethans tended to transfer in their thoughts the primitive savagery of the old stories to historical Greece and Rome, and so produced plays like *Titus Andronicus*.

'bestride me'—'Nothing but a Colossus can do that' (v. i. 124)

The Colossus of Rhodes was famous throughout later antiquity, the Middle Ages and the Renaissance as one of the Seven Wonders of the World. It was a statue of Helios (the Sun), 280 feet high, which stood at the entrance to Rhodes harbour. It was brought down by an earthquake in 222 B.C., having stood for little more than half a century. The memory of it long survived and produced some false beliefs, particularly the belief that ships entering the harbour sailed between its legs. It is to this that Falstaff alludes.[1]

Another king! they grow like Hydra's heads (v. iv. 25)

The heads of the Hydra grew, two in place of one, as they were cut off. Killing the Hydra was one of the Labours of Hercules. In Greek the word means 'watersnake', but it must have looked more like an octopus, as we see from Greek vase-paintings. In fact it is a fabulous monster, defying zoological description.

'Homo' is a common name to all men (II. i. 104)

This is taken from Lily's Latin grammar.

[1] The Colossus is described in Pliny, XXXIV. 7. 18.

Henry IV: Second Part. The Induction, which brings in 'Rumour painted full of tongues', is a relic of the ancient Prologue, which is often spoken by some divine being or by a ghost, as in the *Agamemnon* and *Thyestes* of Seneca. 'Rumour' is, or is suggested by, Virgil's Fama, described in *Aeneid*, IV, that favourite book. See 181 f.:

> monstrum horrendum ingens, cui quot sunt corpore plumae,
> tot vigiles oculi subter (mirabile dictu),
> tot linguae, totidem ora sonant, tot subrigit aures.[1]

> I have read the cause of his effects in Galen (I. ii. 132)

Galen was a native of Pergamum in Asia Minor who spoke and wrote in Greek. He lectured and practised with great applause in Rome in the latter part of the second century, and was a voluminous author on medical and other subjects. Much of what he wrote has survived. In the revival of science which accompanied the revival of classical studies at the Renaissance his 'empirical' system was generally accepted until its weaknesses were exposed by the founders of modern medical science. But in Shakespeare's time Galen was still a household word among laymen as well as physicians, who read such parts of his works as had been translated into Latin.

> You rascally Althaea's dream . . . (II. ii. 93)

There is confusion here. The story of Althaea, the mother of Meleager, is told in *Metamorphoses*, VIII. 451 f. When her son was born, it was prophesied to her that he would live no longer than the brand that was then burning on the hearth. This brand therefore she seized and quenched in water. It was not Althaea but Hecuba who *dreamed* that she gave birth to a firebrand, which was Paris. Cf. 2 *Henry VI.* I. i. 234, 'the fatal brand Althaea burned'. But this refers to the revenge of Althaea upon her son, when in her rage against him she took the half-burned brand and burned it out.

---

[1] 'a monster with as many eyes at watch in her under parts, as many noisy tongues and mouths—wonderful to say—as many ears pricked up, as there are feathers on her body.'

I will imitate the honourable Romans in brevity (II. ii. 135)

It is not true that Shakespeare's Romans are just Elizabethans with Latin names. He had formed to himself a distinct idea of the Roman national character, a laconic bluntness of speech being one of its traits.

> From a god to a bull? ... It was Jove's case (II. 192)

The allusion is to the story of Europa—one of the Shakespearian myths.

> the hook-nosed fellow of Rome (IV. iii. 45)

Julius Caesar. There is no evidence that the historical Caesar had a noticeably aquiline nose. Falstaff's notion is that so great a Roman must have had a great 'Roman' nose.

> May this be wash'd in Lethe, and forgotten? (V. ii. 72)

Shakespeare often mentions Lethe. He and his contemporaries would know it best from Virgil, who says of the souls in Hades that, at a certain stage of their experience, 'Lethaei ad fluminis undam | securos latices et longa oblivia potant' (*Aeneid*, VI. 714, 715).[1] By a natural association of ideas Lethe is regarded by Shakespeare as a sluggish stream.

> Shall dunghill curs confront the Helicons? (V. iii. 108)

The Muses are often called Heliconiades in ancient poetry, and Pistol may be thinking of them, confusing noun and adjective. Helicon of course was the Greek mountain sacred, as poets knew, to the Muses. (It should be distinguished from Parnassus, which was sacred to Apollo.) Here and elsewhere Pistol's rodomontade is garnished with classical allusions, although he very often gets them wrong. It reflects his favourite literature, which was drama of the *Tamburlaine* type. One imagines him an Alleyne 'fan'.

> 'Tis 'semper idem' for 'obsque hoc nihil est' (V. v. 30)

What Pistol meant by this I do not know; neither, one suspects, did he.

[1] 'At the wave of Lethe river they quaff care-free waters and long forgetfulness.'

Rouse up revenge from ebon den with fell Alecto's snake (v. v. 39)

This is altogether in the manner of the Revenge plays. Though Shakespeare uses Pistol to make fun of them, it is as Cervantes makes fun of the romances that crazed Don Quixote. . . . Alecto (Allecto) is described by Virgil, *Aeneid*, VII. 324 f. . . . For the snake see line 329: 'tot pullulat atra colubris', 'so many are the blackening snakes that sprout from her.'

> trumpet-clangor sounds (v. v. 41)

Is this an echo of *Aeneid*, II. 313, 'clangor tubarum' ?

Henry V.

Prologue. Enter *Chorus.*

A Greek Chorus normally consisted of fifteen dancers. Its function is to sing as well as dance; if it speaks at all, it is through the mouth of its leader. This convention made it easier to think of a single person as Chorus. In *Henry V* we find a single person speaking the Prologue, but he ought not to be called *Chorus*, because the Prologue of a tragedy is 'that part which precedes the entry of the Chorus'. This definition is in all the critics, and one may perhaps infer that Shakespeare had not troubled to read them, at least with attention.

> The Gordian knot of it he will unloose. (I. i. 46)

The incident of the Gordian knot, which Alexander the Great loosened by cutting it with his sword, is related in Plutarch's *Alexander*, in Curtius, III. i. 15 f., and Justin, XI. vii. 11. It struck the Renaissance imagination, and 'the Gordian knot' became proverbial.

> for so work the honey bees . . . (I. ii. 187 f.)

The probable germ of this passage (in Elyot) has been discussed by Dover Wilson in his edition of the play. On the subject of bees the literary tradition in Renaissance times goes back to Virgil (*Georgics IV*), who like all the ancients (except Xenophon) thought the queen was a king. Otherwise Virgil's account is much more scientific than Shakespeare's, and there is no direct influence.

vasty Tartar (II. ii. 123)

'Tartar' is Tartarus, the classical Hell, best known to the Renaissance from the sixth book of the *Aeneid*, 547 f.

> Were but the outside of the Roman Brutus,
> Covering discretion with a coat of folly. (II. iv. 37, 38)

It is the earlier Brutus, the expeller of the Tarquins, that is meant. To escape the jealousy and suspicion of the king, he pretended to be mad or half-witted. The most probable source for Shakespeare, apart from some English book or some lexicon, is Ovid, *Fasti*, II. 559–562. But the 'madness' of Brutus is mentioned by other classical authors, such as Livy and Plutarch (*Life of Brutus*).

> giddy Fortune's furious fickle wheel,
> That goddess blind,
> That stands upon the rolling, restless stone. (III. vi. 27 f.)

Fortune, with all these attributes (explained in Fluellen's commentary) was an exceedingly familiar figure to Elizabethans. Although she was a very important deity while the Roman empire lasted, it was in the Middle Ages, with their love of allegorical and symbolic figures, that Fortune was most completely visualized. What 'poet' Fluellen had in mind is not clear (perhaps even to himself); but many poets, since Boethius and even earlier, had celebrated, and many artists depicted, her. It is likely enough (though we do not know) that the Fortune theatre, built in 1600, was adorned by a figure of the goddess standing on her ball. In the Kenilworth inventory (1584) there is the description of a salt in the form of a ship on the stern of which was 'the image of Dame Fortune standing on a globe'.

'The basest horn of his hoof is more musical than the pipe of Hermes.' (III. vii. 14)

The pipe of Hermes, which he used to lull Argus asleep, is described in the *Metamorphoses*, 1. 677 f. But in that passage Ovid does not call him Hermes but Mercurius. Of course the name Hermes occurs often enough in Latin literature, but Shakespeare must have the credit of knowing that Hermes and Mercury were the same.

> It is a beast for Perseus: he is pure air and fire (III. vii. 22)

As we remarked, it was not Perseus but Bellerophon who rode Pegasus. But Shakespeare was not the first (or last) to fall into this misunderstanding.

> Doth rise and help Hyperion to his horse (IV. i. 292)

Shakespeare may have got Hyperion from Ovid. Strictly speaking Hyperion was the father of the Sun, but Latin poets often confound them. Nowhere, however, in the classical poets does the Sun ride upon a horse; he drives a chariot, as Shakespeare might have remembered from the story of Phaethon.

> There is a river in Macedon (IV. vii. 24)

The Strymon (modern Struma). Fluellen, an officer of some reading in the ancient wars, might know this. But would Shakespeare?

> 'Alexander . . . in his rages . . . and also being a little intoxicates . . . did kill his best friend Cleitus.' (IV. 7. 39)

Shakespeare may have taken this from North. But the story was well enough known, before Plutarch was translated, from Curtius Rufus, a favourite author with Renaissance readers. There was a translation of Curtius, published in 1553, from the hand of John Brende. It is interesting that Shakespeare's Alexander is the historical king of Macedonia and not the half-mythical being of medieval legend, as we find him in the Pseudo-Callisthenes and the verse romances dependent on that.

> dost thou thirst, base Trojan,
> To have me fold up Parca's fatal web? (v. i. 20. Cf. 32)

There were, according to the usual account, three Parcae or Fates, not one, as Pistol seems to think; and they did not weave, they spun. It was usually the Greeks, not the Trojans, who were regarded as 'base'. But it is all one to mine Ancient.

> all hell shall stir for this (v. i. 70)

Was this perhaps suggested by the famous words of Juno in *Aeneid*, VII. 312?

> flectere si nequeo superos, Acheronta movebo.[1]

'Praeclarissimus filius' etc. is of course diplomatic Latin (v. 2). The only other Latin in the play worth mentioning is in II. iii. 54:

> Caveto be thy counsellor.

This has a proverbial ring. In any case *caveto* is a word that might easily be picked up by someone who was not a latinist.

Henry VIII.

> Orpheus with his lute made trees ... (III. i. 3 f.)

Compare Virgil, *Georgics*, 510 (of Orpheus): 'mulcentem tigres et agentem carmine quercus', 'soothing tigers and drawing oaks by his song'. But references to Orpheus are innumerable both in ancient and in Renaissance literature.

In *Henry VIII* a number of Latin words and phrases are quoted. Some like 'cum privilegio' and 'viva voce' are trite. 'In limbo Patrum' (v. iv. 67), 'in the Limbus of the Fathers', appears to mean what, since Dante, we call Limbo, which is merely the Italian for limbus. At any rate this is hardly a classical allusion. . . . 'Ego et rex meus' (III. ii. 314) is quoted, as usual, to prove Wolsey's arrogance. Arrogant no doubt he was, but this quotation does not prove it; rather it proves that Wolsey was a better Latin scholar than his critics. In Latin the important person in a list is mentioned last. . . . The Latin attributed to Wolsey in III. i. 41 f.: 'Tanta est erga te mentis integritas, regina', etc., is in good classical style. . . . Since the play is thought to be mainly the work of Fletcher, we can only guess at the extent of Shakespeare's contribution. It is of course not baseless guessing, but

---

[1] 'If I cannot bend the gods of Heaven, I will stir up Hell.'

certainty is unattainable. We cannot say then that any of this Latin is Shakespeare's. Fortunately it would not affect our estimate, if it all was his. For none of it is significant.

We may now take a group of comedies which belong to Shakespeare's middle period: *Much Ado About Nothing, The Merry Wives of Windsor, As You Like It.*
Much Ado About Nothing.

In time the savage bull doth bear the yoke (I. i. 260)

This is a translation, or rather a summary, of a couplet in Ovid, *Tristia*, IV. 6. 1, 2.

tempore ruricolae patiens fit taurus aratri,
praebet et incurvo colla premenda iugo.[1]

born under Saturn (I. iii. 12)

Astrology originated in Babylonia, chiefly, and was little known or regarded by the Greeks until they came in contact with the East through the conquests of Alexander. But after that it took some hold of the Western mind. The new interest found expression in the *Astronomica*, a long poem by Manilius, written in the first quarter of the first century. But only scholars could read the *Astronomica*, and that with extreme difficulty, and the ordinary man was content with a few 'rules' of the pseudo-science and the hope that there might be something in it. He did not clearly distinguish between astronomy and astrology. The history of the subject is important, though it is largely the history of nonsense. Quintilian says that one cannot understand the poets without some knowledge of the stars, and this is true of English literature up to and including Dryden.

My visor is Philemon's roof; within the house is Jove.
HERO. Why then your visor should be thatched. (II. i. 99 f.)

This is to be explained from the story of Baucis and Philemon in *Metamorphoses*, VIII. 626–724—in Golding's version, as the metre

---

[1] 'In time the bull becomes patient of the farmer's plough and offers his neck to be pressed by the curving yoke.'

indicates. Baucis and Philemon were an old married couple, very poor, who lived by themselves in a mean cottage *stipulis et canna tecta palustri*, 'thatched with straw and reeds from the mere'. Golding translates 'The roofe thereof was thatched all with straw and fennish reede', and this was in Shakespeare's mind when he used the word 'thatched'. Jupiter and Mercury were in disguise when they visited the cottage.

> an embassage to the Pigmies (II. i. 278)

Although the Pigmies (rather Pygmies) are mentioned in Homer, the Renaissance gets its information about them in the main from Pliny, e.g., VI. xxx. §35. 188; IV. ii. §18. 44; V. xxix. §29. 109. Ovid mentions them twice.

> How now! Interjections?... (IV. i. 21)

The mocking reference is to Lily's grammar, which deals with 'interjections'.

> For there was never yet philosopher
> That could endure the toothache patiently,
> However they have writ the style of gods
> And made a push at chance and sufferance (V. i. 36 f.)

The kind of philosopher here meant is a Stoic of the type depicted in the philosophical works of Cicero and Seneca. The Stoic held that pain was of no importance in itself, and that the good man was independent of fate and chance. By 'writ in the style of gods' Shakespeare is not describing the literary style of philosophers but their way of writing as if they were more than mortal beings. It was not necessary for him to read the Latin sages in order to form this opinion about them.

> And Hymen now with luckier issue speeds (V. iii. 32)

Hymen was the classical god of marriage. He was represented as a youth wearing a saffron dress and carrying a torch. A great figure at Renaissance marriage festivities.

> I think he thinks upon the savage bull.
> Tush, fear not, man; we'll tip thy horns with gold,

> And all Europa shall rejoice at thee,
> As once Europa did at lusty Jove,
> When he would play the noble beast in love (v. iv. 42 f.)

The 'savage bull' alludes to the couplet already quoted from *Tristia*. The Europa story is in *Metamorphoses*, II. 835–III. 2. It was an ancient custom, as old as Homer, to tip with gold the horns of a sacrificial victim. Shakespeare evidently knew this—rather surprisingly, perhaps.

The Merry Wives of Windsor.

> Shall I Sir Pandarus of Troy become? (I. iii. 83)

Although Pandarus appears in Homer, his character as pander is not ancient. For English readers it was stamped upon him by Chaucer, almost the only medieval poet for whom the Elizabethans cared, although they used Lydgate for his matter.

> lie under Mount Pelion (II. i. 81)

The Thessalian mountain on which the sons of Aloeus were for piling Ossa, and Ossa on Olympus. This is the Homeric form of the story. In later poets it is the Giants who essay the feat. The most celebrated text for Renaissance writers was Virgil, *Georgics*, I. 281 f.

> Like Sir Actaeon he, with Ringwood at thy heels (II. i. 122)

The story of Actaeon we have already noted as Shakespearian. 'Ringwood' is the name of one of Actaeon's hounds in the translation of Golding, who substitutes it apparently for Ovid's *Hylactor* ('Barker'). Here we have incontestable evidence of Shakespeare's using the translation instead of consulting the original.

> 'What says my Aesculapius?' (II. iii. 29; cf. 66)

Aesculapius, the god of medicine, Shakespeare could read about in the *Metamorphoses*, xv. 622 f. or in *Fasti*, 651 f., a passage in which it may be remarked that Diana is called Dictynna. No doubt he read what Spenser has said about Aesculapius in *The Faerie Queene*, I. v. 36 f. But Aesculapius, with his snake-encircled rod, had been adopted by the medical profession as, so to speak, their patron saint and would be known to Shakespeare from that circumstance.

> Knowledge in Hibocrates and Galen (III. i. 64)

Galen was known to every Elizabethan as the most celebrated of physicians. But Hippocrates, the founder of medical science, a native of the Greek island of Cos, was a mere name to Shakespeare and his audience, though as a name familiar enough, largely because he is constantly being mentioned by Galen.

> 'William, how many numbers is nouns?'
> 'Two. . . .'
> 'What is "lapis", William?'
> 'A stone.' (IV. i. 21 f.)

I quote from Lily's grammar. 'In Nounes be two Numbers, the Singular, and the Plurall. The Singular Number speaketh of one: as *Lapis*, a stone, The Plurall Number speaketh of mo than one; as *Lapides*, Stones.'

> 'What is "fair", William?'
> 'Pulcher.' (*ib.*)

On the same page of Lily we have '*Bonus*, Good; *Pulcher*, Fayre.'

> 'What is he, William, that doth lend articles?'
> 'Articles are borrowed of the pronoun, and be thus declined,
> Singulariter, nominativo, hic, haec, hoc.' (ib. 39 f.)

Lily says: 'Articles are borrowed of the Pronoune, and be thus declined.

> *singulariter. Nominativo* hic, haec, hoc'

Later Sir Hugh elicits from William, who at first ventured 'hinc', that the accusative of *hic* is 'hunc', or, as Lily puts it, *Accusativo, hunc, hanc, hoc.*

> 'What is the focative case, William?'
> 'O,—vocativo, O.'
> 'Remember, William; focative is caret.' (*ib.*)

So Lily: *Vocativo caret.*

Later William correctly gives the genitive plural: *horum, harum, horum.*[1] The whole of this scene then is a lesson in accidence drawn from Lily's Latin grammar, which therefore Shakespeare read and remembered from his school-days. What other explanation is possible? He was not studying Latin grammar when he wrote *The Merry Wives*; he was remembering with humorous malice what he had gone through at school. Has the reader not noticed his unfailing sympathy with schoolboys?

>   ·to speak like an Anthropophaginian (IV. v. 10)

The speaker is thinking of anthropophagus—a word known to Shakespeare. 'Anthropophagian' might just pass.

>   the hot-blooded gods assist me! (v. v. 2)

The loves of the gods form a great part of ancient mythology, as Virgil recognized, *Georgics*, IV. 347, 'aque Chao densos divom enumerabat amores.'[2] Shakespeare knew them from the *Metamorphoses*.

>   You were also, Jupiter, a swan for the love of Leda (v. v. 23)

See, especially, Ovid, *Amores*, I. ii. 3, 4. The *Amores* had been translated by Marlowe.

As You Like It.

fleet the time carelessly, as they did in the golden world (I. i. 125)

The 'golden world' is the *aurea aetas* described by Ovid towards the beginning of the *Metamorphoses*. Cf. *Amores*, III. 8. 35 f. It is the *Saturnia regna* of Virgil's Fourth Eclogue, for in it Saturn was king. Men were innocent then, and the earth brought forth its fruits spontaneously. It was a Garden of Eden existence.

>   And whereso'er we went, like Juno's swans,
>   Still we went coupled and inseparable (I. iii. 77, 78)

---

[1] It is perhaps worth observing that with *Nominativo, Accusativo*, etc., *casu* is to be understood, 'in the nominative, accusative, etc. *case*.'

[1] The bard 'recounted the numerous loves of the gods, beginning with Chaos'.

The swans do not belong to Juno, whose bird is the peacock, but to Venus. See *Metamorphoses*, x. 708, 'iunctisque per aera cygnis', 'through the air, behind her coupled swans'.

> I'll have no worse a page than Jove's own page;
> And therefore look you call me Ganymede (i. iii. 126)

The story of Ganymede is briefly related by Ovid in the tenth book of the *Metamorphoses* (155–61), by Hyginus and others. He plays but a little part in ancient literature, but a great one in the poetry of the Renaissance.

> All the world's a stage . . . (ii. vii. 139 f. Jaques's speech)

T. W. Baldwin has traced this to Palingenius:

> Si recte aspicias, vita haec est fabula quaedam,
> Scena autem mundus versatilis, histrio et actor
> Quilibet est hominum, mortales nam proprie omnes
> Sunt personati et falsa sub imagine vulgi
> Praestringunt oculos: ita dis risumque iocumque
> Stultitiis nugisque suis per saecula praebent.[1] (*Zodiacus Vitae*)

Palingenius may, as Professor Baldwin suggests, have borrowed the idea from Vives, who perhaps got it from Petronius. At least the inscription on the portico of the Globe Theatre (where *As You Like It* is thought to have been produced), 'Totus mundus agit histrionem', 'All the world plays the actor', is adapted from a fragment of Petronius' *Satyricon*: 'totus fere mundus mimum videtur implere . . . non duco contentionis funem, dum constet inter nos quod fere totus mundus exerceat histrionem', 'Almost the whole world is seen to fill a rôle . . . I won't haul upon the rope of controversy, provided that it is agreed between us that almost the whole world plays the actor.' The sentiment then would be familiar to Shakespeare without his reading Palingenius. So far

---

[1] 'If you look at it rightly, this life is a play; the scene is the revolving world, player and actor is every man, for all mortals are truly masked characters, and under a deceptive appearance they dazzle the eyes of the multitude. Thus they furnish the gods with laughter and jest through the ages by their folly and trifling.'

as I have read, the division of life's drama into seven acts is Shakespeare's own.

> thrice crowned queen of night, survey
> With thy chaste eye, from thy pale sphere above,
> Thy huntress' name (III. ii. 2f.)

The Romans identified their Diana with the Greek Artemis, a goddess of the wild, who had in her turn usurped most functions of the Moon-goddess—generally called Cynthia by the Elizabethans—and of the goddess of witches, Hecate, who was also the presiding spirit wherever three roads met. For this or some other magical reason she was often represented with three heads, which might be crowned. The 'sphere above' is not the globe of the moon but the sphere in which it is fixed and which carries it round. It is of course a hollow sphere, while the earth, about which it revolves, is fixed. It is impossible to understand Shakespeare adequately without some knowledge of the old (classical) cosmology.

'Atalanta's better part' (III. ii. 155). Cf. 'Atalanta's heels' (III. ii. 292)

The story of Atalanta, the swift runner, is related to Adonis by Venus in the tenth book of the *Metamorphoses*, 560–704.

'I was never so berhymed since Pythagoras' time, that I was an Irish rat, which I can hardly remember.' (III. ii. 186).

Pythagoras' doctrine of metempsychosis or the transmigration of souls is expounded at great length in the fifteenth book of the *Metamorphoses*. That was the great source of Renaissance information upon the subject. The attribution of the doctrine to Pythagoras is probably correct, although it is only traditional, for Pythagoras left no book. Shakespeare refers more than once to the view of Pythagoras, sometimes to make fun of it. The theologians condemned it as unorthodox.[1]

'It may well be called Jove's tree when it drops such fruit.' (III. ii. 249)

[1] Cf. *Merchant of Venice*, IV. i. 130 f.

A clear reminiscence of the line in *Metamorphoses*, I. 106:

> et quae deciderant patula Iovis arbore glandes.[1]

'O Lord, Lord . . . mountains may be removed with earthquakes and so encounter.' (III. ii. 194)

Perhaps an allusion to a passage in Pliny on earthquakes, *Nat. Hist.* II. 83 (Detlefsen): namque montes duo inter se concurrerunt crepitu maximo adsultantes recedentesque, thus translated by Holland: 'two hilles encountred together, charging as it were, and with violence assaulting one another, yea and retiring againe with a most mightie noise.'

'I am here with thee and thy goats, as the most capricious poet, honest Ovid, was among the Goths.' (III. iii. 7 f.)

The place of Ovid's exile, Tomi or Tomis, was among the Goths (*Getae*). Cf.

> non mea verba legis, qui sum summotus ad Istrum,
> non bene pacatis flumina pota Getis[2] (*Ep. ex Ponto*, IV. 90)

There is of course a pun on 'Goths' and 'goats'; but it is not always observed that 'capricious' is meant to recall its derivation from caper, a he-goat. Shakespeare knew enough Latin to make this joke. But caper is a word that is always recurring in Latin pastoral poetry and therefore one of the first likely to be learned by a schoolboy.

the heathen philosopher (v. i. 35)

A creature of Touchstone's imagination.

Wedding is great Juno's crown (v. iv. 147)

Juno presided over Roman marriages under the epithet of *pronuba*. Shakespeare is aware of her nuptial functions and brings her—if

---

[1] 'And acorns which had fallen from Jove's spreading tree'—the oak. Cf. 3 *Henry VI.*, v. ii. 14.

[2] 'You are not reading the words of me, that have been removed to the Danube, a river drunk by half-tamed Getae.'

it is he that brings her—on the stage in that capacity. No doubt he had seen her in wedding-masques.

Let us now look through the four great tragedies, beginning with the earliest, *Hamlet*.

It has some Senecan characteristics—a ghost seeking revenge, killings within a family—but these are inherent in the story, not imported by Shakespeare, who moreover has softened and humanized them in such a way as greatly to neutralize their quality of horror. It should also be remembered that Seneca did not invent (though he exaggerated) the grim incidents of his plots. The myths on which he worked are traditional and conform to certain laws of the mythopoeic imagination. The Hamlet story, as Gilbert Murray has observed, is comparable to a Greek myth, especially to the myth of Orestes, which cannot be shown to have influenced it. Accordingly we may say that in writing *Hamlet* Shakespeare was dealing with just such material as Aeschylus and Sophocles and Euripides found to their hand when they wrote their tragedies about Orestes. This is a far more interesting fact than any real or supposed indebtedness to the Senecan stage.

> In the most high and palmy state of Rome,
> A little ere the mightiest Julius fell,
> The graves stood tenantless and the sheeted dead
> Did squeak and gibber in the Roman streets (i. i. 113 f.)

See *Julius Caesar*, recently written and still in Shakespeare's mind. The omens before Caesar's death strongly impressed his imagination. In this he showed himself a child of his time. *Hamlet* has been a good deal misunderstood by people who think that the ghost there is only a theatrical device. Shakespeare's audience did not so regard it; nor, for all we know, did Shakespeare.

> like Niobe, all tears (i. ii. 148)

The story of Niobe is told in *Metamorphoses*, VI. 146 f.

> a beast that wants discourse of reason (i. ii. 150)

This distinction between man and beast is Greek. From the Greek philosophers it was received by the Roman, and from the Roman by the modern. Plato and most subsequent Greek philosophers did not deny a soul to animals, but a *reasonable* soul; and the implied question, which hardly anyone now asks himself, profoundly interested and disturbed the old theologians.

Hic et ubique? (I. v. 155)

'Here and everywhere'. Said to be a magical formula. How did Shakespeare come to know it?

Hercules and his load too (II. ii. 379)

Thought to be an allusion to the sign of the Globe theatre, which was a giant carrying a globe on his shoulders. One would naturally take him to be Atlas, but here is Shakespeare calling him Hercules. The identification is possible, because it is part of the legend of Hercules that, when he travelled to the west to win the apples of the Hesperides, he relieved Atlas of his burden until Atlas had fetched the apples.

The rugged Pyrrhus . . . (II. ii. 473 f.)

The matter, or rather the suggestion, of this speech comes from Virgil, *Aeneid*, II. 469 f. Hardly any passage of Virgil, perhaps none, is more frequently alluded to in post-classical literature than this, and it is the chief cause of the medieval and even Elizabethan conception of Pyrrhus as the ruthless warrior *par excellence*. The style of the Shakespearian speech is epic rather than dramatic, the language influenced in part by the speech of Aeneas in Marlowe's *Dido, Queen of Carthage*.

What's Hecuba to him, or he to Hecuba,
That he should weep for her? (II. ii. 586)

I am inclined to think that, when Shakespeare wrote these words, he may have had at the back of his mind a passage in Plutarch's *Life of Pelopidas*, where we are told that Jason, the tyrant of Pherae, wept to behold the sorrows of Hecuba enacted on the stage. See Dover Wilson's edition of *Hamlet*, p. 300.

Tellus' orbed ground (III. ii. 166)

SHAKESPEARE AND THE CLASSICS

The terrestrial globe. Tellus is the (deified) land as opposed to Neptune.

> For thou must know, O Damon dear,
>   This realm dismantled was
> By Jove himself (III. ii. 292 f.)

Damon is a name from pastoral poetry, which frequently cele-brated the Golden Age, 'dismantled' by Jove.

> A station like the herald Mercury
> New-lighted on a heaven-kissing hill (III. iv. 58, 59)

With this has been compared *Aeneid*, IV. 252 (of Mercury alighting on Mount Atlas) 'hic primum paribus nitens Cyllenius alis | con-stitit.[1] Commentators too rarely reflect that Shakespeare may have seen Mercury in this attitude in some or many works of art.

> thy rebellion looks so giant-like (IV. v. 121)

The point of this has been missed. The rebellion of the Giants against the king of the gods was the great classical instance of *lèse-majesté*. See Ovid, *Metamorphoses*, I. 152: 'affectasse ferunt regnum caeleste Gigantas'.[2] There is a fuller account, but less likely to be familiar to Shakespeare, in the *Fasti*, v. 35–42. No subject was more popular with ancient artists, and it was well enough known to Elizabethan poets for Shakespeare to use it here.

> make Ossa like a wart! (v. i. 306)

Compare Erasmus, *Colloquies*, *Naufragium*. *Ad.* 'vidistine um-quam Alpes?' *An.* 'vidi'. *Ad.* 'illi montes verrucae sunt, si con-ferantur ad undas maris'.[3] Shakespeare uses the *Naufragium* again in *The Tempest*.

> I am more an antique Roman than a Dane (v. ii. 352)

The Romans did not condemn suicide in certain circumstances. A good many Stoics (including Cato and Brutus) killed them-selves. Plato on the other hand in his *Phaedo* condemns suicide,

---

[1] 'Here first Mercury took his stand buoying himself on equal wings.'

[2] 'They relate that the Giants aspired to the sovereignty of heaven.'

[3] 'ADOLPHUS. Have you ever seen the Alps? ANTONIUS. Yes. AD. Those mountains are warts, compared to the waves of the sea.'

but the effect of the arguments in that dialogue in favour of the immortality of the soul was to make at least two ancient readers, Cleombrotus and Cato—Addison's Cato—seek the way to immortality through self-slaughter.

Macbeth is in many respects the most classical of all Shakespeare's plays. It employs, more powerfully and overtly than any other, the method of tragic irony, which gets its effects by working on the foreknowledge of the audience—here communicated by the Witches—of what is to come. And the killing of Duncan is, in the Greek manner, done off the stage. It is at least arguable that these affinities are not accidental, for there is, after every abatement has been made, clear evidence that Shakespeare had Seneca a good deal in his mind when he was writing *Macbeth*.

> But in these cases
> We still have judgement here; that we but teach
> Bloody instructions, which, being taught, return
> To plague the inventor: this even-handed justice
> Commends the ingredients of our poison'd chalice
> To our own lips (i. vii. 8 f.)

It has been suggested that these lines are inspired by Seneca, *Hercules Furens*, 735, 736:

> quod quisque fecit patitur: auctorem scelus
> repetit suoque premitur exemplo nocens.[1]

One cannot rule out the possibility of some influence here; but it has to be said that the condition we required in such cases—that the thought should have something original or unusual about it—is not fulfilled. On the contrary the thought is one that often occurs, and so may have occurred to Shakespeare. And the other condition—that the expression of the later passage should reflect the expression of the earlier—is not fulfilled either. But it is said that there is in *Macbeth* another proof that Shakespeare had been

---

[1] 'What each man has done, he suffers; a crime strikes back at its author, and the guilty is crushed by the precedent he set.'

reading the *Hercules Furens*. For the Chorus of that play sings of
Sleep (1065 f.):

> tuque o domitor,
> Somne, laborum, requies animi,
> pars humanae melior vitae,
> volucer, matris genus Astraeae,
> frater durae languide Mortis,
> veris miscens falsa, futuri
> certus et idem pessimus auctor;
> pater o rerum, portus vitae,
> lucis requies noctisque comes . . .[1]

Who can help thinking of Macbeth's cry (II. ii. 35 f.)?

> the innocent sleep,
> Sleep that knits up the ravell'd sleave of care,
> The death of each day's life, sore labour's bath,
> Balm of hurt minds, great nature's second course,
> Chief nourisher in life's feast . . .

To deny any connexion here would argue too negative a frame
of mind. But the point is not easily decided. For there is an
equally striking parallel in Ovid, *Metamorphoses*, XI. 623 f.:

> Somne, quies rerum, placidissime, Somne, deorum,
> pax animi, quem cura fugit, qui corpora duris
> fessa ministeriis mulces reparasque labori.[2]

It is obvious that this is the source of the Senecan passage: so why
may it not be the source of the Shakespearian? The point, it
seems, must be left undecided. Macbeth's is not the only invocation of Sleep in Shakespeare; there is of course the famous speech
of Henry IV. As for *Macbeth*, the murder of sleep is a motif
that runs through the play, whereas the invocation in Seneca is

---

[1] 'And thou, O Sleep, tamer of toils, peace of the soul, the better part of
human life, wingèd one, son of Justice, tired brother of hard Death, mingling
true and false, sure but also most evil teacher of that which is to come, father of
a world, haven of life, rest from the light and companion of Night.'

[2] 'O Sleep, rest of the world, Sleep gentlest of gods, peace of the mind, whom
care flies, who dost soothe bodies worn out by hard services and dost refresh
them for toil.'

a mere piling up of somewhat conventional or derivative epithets
in a choral interlude. Macbeth's imagery is much more subtle
and imaginative, and does not seem in any *vital* way suggested
by Seneca or Ovid. The most striking similarity is in the syntax.
But here again Shakespeare is following a method—the development of a thought in successive parallels—which is his own at
least as much as Seneca's, though its originator for both is, or is
mainly, Ovid. There is a supreme example in this very play:
'Life is a walking shadow, a poor player' and so on. These considerations make me hesitate before accepting the view that
Shakespeare in this place is directly imitating Seneca. I do not
say it is impossible. It is perhaps more likely that he is influenced
merely by Sidney's famous sonnet, *Astrophel*, xxxix.

> Bellona's bridegroom (I. ii. 55)

Mars is the companion but not, in classical authors, the bride-
groom of Bellona.

> have we eaten on the insane root
> That takes the reason prisoner? (I. iii. 85)

This has evidently been suggested by a passage in Plutarch's *Life
of Antony*, where he says, XLV (937) that the Roman army cam-
paigning in the Syrian desert were compelled by hunger to eat
'a certain herb which led through madness to death'.[1]

> witchcraft celebrates
> Pale Hecate's offerings (II. i. 51. Cf. III. ii. 41)

A good commentary on this is what Burton says, *Anatomy of
Melancholy*, Pt. I. sec. 2. mem. 1. subs. 3.

> Will all great Neptune's ocean wash this blood
> Clean from my hand? No, this my hand will rather
> The multitudinous seas incarnadine,
> Making the green one red (II. ii. 60 f.)

Seneca, *Hippolytus*, 715 f. has:

> Quis eluet me Tanais aut quae barbaris
> Maeotis undis Pontico incumbens mari?

---

[1] ἥψαντό τινος πόας ἐπὶ θάνατον διὰ μανίας ἀγούσης

> Non ipse toto magnus Oceano pater
> Tantum expiarit scelus.[1]

Again in *Hercules Furens*, 1323 f. we read:

> Quis Tanais . . .
> Abluere dextram poterit?[2]

These are parallels, certainly; yet may not be models.

> destroy your sight
> With a new Gorgon (II. iii. 76, 77)

The Gorgon is Medusa, whose head, cut off by Perseus, turned to
stone anyone who looked on it. It afterwards appeared on the
shield of Athena (Minerva). See Ovid, *Metamorphoses*, IV.
664–V. 249.

> by the clock 'tis day . . .
> When living light should kiss it (II. iv. 6–10)

There is perhaps some memory here of Seneca's *Agamemnon*,
726, 727:

> fugit lux alma et obscurat genas
> Nox alta et aether abditus tenebris latet.[3]

Cf. *Thyestes* (Chorus), 790–885, where the Sun is described as
turning back in horror at the crimes he saw.

> under him,
> My Genius is rebuked; as, it is said,
> Mark Antony's was by Caesar (III. i. 55 f.)

Shakespeare found this in Plutarch's *Life of Antony*. Caesar here is
Octavius (Augustus), not Julius.

> our monuments
> Shall be the maws of kites (III. iv. 72)

---

[1] 'What Tanais'—the river Don—'or what Maeotis'—the Sea of Azov—
'leaning with its barbarian waves upon the Pontic'—the Black—'Sea will wash
me clean? Not the great father himself with all his Ocean could expiate so
great a crime.'

[2] 'What Tanais'—then follows a list of other waters—'will be able to wash
my hand clean?'

[3] 'The kindly light flees and deep Night darkens her countenance and the
heavens are hidden, buried in the shadows.'

The history of this expression goes back to the Sicilian orator Gorgias (fifth century, B.C.), who spoke of vultures as 'living tombs' (ἔμψυχοι τάφοι). The phrase became famous, and we find Lucretius saying (v. 924), 'viva videns vivo sepeliri viscera busto', 'seeing his bowels buried living in a living tomb.' Spenser has 'entombed in the raven or the kight' (*Faerie Queene*, II. viii. 16). Shakespeare follows Spenser.

> Stones have been known to move and trees to speak (III. iv. 123)

The poet may have been thinking of Polydorus who, incorporated in a tree, revealed the circumstances of his murder to Aeneas (*Aeneid*, III. 22–57). Few passages in Virgil were better known than this.

> Upon the corner of the moon
> There hangs a vaporous drop profound (III. v. 23, 24)

The moon in ancient, as in modern, witchcraft is of sovereign influence. Hecate herself was to some extent identified with the moon-goddess. Witches play a great part in the Latin poets most affected by the Elizabethans. For Shakespeare we may assume that the *locus classicus* was the description of Medea's activities and her invocation in the *Metamorphoses*, VII. 262 f. For the 'vaporous drop' Lucan has *virus lunare*, 'lunar poison-drop', *Phars.*, VI. 669.

> I have lived long enough: my way[1] of life
> Is fall'n into the sear, the yellow leaf;
> And that which should accompany old age,
> As honour, love, obedience, troops of friends,
> I must not look to have (v. iii. 22 f.)

Compare Seneca, *Hercules Furens*, 1258 f.:

> cur animam in ista luce detineam amplius
> morerque, nihil est: cuncta iam amisi bona,
> mentem, arma, famam, coniugium, natos, manus.[2]

[1] May (Johnson).

[2] 'There is no reason why I should keep my existence further in this light and linger on: I have already lost all blessings—mind, arms, reputation, children, hands.'

The form, the syntax, of Shakespeare's lines does seem to be modelled on the Senecan passage. But in the poetical effect, what a difference!

> Cans't thou not minister to a mind diseased? (v. iii. 40)

Seneca has, *Hercules Furens*, 1261 f.

> nemo polluto queat
> animo mederi.[1]

To this I will add an earlier parallel:

> Give sorrow words: the grief that does not speak
> Whispers the o'er-fraught heart and bids it break (IV. iii. 209 f.)

Seneca, *Hippolytus*, 607 has

> curae leves loquuntur, ingentes stupent.[2]

The Senecan line became almost proverbial, and very likely Shakespeare knew it. Otherwise we should have to say that it expresses a commonplace, which might have occurred to Shakespeare independently. But, on the whole, must we not say that this accumulation of parallels conquers scepticism? Shakespeare, before writing *Macbeth*, must have been reading Seneca, being especially struck by the *Hercules Furens*. Of course he may have used a translation. We have no means of proving that he read Seneca in Latin, but it seems more than probable. It almost looks as if, before writing *Macbeth*, he had made a special study of at least one or two dramas of the Latin poet in Latin. I think he did.

In *King Lear* Shakespeare never speaks of God, but of the gods. It is the same in *Cymbeline*—as if he would not forget that the action took place in pre-Christian times.

> None of these rogues and cowards
> But Ajax is their fool (II. ii. 131)

---

[1] 'No one could cure a polluted mind.'
[2] 'Light cares speak, great cares are stunned.'

The stupidity of Ajax is dwelt upon, and exaggerated, by Ulysses in Ovid, *Metamorphoses*, XIII. 128 f. He is not stupid in Homer.

Hysterica passio (II. iv. 57)

Medical Latin; from Harsnett, *Declaration*, etc., 1603. (I take this from Bush.)

> I will do such things,—
> What they are yet I know not; but they shall be
> The terrors of the earth (II. iv. 282 f.)

Compare *Metamorphoses*, VI. 618:

> magnum quodcumque paravi:
> quid sit, adhuc dubito.[1]

> to be worst,
> The lowest and most dejected thing of fortune,
> Stands still in esperance, lives not in fear:
> The lamentable change is from the best;
> The worst returns to laughter (IV. i. 2–6)

Churton Collins compares Ovid, *Epist. ex Ponto*, II. 2. 31, 32:

> fortuna miserrima tuta est,
> nam timor eventus deterioris abest.[2]

The idea however, is one that presents itself to every mind.

> we came crying hither:
> Thou know'st, the first time that we smell the air,
> We wawl and cry. (IV. vi. 182–4)

Anders compares Holland's Pliny, Proem to the Seventh Book:

'man alone ... she (Nature) hath laid all naked upon the bare earth, even on his birth-day, to cry and wraule presantly from the very first houre that he is borne into this world.'[3]

---

[1] 'I have prepared whatever is dreadful; what it is, I am still doubtful.'
[2] 'The most wretched fortune is safe, for the fear of a worse issue is absent.'
[3] hominem tantum nudum et in nuda humo natali die abicit (Natura) ad vagitus statim et ploratum (*Nat. Hist. VII*, Sect. 1).

Othello.

> the Cannibals that each other eat,
> The Anthropophagi and men whose heads
> Do grow beneath their shoulders (I. iii. 143 f.)

The Anthropophagi are in Pliny, IV. 12. §26. 88; VI. 17. §20. 53; 30. §35. 195. Philemon Holland's translation came out in 1601. Pliny influenced the imagination of explorers, whose narratives may have influenced Shakespeare.

> the tyrant custom (I. iii. 230)

Compare Erasmus, *Colloquies*, II, *Synodus Grammaticorum*: 'consuetudo quovis tyranno potentior', 'custom mightier than any tyrant'. Since Shakespeare knew the *Colloquies*, he may have remembered this phrase.

> let the labouring bark climb hills of seas
> Olympus high and duck again as low
> As hell's from heaven! (II. i. 189 f.)

In *Metamorphoses*, XI. 503 f. we find:

> et nunc sublimis veluti de vertice montis
> despicere in valles imumque Acheronta videtur:
> nunc, ubi demissam curvum circumstetit aequor,
> suspicere inferno summum de gurgite caelum.

The subject is a ship. Golding thus translates:

> One while as from a mountaines top it seemed downe to looke,
> To vallies and the depth of hell, another while beset
> With swelling surges round about which neere above it met
> It looked from the bottome of the whirlpoole up aloft,
> As if it were from hell to heaven.

Cf. *Tristia*, I. ii. 18–22 and Erasmus, *Colloquies*, *Naufragium*: 'quoties tollebamur in altum, licuisset lunam digito contingere, quoties demittebamur, videbamur dehiscente terra recta ire in Tartara'.[1] Since there is little doubt that Shakespeare had read both passages, we may believe their words had lingered in his memory.

---

[1] 'As often as we were heaved on high, we might have touched the moon with a finger: as often as we were sent down, we seemed to be going straight to hell, the earth yawning for us.'

That does not prove that he would have expressed himself differently if he had read neither. For what confronts us in the words of Shakespeare is no more than an example of rhetorical 'amplification', which is characteristically Elizabethan, while the idea expressed is a commonplace of sea-literature.

> Chaos is come again (III. iii. 92)

Renaissance ideas of Chaos were mainly derived from the description which begins the *Metamorphoses*. What characterizes the ancient Chaos is not so much confusion as formlessness; it was the state of things before the elements were separated from one another.

> like to the Pontic sea,
> Whose icy current and compulsive course
> Ne'er feels retiring ebb, but keeps due on
> To the Propontic and the Hellespont . . . (III. iii. 453 f.)

This comes from Pliny, II. 919: Et Pontus semper extra meat in Propontidem, introrsus in Pontum numquam refluo mari. The words are translated adequately, if a little verbosely, by Philemon Holland: 'And the sea Pontus evermore floweth and runneth out into Propontis, but the sea never retireth backe againe within Pontus.' This of course is what Shakespeare read. I should myself greatly doubt if he ever handled a Latin Pliny at all, for the *Historia Naturalis* is an enormous book, very heavy and expensive, and by no means written in an easy style.

Let us now take *Twelfth Night*, *Measure for Measure*, *All's Well that Ends Well*, *The Winter's Tale*, *Cymbeline*, *The Tempest*, *Pericles*. Beginning with *Twelfth Night*, we find:

> like Arion on the dolphin's back (I. ii. 15)

The story of Arion is best told (after Herodotus) by Ovid in his *Fasti* (II. 79 f.). But Shakespeare did not need to search in the *Fasti* for so familiar a tale. Readers of *Kenilworth* will remember the episode there of Arion and the dolphin.

Now Mercury endue thee with leasing (I. v. 108)

Mercury, as the patron god of cheating, thieving and lying—a function of his as old as the Homeric *Hymn to Hermes*, and of course much older—was known to the Elizabethans chiefly from Ovid (*Fasti*, v. 625-38) or from the mythographers dependent on Ovid.

the Myrmidons are no bottle-ale houses (II. iii. 29)

The Myrmidons were originally the tribesmen and subjects of Achilles, as they are in *Troilus and Cressida*, but in time they came to represent a type. They shared the medieval unpopularity, and to some extent reflected the character, of their chief. (We still speak of 'the myrmidons of the law', when we wish to be disrespectful to the police.)

'diluculo surgere', thou know'st (II. iii. 3)

The Latin is from Lily. It means of course 'to rise at day-break'.

Good night, Penthesilea (II. iii. 190)

Penthesilea was the warrior-queen of the Amazons slain before Troy by Achilles. Although she is not in Homer, she played a considerable part in the Tale of Troy as it was developed in the ancient epics (now lost) which dealt with the events that followed the funeral of Hector. From these epics she passed into Latin literature, ancient and medieval. The third book of the *Ars Amatoria* begins with the mention of Penthesilea, who is taken as representing women who think themselves a match for men. That is perhaps the idea behind Sir Toby's good-night. But Penthesilea was also known from Virgil, *Aeneid*, XI. 662 and (particularly) I. 490 f., where she is one of the characters depicted in the wall-painting of Trojan scenes—a passage which Shakespeare must have known, if it suggested the painting in *Lucrece*.

music from the spheres (III. i. 121)

This perhaps everyone knows to be a Pythagorean idea; but it is not sufficiently understood that it was not, originally, a poetical fancy but a scientific hypothesis, developed from Pythagoras's discovery of the elementary principles of harmonics.

'Like to the Egyptian thief at point of death,
Kill what I love (v. i. 121)

The allusion is to the episode in the *Aethiopica* of Heliodorus,
which had been translated by Underdowne. Thyamis, the
'thief', did not in fact kill Chariclea, but only thought he had
killed her.

There is very little for us in *Measure for Measure*.

'if I do, Pompey, I shall beat you to your tent, and prove a shrewd
Caesar to you' (II. i. 261). 'How now, noble Pompey? What, at
the wheels of Caesar? art thou led in triumph?' (III. ii. 45 f.).

Pompey was 'beaten to his tent', quite literally, by Caesar at the
battle of Pharsalus. This was something known to every educated
Elizabethan, whether he had read Plutarch and the *Bellum Civile*
of Caesar or not. On the other hand it is not true that Pompey
was 'led in triumph' or 'at the wheels of Caesar'. Of course
Shakespeare does not imply that it is.

'What, is there none of Pygmalion's images, newly made woman,
to be had now?' (III. ii. 47)

Another evidence of Shakespeare's familiarity with the *Metamorphoses*. The story occupies x. 243–97.

cucullus non facit monachum (v. i. 263)[1]

Shakespeare seems fond of this adage or proverb, which of course
is not classical.

There is not much more in *All's Well that Ends Well*.

Ere twice in murk and occidental damp
Moist Hesperus hath quench'd his sleepy lamp (II. i. 167, 168)

Hesperus is the Latin Vesper, the Evening Star. Shakespeare
would find him—for the Evening Star is masculine in Latin and

---

[1] 'It is not the cowl that makes a monk.'

Greek—in *Metamorphoses*, v. 441. An often-quoted line about Hesperus is in Virgil, *Eclogue* x. 77:

> ite domum saturae, venit Hesperus, ite, capellae.[1]

> I, his despiteful Juno (III. iv. 13)

Juno is 'despiteful' throughout the *Aeneid* and in much of the *Metamorphoses*. Even in Homer she has this character. But it is evidently the Ovidian Juno who speaks here, and her quarrel with Jupiter is due to his amours rather than his refusal to share her anti-Trojan sentiments.

> for rapes and ravishments he parallels Nessus (IV. ii. 281)

Nessus was the Centaur who would have ravished Dejanira, the bride of Hercules (*Metamorphoses*, IX. 101–34). I cannot remember any other rape or ravishment committed by Nessus; but he was a Centaur, which was a presumption of guilt in such matters. Shakespeare would remember the Centaurs' conduct at the marriage of Pirithous and Hippodamia.

> Plutus himself,
> That knows the tinct and multiplying medicine,
> Hath not in nature's mystery more science (v. iii. 102 f.)

Plutus was the god of wealth. As such he might be regarded as the protector of alchemists, who sought the philosophers' stone, which could turn lead into gold. But the true patron of the alchemist was Hermes (Mercury), not Plutus, who seems to be rather a personification of wealth than a genuine god of the Greek people. There was a tendency to confound him with Pluto, the god of the dead; and in fact the names appear to have the same etymology. Plutus was known to the Elizabethans from the Platonic myth in the *Symposium* (where Poros was understood to be Plutus) but chiefly from Aesop, that is Phaedrus, *Fables*, IV. 12.

The plot of *The Winter's Tale* is largely indebted to Greene's *Dorastus and Fawnia* (earlier *Pandosto*), who used motifs from the

---

[1] 'Go home satisfied—Hesperus comes—go home, my goats.'

Greek 'novelists', especially that favourite motif of oracles. The oracle interpreted at the end of *The Winter's Tale* is almost identical with Greene's. The most influential of the Greek *romanciers* on Greene and his contemporaries was Heliodorus, whose *Aethiopica*, crammed full of surprising turns of fortune and written without distinction of style, is prophetic of the modern 'best-seller'.

> I have tremor cordis on me (I. ii. 110)

Shakespeare has some knowledge of medical and legal Latin, but no deep acquaintance with either. In his time Latin was still the medium for all medical literature, as it still is for medical prescriptions.

> To sacred Delphos, to Apollo's temple (II. i. 183)

The error of Delphos for Delphi, however it originated, had established itself before Shakespeare. Even Milton has it—the young Milton of the Nativity Ode.

> carry
> This female bastard hence and that thou bear it
> To some remote and desert place quite out
> Of our dominions ... (II. iii. 175 f.)

This and similar passages in the play are suggested by *Pandosto*. They follow a literary tradition which begins very early. Indeed the story of the exposed baby, miraculously saved and turning out to be of royal or divine birth, is of immemorial antiquity. In classical literature it is told of Oedipus, of Cyrus the Great and others. It naturally lends itself to dramatic treatment, giving the plot of Euripides' *Ion* and a number of comedies. The motif therefore was not invented but inherited by Heliodorus, from whom Greene borrowed it, for Shakespeare to borrow from Greene.

'My father named me Autolycus; who being, as I am, littered under Mercury, was likewise a snapper-up of unconsidered trifles' (IV. iii. 25)

Autolycus appears first in the *Odyssey* (XIX. 392 f.), but it was in Ovid that Shakespeare found him (*Metamorphoses*, XIX. 310 f.).

> alipedis de stirpe dei versuta propago
> nascitur Autolycus, furtum ingeniosus ad omne:
> candida de nigris et de candentibus atra
> qui facere adsuerat, patriae non degener artis.[1]

> no shepherdess, but Flora
> Peering in April's front . . .
> And you the queen on't (IV. iv. 2 f.)

For an account of Flora see Ovid's *Fasti*, v. 195 f. Her festival was in April.

> Neptune
> A ram (IV. iv. 28)

See the *Metamorphoses*, VI. 115 f. (*Neptune*), *aries Bisaltida fallis*.[2] Cf. Hyginus, *Fables*, 188.

> Golden Apollo, a poor humble swain (IV. iv. 30)

Ovid, *Metamorphoses*, II. 680 says (of Apollo):

> illud erat tempus, quo te pastoria pellis
> texit, onusque fuit baculum silvestre sinistrae[3].

> O Proserpina,
> For the flowers now, that frighted thou let'st fall
> From Dis's waggon! (IV. iv. 116 f.)

See *Metamorphoses*, V. 391–400; *Fasti*, IV. 351–88; Claudian, *de raptu Proserp*. The flowers that Perdita mentions are however different from those let fall by Proserpina.

> Far than Deucalion off (IV. iv. 441)

For Deucalion see *Metamorphoses*, I. 313 f. He was the Noah of Greek mythology.

> The crown will find an heir: great Alexander
> Left his to the worthiest (v. i. 48, 49)

---

[1] 'There is born of the stock of the wing-footed god'—Mercury—'a versatile scion, Autolycus, clever at every form of theft; true inheritor of his father's skill, he was wont to turn white black and black white.'

[2] 'As a ram you'—Neptune—'are the deceiver of Bisaltis'—the Bisaltian maid, Theophane.

[3] 'That was the time when you were covered by a pastoral skin and your left hand was weighted with a staff from the wood.'

Evidently from Justin, XII. 15. 'cum deficere eum amici viderent, quaerunt, quem imperii faciat heredem: respondit, Dignissimum'.[1] Curtius has *optimus*, Arrian ὁ κράτιστος.

Cymbeline, though the action takes place in the reign of Augustus, is a very unclassical play.

> Or, like the Parthian, I shall flying fight (I. vi. 20)

Shakespeare could read about the Parthian mode of fighting in Plutarch's *Life of Crassus* and *Life of Antony*. But it is a constant object of allusion in Ovid and other Roman poets, and in this way had come into Renaissance poetry.

> as common as the stairs
> That mount the Capitol (I. vi. 105)

Shakespeare thought of the Capitol as a place of much resort. It was in fact a consecrated building on a height and not frequented except on ceremonial occasions. There is the same misconception in *Julius Caesar*, where the Capitol is evidently regarded as the Roman equivalent of the Tower of London, which in Tudor and Stuart times dominated London life in a way now hard to imagine. There was probably some confusion made between 'Capitol' and 'capital'.

> This your king
> Hath heard of great Augustus (II. iv. 10)

This dates the action of the play, although the embassy from Augustus is entirely unhistorical. Cymbeline is Cunobelinus, the Latin form of the name of a historical British *regulus*. His uncle— 'Cassibelan, thine uncle' (III. i. 5)—is Caesar's Cassivelaunus. It is not improbable that Shakespeare at one time or another read those chapters of the *Gallic War* in which Caesar describes his two invasions of Britannia. But he is not very clear on the subject.

---

[1] 'When his friends saw that his strength was leaving him, they asked whom he made heir of his authority, he answered "The worthiest".'

our countrymen
Are men more order'd than when Julius Caesar
Smiled at their lack of skill, but found their courage
Worthy his frowning at (II. iv. 20 f.)

Caesar in the *Gallic War* neither smiles at their lack of skill nor
remarks on their courage. But *Cymbeline* is a very patriotic play,
Shakespeare like other Elizabethans looking on the Britanni as
the ancestors of the English.

Proud Cleopatra, when she met her Roman,
And Cydnus swell'd above the banks. (II. iv. 70)

This scene from Plutarch's *Life of Antony* made an abiding impression on Shakespeare's imagination.

Caesar's ambition,
Which swell'd so much that it did almost stretch
The sides o' the world (III. i. 47 f.)

Shakespeare accepted from Plutarch the view that ambition was
the ruling passion of Julius Caesar. This is very likely to be true
and it is, I think, the key to the understanding of *Julius Caesar*.

I love and hate her (III. v. 70)

This is the *odi et amo* of Catullus, whether Shakespeare knew it or
not.

Thersites' body is as good as Ajax' (IV. ii. 252)

The best commentary on this is not in any classical author; it is
Troilus and Cressida.

All curses madded Hecuba gave the Greeks (IV. ii. 313)

See *Metamorphoses*, VIII and Seneca, *Troades* (IV and V). Hecuba
cursed the Greeks, went mad and was changed into a dog.

Lucina lent me not her aid (V. iv. 43)

Lucina was the Roman goddess of childbirth.

The vision that appears to the sleeping Posthumus (V. iv.
30–313) is not at all likely to be the work of Shakespeare. In any
case the classical allusions in it are trite. But scenes of this kind,

whether in dumb-show or not, were a source of instruction in mythology to Elizabethan audiences, who in this way picked up a good deal of superficial knowledge about classical gods and myths.

> Mount, eagle, to my palace crystalline (v. iv. 113)

Jupiter does not *ride* on an eagle in classical story, although the eagle is his sacred bird. He is represented here as dwelling apparently in the primum mobile, which was made of crystal.

> When as a lion's whelp. . . (v. iv. 138 f.)

This is a good imitation of a kind of oracle that is frequent in Heliodorus.

The means by which the lineage of Guiderius and Arviragus is established—birth-marks, objects left with the child, etc.—are traditional, going back to Euripides and earlier (v. v. 360 f.). The exposition of the oracle (440 f.) also follows traditional lines; and the etymologies offered, though absurd, are not more absurd than many that passed current in Shakespeare's time. For instance:

> The piece of tender air, thy virtuous daughter,
> Which we call 'mollis aer'; and 'mollis aer'
> We term it 'mulier' (446 f.)

In Caxton's *Game of Chesse* (Bk. 3, ch. 5) we read: 'she is callid mulier whyche Is as moche to saye in latyn as mollys ær. And in english soyfte ayer.' The *Etymologiae* of Isidore of Seville, who died about 636, filled the Middle Ages with similar explanations of words and things.

The Tempest has so far defied the efforts of scholarship to find a source for its plot, though it has been influenced by an event which occurred in the Bermudas in 1609. The problem does not concern us, but we must take account of the fact that the tempest, which gives its title to the play, is described with details that are taken from the *Naufragium* of Erasmus. The *Naufragium* is a brilliant piece of writing and in the sixteenth century was admired as it deserves to be. It has been imitated by one writer

after another from Rabelais to Charles Reade; and we must
include Shakespeare. The first scene is his own, although he may
have had in his mind the situation envisaged in these words of
the *Naufragium*: 'nautis frustra luctantibus cum tempestate tandem
nauclerus totus pallens nos adiit. . . "Amici", inquit, "desii esse
dominus navis meae; vicere venti: reliquum est ut spem nostram
collocemus in Deo, et quisque se paret ad extrema".'[1] But in
Scene 2, when Ariel relates the part he played on the wrecked
ship, we observe, as Dover Wilson perceived, plain traces of
imitation. For instance, Erasmus tells what happened to the
look-out man, 'huic coepit adsistere sphaera quaedam ignea . . .
nauclerus . . . "Socie", inquit . . . "videsne quod sodalitium tibi
claudat latus?" "video", respondit ille; "et precor ut sit felix".
mox globus igneus delapsus per funes devolvit sese usque ad
nauclerum . . . ibi paullisper commoratus volvit se per margines
totius navis: inde per medios foros dilapsus evanuit.'[2] Here
is what Ariel says (I. ii. 196 f.):

> I boarded the king's ship; now on the beak,
> Now in the waist, the deck, in every cabin,
> I flamed amazement: sometime I'ld divide,
> And burn in many places; on the topmast,
> The yards and bowsprit, would I flame distinctly,
> Then meet and join.

> This Tunis, sir, was Carthage (II. i. 83)

It is not clear where Shakespeare found this piece of information;
but it is true.

> 'His word is more than the miraculous harp; he hath raised the walls
> and houses too.' (II. i. 86)

---

[1] 'While the mariners wrestled vainly with the tempest, at last the master
came to us as white as a sheet. . . . "Friends," says he, "I have ceased to have
any control over my vessel; the winds have got the better of me: it only remains to put our trust in God and for everyone to prepare for the worst." '

[2] 'A ball of fire began to settle upon him. . . . "Mate," said the master, "do
you see what companionship you have supporting you?" "Yes," said the other,
"and I hope it is lucky." Presently the ball of fire slipped along the rigging and
rolled up to the master. . . . There it stayed a little, and then rolled by the
bulwarks of the whole ship; then it glided through the scuppers and vanished.'

Shakespeare must be thinking of Amphion, who raised the walls of Thebes by his harping, for which see *Metamorphoses*, VI. 178, 'fidibusque mei commissa mariti moenia,' 'the walls brought together by the harp-strings of my husband.' It is Niobe who speaks of Amphion.

'*Enter* ARIEL, *like a harpy; claps his wings upon the table; and, with a quaint device, the banquet vanishes.*' (III. iii. 52)

As the exquisitely composed stage directions for the *Tempest* very probably come from Shakespeare himself, we ought to take them into account. The classical description of Harpies was, for the Renaissance, *Aeneid*, III. 210 f. They were bird-like creatures with 'maiden faces' (*virginei volucrum voltus*), who defiled the food they did not steal. The expression 'claps his wings' was perhaps suggested by *magnis quatiunt clamoribus alas*, 'they shake their wings with loud cries'.

> her peacocks fly amain (IV. i. 74)

Probably suggested by Ovid, *Metamorphoses*, II. 532 f.:

> habili Saturnia curru
> ingreditur liquidum pavonibus aethera pictis.[1]

The peacock was the sacred bird of Hera (Juno), especially at her ancient shrine in Samos.

> since they did plot
> The means that dusky Dis my daughter got,
> Her and her blind boy's scandal'd company,
> I have forsworn (IV. i. 88 f.)

The explanation of these lines, as of so many others in Shakespeare, is to be found in Ovid's *Metamorphoses*. The relevant passage is V. 359-380. Venus and Cupid had plotted between them the abduction of Proserpine by Dis.

> PROS. Ye elves of hills, brooks, standing lakes and groves,
> And ye that on the sands with printless foot
> Do chase the ebbing Neptune and do fly him

---

[1] 'With managed car Saturnia'—that is, Juno—'enters the clear sky with her painted peacocks'—that is, the managed peacocks drew the car.

When he comes back; you demi-puppets that
By moonshine do the green sour ringlets make,
Whereof the ewe not bites, and you whose pastime
Is to make midnight mushrooms, that rejoice
To hear the solemn curfew; by whose aid,
Weak masters though ye be, I have bedimm'd
The noontide sun, call'd forth the mutinous winds,
And 'twixt the green sea and the azured vault
Set roaring war: to the dread rattling thunder
Have I given fire and rifted Jove's stout oak
With his own bolt; the strong-based promontory
Have I made shake and by the spurs pluck'd up
The pine and cedar: graves at my command
Have waked their sleepers, oped, and let 'em forth
By my so potent art (v. i. 33–50)

It was observed by Richard Farmer that the language of this passage is clearly influenced by Golding's translation of Medea's invocation in Ovid's *Metamorphoses*, VII. 197 f. But Ovid is the original; so I quote here the relevant words of Medea.

auraeque et venti montesque amnesque lacusque,
dique omnes nemorum, dique omnes noctis adeste:
quorum ope, cum volui, ripis mirantibus amnes
in fontes rediere suos, concussaque sisto,
stantia concutio cantu freta, nubila pello
nubilaque induco, ventos abigoque vocoque. . . .
                              iubeoque tremescere montes
et mugire solum, manesque exire sepulchris.[1]

It will repay study to examine how Shakespeare has transformed this passage; how (partly under Golding's influence) the classical gods have become English fairies, and what Matthew Arnold called 'natural magic' has been added to the original. (Not that I would deny all feeling for natural magic in Ovid.)

[1] 'Ye breezes and winds, mountains and rivers and lakes, all ye gods of the woodland, all ye of the night, assist me: by whose aid, when I willed it, the rivers, to the wonder of their banks, have gone backward to their sources, and I stay by my incantation the storm-vexed sea, and the calm sea vex with storm, drive off the clouds and bring them on, dispel and summon the winds. . . . I bid the mountains shake and the earth bellow and the ghosts to come forth from their graves.'

His mother was a witch, and one so strong
That could control the moon (v. i. 269)

Shakespeare, I imagine, is still thinking of Medea, who in her invocation says (207) 'te quoque, Luna, traho', 'Thee also, O Moon, I draw down.' Witches were thought to have this power, e.g., Ovid, *Amores*, III. 1. 23: 'carmine sanguineae deducunt cornua Lunae, 'By a charm they draw down the horns of the blood-red moon.'

The story dramatized in *Pericles, Prince of Tyre* has been traced back to a hypothetical Greek romance, written perhaps early in the third century. It was a mere romance without any genuine roots in history, and the Latin version which has survived, a product perhaps of the Dark Ages, is, like *Titus Andronicus*, classical only in appearance. *Pericles* therefore is best treated along with *Cymbeline* and not with the plays based on Plutarch, which have an essentially different origin and character. What is chiefly classical in it is the story itself, which is much in the manner of the earlier Greek novelists—earlier, that is to say, than Heliodorus. Another classical feature is the Chorus, which however comes from ancient drama, not the ancient novel. The names of places and persons are Greek. All this Shakespeare would find in his sources, although it may have been he who was responsible for bringing in Gower to act as Chorus. But this is not very likely, and Gower does not use Shakespearian language. I am very willing to accept the general opinion of scholars that Shakespeare had little to do with *Pericles*; but the play will be treated here as if it were substantially his work. If Shakespeare did write the Gower passages, we must attribute to him the knowledge of a Latin phrase quoted by the old poet on his first appearance: 'Et bonum quo antiquius, eo melius.'[1] But it is just a 'tag'.

Before thee stands this fair Hesperides,
With golden fruit, but dangerous to be touch'd;
For death-like dragons here affright thee hard (I. i. 27 f.)

[1] 'And a good thing, the older it is, the better.'

The author seems to think that Hesperides is in the singular, nor is it clear whether he regards her as a nymph or an island. The story of the tree bearing golden apples and guarded by a sleepless dragon must be admitted to be one of the Shakespearian myths. But everybody at that time knew it.

> We have heard your miseries as far as Tyre (I. iv. 88)

A reminiscence of *Aeneid*, IV. 565 f.:

> quis genus Aeneadum, quis Troiae nesciat urbem
> virtutesque virosque aut tanti incendia belli?
> non obtusa adeo gestamus pectora Poeni,
> nec tam aversus equos Tyria sol iungit ab urbe.[1]

> these our ships, you happily may think,
> Are like the Trojan horse was stuff'd within
> With bloody veins, expecting overthrow. (I. iv. 92 f.)

Consult *Aeneid*, 13–20, 31–53, 183–94, 232–47, 257–67.

The Latin mottoes in II, i were not composed by Shakespeare.

> immortality attends the former
> Making a man a god (III. ii. 30)

A Greek, not a Christian, belief.

> Shall's go hear the vestals sing? (IV. v. 8)

The Vestals were priestesses of Vesta and could not leave Rome. Nor did they sing like a church choir.

> She is able to freeze the God Priapus (IV. vi. 4)

Priapus is mentioned by Virgil and Ovid, and he speaks a short poem in Horace. But the Renaissance would learn most about him from the *Priapea*, a collection of short poems of which he is the subject.

---

[1] 'Who could be ignorant of Aeneas' race and the city of Troy, the brave deeds and the heroes or the blaze of such a war? Not so dull as that are the hearts we Phoenicians bear, not so much does Phoebus turn his back on the Tyrian city'—Carthage—'when he yokes his horses'.

Troilus and Cressida stands in a manner between such plays as *Titus Andronicus*, *Pericles* and *Cymbeline* on the one hand and the truly historical plays of classical antiquity, such as *Julius Caesar*, on the other. It is appropriate then to consider it now.

It is the dramatization of a story with almost no ancient tradition behind it, being in fact the invention of successive medieval and earlier romancers. This is not the place to consider how Shakespeare dealt with his two main and almost contradictory sources, which were evidently Caxton's *Recuyell*,[1] and Chapman's *Seaven Bookes of the Iliades*. But we may note in passing that the diction of *Troilus* contains a larger Latin element than we find in the rest of Shakespeare's theatre, as if he considered this appropriate to a play on a classical subject. If that was his idea, he gave it up.

Troilus opens, like a Senecan tragedy, with a Prologue, composed somewhat in the quasi-epic manner of the Pyrrhus speech in *Hamlet*. Towards the end of it we read (27 f.):

> our play
> Leaps o'er the vaunts and firstlings of those broils,
> Beginning in the middle . . .

This recalls the famous lines in Horace where he praises Homer for plunging at once *in medias res*. Shakespeare would know so celebrated a *locus criticus* or, if he did not, he would hear about it.

> A gouty Briareus, many hands and no use (I. ii. 29)

Briareus is mentioned in Virgil (*Aeneid*, VI. 287) with the strange epithet *centumgeminus*, which can only mean 'with a hundred arms.'

The speech of Ulysses, beginning:

> Troy, yet upon his basis, had been down . . . (I. iii. 75 f.)

This magnificent oration embodies certain typically classical ideas. Ulysses argues from two main positions (1) that the world is a *cosmos*, that is, an ordered system pervaded by a harmony which keeps different and opposing elements in their due place;

---

[1] *The Recuyell of the Historyes of Troye*, a translation from the French.

(2) that the physical order is inseparably connected with the moral order, so that a breakdown in the one entails a breakdown in the other. Both of these conceptions go back to Pythagoras or the Pythagoreans, and were in the main accepted by Platonists and Stoics. Since a good political system reflects or should reflect the moral order of the world (which the Stoics defined as 'living according to Nature'), a sound political philosophy must assume the two positions I have indicated. The classical evidence is too long to quote, but the authorities most influential on the Renaissance and indeed the medieval mind were in this matter these three: the *Timaeus* of Plato, the *Somnium Scipionis* of Cicero with the Commentary of Macrobius, and the second book of Pliny's *Natural History*. The conception of the universe as a *cosmos*, that is a beautifully ordered arrangement of interconnected and interacting parts, is originally and characteristically Greek, and is fundamental to all Greek thought—to the philosophy of Aristotle as completely as to the philosophy of Plato. It should not be thought of as, even in Aristotle, a purely physical hypothesis. Both Plato and he consider it as the best proof of the intelligence and goodness of God. From them the conception passed to the Stoics and so to the Romans, from the Romans to later times. Of this *cosmos*, or as the Romans called it *mundus*, the earth is the stationary centre, round which the heavenly bodies are carried at varying speeds by translucent, and so invisible, concentric spheres of varying size. Of these heavenly bodies the Sun is the apparent monarch. Since Shakespeare emphasizes this, I will quote two passages, one from Cicero, the other from Pliny. Cicero makes the spirit of Africanus say: 'subter mediam fere regionem sol obtinet, dux et princeps et moderator luminum reliquorum, mens mundi et temperatio, tanta magnitudine ut cuncta sua luce lustret et compleat. *Som. Scip*, 4.[1] Pliny says, *Nat. Hist.*, II. 5 (Detlefsen): Eorum medius sol fertur amplissima

---

[1] 'Roughly under the middle region the Sun holds his station, the leader, chief and governor of the other luminaries, the mind and rule of the world.'— Cf. Milton, *Paradise Lost*, v. 171. 'Thou Sun! of this great world both eye and soul!'—'of such magnitude that with his light he illuminates and fills the whole.'

magnitudine ac potestate, nec temporum modo terrarumque sed siderum etiam ipsorum caelique rector. Hunc esse mundi totius animum ac planius mentem, hunc principale naturae regimen ac numen credere decet opera eius aestimantes. Hic lucem rebus ministrat aufertque tenebras, hic reliqua sidera occultat inlustrat, hic vices temporum annumque semper renascentem ex usu naturae temperat, hic caeli tristitiam discutit atque etiam humani nubila animi serenat. . . .[1]   The astronomy of Ulysses, though plainly derived from classical sources, is to some extent affected by astrology, which came originally from Babylonia and did not affect Western science until so-called Hellenistic times. But we see it at work in the *Astronomica* of Manilius (first half of the first century) and in the commentary of Macrobius (beginning of the fifth century) on Cicero's *Somnium Scipionis*. This commentary had much influence in medieval times and is a really learned, though not very wise, production. The 'ill aspects of planets evil' and the 'medicinable eye' of the Shakespearian passage belong to astrology rather than astronomy. But, as Macrobius points out, the Sun was often identified with Apollo; and Apollo was the ancient god of healing. As for the vital connexion between the physical and the moral order, that is quite in accordance with much ancient thought. So is the connexion between the ordered soul and the ordered state. Thus Plato, in the *Republic*, proceeds on the principle that we cannot discover what is justice in the individual until we have discovered what is justice in the state. Thus none of the ideas in Ulysses' speech is new, although on the political side they had received some development by Shakespeare's time. The speech ought to be considered in connexion with More's speech to the rioters in *The Booke of Sir*

---

[1] 'In the midst of them the sun is carried, of vast size and influence, the ruler not only of seasons and lands but also of the very stars and the heavens. Him, when we contemplate his works, it is fitting that we should believe to be the mind or, more definitely, the intellect (reason) of the whole universe, the chief government and divinity of nature. He furnishes light and takes away darkness from things, he conceals and illuminates the other stars, he orders the changes of the seasons and the year as it is ever reborn in the course of nature, he dispels the gloom of the sky and even enlightens the cloudy thoughts of the human spirit.'

143

Thomas More. The ideas were 'in the air', and Shakespeare need not have read Latin books to find them. At the same time it must be acknowledged that he puts them with an eloquence and cogency which prove that he had reflected deeply upon them.

> The tongue of roaring Typhon (I. iii. 160)

Typhon is mentioned by Ovid, *Fasti*, II. 471. He is apt to be confused with Typhoeus, for whom see *Metamorphoses*, V. 346–58. Perhaps indeed they were the same. Both were inclined to 'roar'.

> were his brain as barren
> As banks of Libya (I. iii. 328)

From the context it would appear that Nestor is thinking of the Libyan desert rather than the Syrtes. Lucan is voluminously eloquent upon both, and he is the great literary source of Renaissance notions about North Africa. But by Shakespeare's time there was a considerable body of knowledge about the region acquired by travellers, seamen, escaped or ransomed Christian captives and others.

> young men, whom Aristotle thought
> Unfit to hear moral philosophy (II. ii. 166)

In the *Nicomachean Ethics*, I. iii. 5, Aristotle observes that young men are unfit to hear political science. Erasmus, remembering that the observation occurs in the *Ethics*, and not verifying his quotation, gave it in the form repeated by Shakespeare. Since Aristotle regards ethics as a branch of politics, he is not seriously misrepresented. But the origin of the mistake was a very natural *lapsus memoriae* on the part of Erasmus, less excusably perpetuated by others, who copied him without question. 'To hear' preserves the original expression of Aristotle, who calls a student attending lectures a 'hearer' (ἀκροατής).

> Bull-bearing Milo (II. iii. 258)

Another anachronism. Milo was an athlete of Croton in Magna Graecia (south Italy), who, among other feats, was said to have carried a bullock round the stadium at Olympia. There is an account of him in Pliny, VII. 20. §19. 83, but he is also mentioned by Cicero, Seneca and others. Whether he was really stronger than other athletes or not, he created a legend about himself as the typical 'strong man' and as such is often mentioned in Renaissance literature.

> to be wise and love
> Exceeds man's might; that dwells with gods above (III. ii. 163, 164)

One of the apophthegms attributed to Syrus runs:

> amare et sapere vix Deo conceditur.[1]

Shakespeare might learn this at school as a *puerilis sententia*.

> Outswell the colic of puff'd Aquilon (IV. v. 9)

Aquilo (gen. *Aquilonis*) is the north wind in Latin, the Greek Boreas. He is generally represented by ancient poets as a storm-wind. Shakespeare might know this in a literary way, but he may have seen Aquilo blowing with puffed cheeks in some tapestry or picture, as we see him in Botticelli's 'Birth of Venus'.

> Admits no orifex for a point as subtle
> As Ariachne's broken woof to enter (v. ii. 151 f.)

Ariachne is a mistake for Arachne, perhaps suggested by Ariadne. Shakespeare had read about Arachne in the *Metamorphoses*, VI., 1–145. She was a weaving-girl who was changed by the jealous Minerva into a spider, so that by 'Ariachne's broken woof' Shakespeare probably means the filaments of a spider's web. As for 'orifex' it appears to mean an 'orifice'. As 'artifex' means the maker of an 'artificium', so 'orifex' should mean the maker of an 'orificium' or orifice. It is, I suppose, a blunder, but it is not a bad or ignorant one.

We come now to the dramas based on Plutarch. They are *Julius Caesar*, *Antony and Cleopatra*, *Coriolanus* and *Timon of Athens*. They were not written consecutively, and *Julius Caesar* is as early as 1599. But they form a class by themselves and raise a new series of problems. The problems will be considered in

---

[1] 'To love and to be wise is scarcely granted to God.'

due course. Here I content myself with recording such indications of classical knowledge as are not provided by Plutarch,
whom no one supposes Shakespeare to have read in Greek.

> The Genius and the mortal instruments
> Are then in council; and the state of man,
> Like to a little kingdom, suffers then
> The nature of an insurrection (II. i. 66 f.)

This is a difficult passage, and there may be some confusion between the 'genius' of a man, in the sense of his 'angel' or alter
ego, and genius in the sense of the intellect, which is one of the
meanings of the word in Latin. According to the psychology
which Plato evidently took over from the Pythagoreans and
handed on (with large modifications of his own) to Aristotle,
who modified it in his turn, reason or pure intelligence, *nous*, is the
ruling principle of the *psyche*, which is the incorporeal part of a
man, whereby he thinks and feels. This principle Shakespeare
here seems to personify, calling it 'the Genius'. Although we
generally translate the word *psyche* (ψυχή) by 'soul', we must not
think of it in terms of Christian theology. It is not a unity and it
is not all immortal. The only immortal part of it is *nous* or
logos—Reason or Pure Intelligence—and this can be distinguished,
as Shakespeare distinguishes it, from 'the mortal instruments',
that is, those physical capacities and bodily passions which it
seeks to use and govern. Now in this psychology Reason is
absolutely sovereign; Plato and Aristotle are insistent upon that.
Accordingly 'the mortal instruments' have no business to be 'in
council' with Reason at all; theirs not to reason why. When
they forget this they are in rebellion. The 'kingdom' suffers the
nature of an insurrection, a rising of the governed against their
governor. As for the conception of man as a microcosm, a
'little cosmos', which, since the cosmos as a whole is governed by
God as King thereof, may also be called a 'little kingdom', that
too is classical. There is no use in asking where Shakespeare
found these ideas, but they were familiar enough all through the
Renaissance, particularly among the 'Platonists'.

> et tu, Brute (III. i. 77)

This is not in Plutarch, and it is not clear where Shakespeare got it, though this matters little, since the words had been attributed to Caesar before they were used by Shakespeare. In Suetonius' *Life of Caesar* it is stated that, according to certain persons, when Brutus attacked Caesar, the dictator cried out καὶ σύ, τέκνον, 'thou also, my son'. The Latin for this would be 'et tu, mi fili'. It may be supposed that 'Brute' was substituted for 'mi fili' because of a story that Brutus was the son of Caesar, who would then (on this supposition) be alluding to that fact in his last cry. It should have been considered that, even if Caesar did address Brutus as 'my son', it was quite natural from an older to a younger man with whom he was on terms of intimacy. Nothing is commoner in ancient literature, nor for the matter of that in Elizabethan.

> Dearer than Plutus' mine (iv. iii. 102)

The Folio has 'Pluto's mine', which is not improbably what Shakespeare wrote, the confusion between Plutus and Pluto being not uncommon.

> You know that I held Epicurus strong
> And his opinion (v. i. 76)

This is taken from Plutarch, perhaps without much reflection on what the 'opinion' was. Epicurus did not deny the existence of gods or even of apparitions. But he believed that the gods took no interest in human affairs and that the apparitions, which are included under the term of *simulacra*, were purely optical phenomena with nothing ominous or supernatural about them. The word *simulacra* does not come from Epicurus, who wrote in Greek, but from his follower, the great Roman poet Lucretius. In the seventeenth century three classical authors, Epicurus, Lucretius and Lucian, were violently attacked by orthodox persons as enemies of religion; and Shakespeare would hear some echo of these controversies.

> O Julius Caesar, thou are mighty yet!
> Thy spirit walks abroad, and turns our swords
> Into our proper entrails (v. iii. 94 f.)

Lucan has been compared, I. ii. 3.:

> populumque potentem
> in sua victrici conversum viscera dextra.[1]

I do not believe there is anything in this. The words of Brutus
are what he would utter in the circumstances without suggestion
from Lucan or anyone else. Why he utters them I hope to explain
in a later place. The thought behind them comes from Plutarch,
not Lucan.

The next of the classical plays after *Julius Caesar* was probably
Antony and Cleopatra.

> by the fire
> That quickens Nilus' slime (I. iii. 69)

It is likely enough that this was suggested by some lines in the
Faerie Queene:

> As when old father Nilus gins to swell
> With timely pride above the Aegyptian vale,
> His fattie waves doe fertile slime outwell,
> And overflow each plaine and lowly dale. (I. i. 21 f.)

But the 'fire' has a better parallel in a line of Ovid, namely
Metamorphoses, I. 424: 'aetherioque recens exarsit sidere limus',
'and his'—that is Nile's—'fresh slime has been heated by the
heavenly luminary', namely of course the sun. But the over-
flowing of the Nile and the fertility of its mud had long been
general knowledge.

A little before we read:

> What says the married woman? You may go:
> Would she had never given you leave to come! (I. iii. 20 f.)

Shakespeare is evidently remembering a line in Dido's letter to
Aeneas (*Heroides*, VII. 139):

> sed iubet ire deus. vellem vetuisset adire.[2]

[1] 'And a mighty people turning with victorious right hand against its
entrails.'

[2] 'But, you say, the god bids you go. I wish he had bidden you not to come.'

What Venus did with Mars (i. v. 17)

Related by Ovid, *Ars Amat.*, ii. 561–92; also *Metamorphoses*, iv. 167–255.

broad-fronted Caesar (i. v. 29)

Shakespeare evidently had a mental picture of Julius Caesar—broad forehead, Roman nose. Doubtless he was influenced by the artistic tradition, but how that arose is not clear. In the iconography of the Roman emperors, among whom Julius was apt to be included, the 'Roman nose' is fairly predominant. Rather strangely we possess no certainly authentic representation of Caesar; the most convincing-looking is a statue in the Palazzo dei Conservatori.[1]

I wore his sword Philippan (ii. v. 24)

The sword he wore at Philippi. It should be 'Philippian'.

Thou should'st come like a Fury crown'd with snakes (ii. v. 40)

The Furies were represented with snakes in, or composing, their hair. See *Aeneid*, vii. 328, 329; *Metamorphoses*, iii. 370–510; Seneca often; all borrowing the conception from Greek art and literature.

they take the flow o' the Nile
By certain scales i' the pyramid (ii. vii. 20, 21)

This of the Nilometer comes originally from Pliny, *Nat. Hist.*, v. ch. 9. Holland's translation was now available.

The shirt of Nessus is upon me (iv. xii. 43)

The 'shirt', smeared with the poisoned blood of Nessus the Centaur, which consumed the flesh of Hercules. The chief Latin authorities would be Ovid, *Heroides*, ix and Seneca, *Hercules Oetaeus*. But it was a current story.

he is more mad
Than Telamon for his shield (iv. xiii. 1, 2)

[1] An excellent photograph of the head is reproduced as frontispiece to the 'New Shakespeare' edition of *Julius Caesar*. The forehead is sufficiently 'broad', the nose unfortunately has been restored. The 'British Museum' bust, now prudently withdrawn, is modern.

Shakespeare cannot mean Telamon, the father of Ajax, but Ajax himself, who is called Telamonius. One cannot but suspect another confusion. While it is true that Ajax had a famous shield of his own, what drove him mad was the rejection of his claim to the shield of the dead Achilles.

> the seven-fold shield of Ajax (IV. xiv. 38)

Ovid, *Metamorphoses*, XIII. 1: 'clipei dominus septemplicis Aiax', 'Ajax, lord of the sevenfold shield'. It is described in a celebrated passage in the *Iliad* (VII. 220 f.).

> ANTONY.   Peace!
> Not Caesar's self hath o'erthrown Antony,
> But Antony's hath triumph'd on itself.
> CLEOP.   So it should be, that none but Antony
> Should conquer Antony (IV. xv. 14 f.)

This was evidently suggested by a line (390) of *Metamorphoses*, XIII, a book which Shakespeare had evidently been reading:

> ne quisquam Aiacem possit superare nisi Ajax.[1]

We may next take *Coriolanus*.

> You would be another Penelope, etc. (I. iii. 92 f.)

The original story is of course in the *Odyssey*, but it was epitomized in Hyginus and is often alluded to in Latin authors more familiar to the seventeenth century than Homer.

> the most sovereign prescription in Galen is but empiricutic (II. i. 129)

An anachronism, since Galen belongs to the age of the Antonines. But Shakespeare knows that he was the great champion of the empiric system in medicine. 'empiricutic' is hardly the mistake of a scholar.

> Hear you this Triton of the minnows? (III. i. 88)

Shakespeare may have had in his mind the description of Triton

---

[1] 'That no one should be able to conquer Ajax but Ajax.'

in *Metamorphoses*, I. 333 f. But Triton with his conch was familiar from the masques.

> as Hercules
> Did shake down mellow fruit (IV. vi. 99)

A reference to the apples of the Hesperides. Shakespeare will have it that Hercules gathered the fruit himself, even climbing the tree to do it.

Lastly, *Timon of Athens*.

Plutarch is not the only source; a good deal comes from Lucian's dialogue called *Timon or The Misanthrope*. Much in the play has an unfinished appearance. The anachronism involved in giving some of the characters Latin (not Latinized) names is not peculiar to Shakespeare and is committed by dramatists and story-tellers with greater pretensions to scholarship. According to the practice we have been following it will be assumed that Shakespeare is the sole author.

> You're a dog (I. i. 203)

This is addressed to Apemantus, who is a Cynic philosopher, the word 'Cynic' being derived from the Greek for a dog. In fact a Cynic philosopher was often designated 'dog' *sans phrase*. It is not just an insult or term of abuse, though Shakespeare doubtless took it for one. The Cynics believed that the virtuous life could be lived best by a man who reduced his wants to a minimum. In modern language they advocated living the simple life. The dog was an illustration of how little the human animal actually needed.

> ira furor brevis est (I. ii. 27)

A very common quotation; from Horace, *Epist.*, I. ii. 62.

> I am Misanthropos, and hate mankind (IV. iii. 53)

ὁ μισάνθρωπος is the title of Lucian's dialogue. It means of course 'the hater of mankind'. Shakespeare got the word from the margin of North's Plutarch (*Life of Antony*).

> Be as a planetary plague, when Jove
> Will o'er some high-viced city hang his poison
> In the sick air (IV. iii. 108 f.)

One may compare Burton, *An. Mel.*, Pt. I. sec. 2. mem. 1. subs. 2.
'those aerial devils that corrupt the air and cause plagues, thunders,
fires, etc.' The belief that plague came from a corruption or
poisoning of the air was ancient. See, *inter alia*, Virgil *Georgics*,
II. 478–end. (He uses the expression *morbo caeli*, 479.) The idea of
being 'struck' by one of the planets or stars was also common in
Shakespeare's time and can be traced back to antiquity.

> You perpetual-sober gods (IV. iii. 503)

This was Epicurean doctrine; yet in a sense all ancient philosophers to a greater or less degree accepted it. They left it to the
'vulgar' to believe that the gods were subject to human passions.

> I have a tree etc. (V. i. 208 f.)

From Plutarch's *Life of Antony*.

> Here lies a wretched corse, of wretched life bereft:
> Seek not my name: a plague consume you wicked caitiffs left!
> Here lie I, Timon; who, alive, all living men did hate:
> Pass by and curse thy fill, but pass and stay not here thy gait.
>
> (V. iv. 70 f.)

This is all taken from North, who has 'wretches' for 'caitiffs'.
But Shakespeare has heedlessly run together two distinct epi-
taphs: the first (70, 71) ascribed to Timon himself, the second
(73, 74) by the Greek poet Callimachus. They may be sought in
the Palatine Anthology.

I have now in this cursory, but perhaps sufficient, way reviewed
the clear or reasonably clear evidence for Shakespeare's classical
scholarship. It does nothing in my opinion to destroy or even
seriously to weaken the testimony of his contemporaries, cor-
roborated by the admissions in the Sonnets. This I think is not

now the prevailing view among Shakespearian scholars. Thus I could not help being impressed by the learning and fairmindedness of Professor T. W. Baldwin in the two large volumes of his book entitled *William Shakspere's Small Latine and Lesse Greek* (1944). In these he tells us in very great detail what Shakespeare *could* have learned at school. But the hard fact is that we do not know what amount of schooling Shakespeare had, and my object in this book has been to deal as little in surmise as possible. Moreover I cannot believe that Professor Baldwin has sufficiently considered that a practised man of letters is continually picking up information—even information contained in books—from other people. I hope it will not be suggested that I am accusing Shakespeare of illiteracy. On the contrary I get the impression that he read a good deal, though rapidly and (if I may say so without profanity) not infrequently with an eye to what he could use. But scholarship implies critical reading, and evidences of that elude me. Nor am I impressed by the mere accumulation of possible allusions. I am haunted by a passage in one of Tennyson's letters quoted in the first volume of the old *Life* which I think all of us must take to heart, though none of us, I hope, deserves to be described in Tennyson's words. 'There is, I fear, a prosaic set growing up among us, editors of booklets, book-worms, index-hunters, or men of great memories and no imagination, who *impute themselves* to the poet, and so believe that *he*, too, has no imagination, but is for ever poking his nose between the pages of some old volume in order to see what he can appropriate. They will not allow one to say "Ring the bell" without finding that we have taken it from Sir P. Sidney, or even to use such a simple expression as the ocean "roars" without finding out the precise verse in Homer or Horace from which we have plagiarized it.' Tennyson was over-sensitive to criticism, but when it took this form he had reason to complain. How much more reason has Shakespeare!

It may be thought that I should have taken into consideration Shakespeare's command of rhetoric and the five-act structure of plays, for this rhetoric and this structure derive from the classics. On these points I again acknowledge Baldwin as our chief authority. But I cannot bring myself to believe that Shakespeare made a special study of rhetoric and dramatic structure in the Latin classics. It was not necessary. His sense of style, his feeling for the architectonics of a play appear to me a sufficient explanation. There is hardly a greater master of rhetoric in English prose than Cobbett, and Cobbett, you might say, had no education at all. I can only express my own, perhaps old-fashioned, conviction that Shakespeare was in the most important matters his own teacher. That he may have learned a good deal indirectly from Terence, I do not deny; especially as the world was full of Terentian imitations. Nor do I deny that he may have read some Terence in Latin. But I do not think that he could have made a close study of the Latin because, if that were so, there would almost inevitably be some trace of this in the language of Shakespeare. And this I have not been able to find.

Nevertheless some Latin, apart from mere schoolbooks, he must evidently have read. For instance I think he read the *Colloquies* of Erasmus, or some of them. Undoubtedly he read a certain amount, perhaps a good deal, of Ovid in Ovid's words. It appears from *Macbeth* that he had read the tragedies of Seneca, here and there, in Latin before writing the play; and this is interesting because it suggests an effort on Shakespeare's part to revive his study of Latin in view of a drama which was to have so much of the Greek tragic spirit in it. And there are other possibilities. But it seems to me that a judge, not excited by his own discoveries, would decide on the evidence that Shakespeare was but a perfunctory reader of the classics, and that like most of us who are not Latin scholars he used translations when they came to hand, and only turned to the original when his interest or curiosity was aroused. I ask this question: how could a man, who read Ovid's Latin with ease and pleasure, bear to read Golding instead?

I may be asked a question in turn. If Shakespeare was no classical scholar, how did it happen that he came before the world as an author who deliberately chose classical subjects? The answer, I think, is that he was ambitious to distinguish himself, and that classical subjects were the fashion of the time. Both *Venus and Adonis* and *The Rape of Lucrece* are long poems, and both are written with such elaboration and refinement of language that no reader could doubt that they formed the challenge of a new author to the established masters, such as Spenser. The motto prefixed to *Venus* is the clear expression of this challenge. Others of course made similar claims. The Roman poets had made them, and therefore Renaissance poets made them too. But they are more significant—in the motto and in the Sonnets—in Shakespeare than in another, for he seems to have had as little literary vanity as Sir Walter Scott. He did not, like Jonson, publish his 'works'. It would seem he let Middleton foist his own stuff into *Macbeth*. In any case the *Venus* motto is not a mere *exegi monumentum*. It is rather an aspiration than a claim. Yet a poet does not offer up an aspiration as the prelude to some work, unless he attaches to that work a serious importance. In view of this the tendency of some to treat both the *Venus* and the *Lucrece* as *juvenilia*, not to be taken too seriously, cannot be defended. The author was a man of about thirty, more ingenious than ingenuous, and a finished master of rhymed verse. Do the *Venus* and *Lucrece* not seem important to us now? They were important enough to Shakespeare. To the end of his life his reputation as a poet rested largely on them. We must adjust our minds to that fact. But what does it mean? It means that Shakespeare was regarded by his contemporaries as the most brilliant master in a school of *classical* art. He was the new Ovid—one of the new Ovids—of his time. Thus we find Francis Meres saying in his *Palladis Tamia* (1598), in a passage where he is comparing English poets with Greek, Latin and Italian: 'As the soul of *Euphorbus* was thought to live in *Pythagoras*, so the sweet, witty soul of Ovid lives in mellifluous and honey-tongued *Shakespeare*; witness his *Venus and Adonis*, his *Lucrece*, his sugared Sonnets among his private friends, etc.' Even after his death, when his fame as a dramatist might be expected to have obscured this early reputation, we find Thomas Fuller[1] describing Shakespeare as a

[1] *Worthies, Warwickshire*, 126.

combination of Martial—a punning jest on the name Shake-spear and therefore not to be taken in evidence—of Plautus and of Ovid. That is to say Shakespeare is like Plautus in his comedies and like Ovid in his poems. This was published in 1662. And there is other evidence to the same effect.

One may go farther. It is possible to make out a case that not merely as a poet but as a dramatist Shakespeare makes his first appearance in the character of a classicizing author. The uncertainty of Shakespearian chronology prevents us from deciding the matter; but hardly anyone doubts that the *Comedy of Errors* and *Titus Andronicus* were the first, or among the first, dramas of which he was the exclusive or predominant author. But what are these? The first is a Plautine comedy, the second a Senecan tragedy. It follows that about the year 1594 or 1595 the reputation which attached to Shakespeare must have been that of a new writer who was specially attracted to classical subjects. That being so, it was inevitable, in an age that set so high a value on classical scholarship, that his credentials should be scanned, at least by those who had themselves attempted classical subjects with less applause. The criticisms which I now proceed to quote are almost too familiar to bear repetition. Yet the interpretation of them is still, in places, a matter of dispute. The first criticism (if that is not too complimentary a term to be applied to what is mere railing) appeared in Greene's posthumous *Groatsworth of Wit*, published under a fuller title in 1592. 'For there is an upstart Crow, beautified with our feathers, that with his *Tiger's heart wrapt in a Player's hide*, supposes he is as well able to bombast out a blank verse as the best of you; and being an absolute *Johannes factotum*, is in his own conceit the only Shake-scene in a country. O that I might entreat your rare wits to be employed on more profitable courses, and let those Apes imitate your past excellence, and never more acquaint them with your admired inventions.' There is no question that this is an attack on Shakespeare. But what is the ground of the attack? In a problem of this kind some illumination is nearly always gained by considering the audience. Now in this passage Greene was addressing, at least ostensibly, his 'fellow-scholars'—observe that phrase—who were Peele, Marlowe and, probably, Nashe. They are warned against Shakespeare as one who is not a scholar like themselves, but makes use of them to their detriment and his own advantage.[1]

What concerns us most in this passage is the assertion or insinuation that Shakespeare is no scholar. Since Professor Alexander wrote upon the question it has been generally agreed that in his attack Greene is thinking of Shakespeare as a player. It is evident that the University Wits (of whom Greene was one) considered themselves socially and intellectually superior to the players who acted in their dramas. It is an attitude which cannot have been easy to maintain, since the Wits lived on what the companies gave them for their plays. Moreover by Greene's own confession he had been on terms of special intimacy with the actors until he had been 'deserted' by them. No doubt it was these very circumstances that made poor, disreputable Greene hang on the more desperately to his fancied superiority. He could at least aver that to write dramas was a higher function than to act in them. Alexander quotes evidence which proves that actors were addressed in the very terms in which Shakespeare is attacked by Greene.[2] It is a special aggravation in Shakespeare's

---

[1] I subjoin the whole context in the original spelling, that the reader may satisfy himself that, whatever other interpretations may be put on it, that which I have put is natural and even necessary. 'Base minded men all three of you, if by my miserie you be not warnd: for vnto none of you (like mee) sought those burres to cleaue: those Puppets (I meane) that spake from our mouths, those Anticks garnisht in our colours. Is it not strange, that I, to whom they all haue been beholding, shall (were yee in that case as I am now) bee both at once of them forsaken? Yes trust them not: for there is an upstart Crow, beautified with our feathers, that with his *Tygers hart wrapt in a Players hyde*, supposes he is as well able to bombast out a blanke verse as the best of you: and beeing an absolute *Iohannes fac totum*, is in his owne conceit the onely Shake-scene in a countrey. O that I might intreat your rare wits to be imploied in more profitable courses: & let those Apes imitate your past excellence, and never more acquaint them with your admired inuentions. I knowe the best husband of you all will neuer proue an Usurer, and the kindest of them all will neuer proue a kind nurse: yet, whilest you may, seeke you better Maisters: for it is pittie men of such rare wits, should be subiect to the pleasure of such rude groomes.'

[2] 'Shakespeare's *Henry VI* and *Richard III*', p. 43 ff.

case (so Alexander presents the thought of Greene) that he writes plays himself—bad plays of course, with lines in them like

O tiger's heart wrapp'd in a woman's hide.

If this interpretation be correct, we should not be entitled to infer from Greene's words that he was accusing Shakespeare of plagiarism; he may only be accusing him of presumptuous vanity.

To support this argument Professor Alexander quotes a passage from a pamphlet of Greene's, *Never too Late*, of which the date is 1590, in which an actor—it is not suggested that he is Shakespeare —is attacked in these terms:

'Why *Roscius*, art thou proud with *Esops* Crow, being pranct with the glorie of others feathers? Of thy selfe thou canst say nothing, and if the Cobler hath taught thee to say *Aue Caesar*, disdain not thy tutor, because thou pratest in a King's chamber.'

The source of the first sentence of this passage is clear. It comes from the Latin Aesop.

'De Cornice superbiente aliarum avium pennis. Cornicula collectas pennas de reliquis avibus sibi commodaverat, et superba varietate illa reliquas omnes prae se aviculas contemnebat. Tum forte hirundo notata sua penna advolans illam aufert, quo facto et reliquae postea aves quaeque suam ademere cornici: ita illa risum movit omnibus, furtivis nudata coloribus, ut ait Horatius.—Significat fabula, commendicatam speciem neque diu durare et perlevi momento dissolvi.'[1]

This fable, as the quotation suggests, is taken from Horace; it does not come from Phaedrus, who might be described as the classical fabulist.[2] According to Phaedrus—and this is the best known form of the story—the thief was not a 'crow' (*cornicula*)

[1] '*Of the Crow who was proud with the feathers of other birds.* A crow had collected feathers from the other birds and had fitted them to herself, and made proud by those varied hues she despised all the other birds in comparison with herself. Then by chance a swallow recognized its own feather and flying up carried it away. When this happened the other birds also afterwards took away each its own (feather) from the crow. So she moved them all to laughter, "stripped of her stolen colours", as Horace says.—The fable signifies that a borrowed beauty does not last long and is destroyed in an instant.'
[2] He wrote in Rome in the first century A.D.

but a 'jackdaw' (*graculus*), and the feathers it took had fallen
from peacocks. The picture then is that of a jackdaw—if that
is how to translate *graculus*—strutting about in peacocks' feathers,
not that of a crow dressed up in a variety of feathers from other
birds, among which is mentioned a swallow but not a peacock.
We are thus led to Horace's version, which is to be found in
the first book of his *Epistles* (III. 15–20).

> quid mihi Celsus agit, monitus multumque monendus
> privatas ut quaerat opes, et tangere vitet
> scripta Palatinus quaecumque recepit Apollo,
> ne, si forte suas repetitum venerit olim
> grex avium plumas, moveat cornicula risum
> furtivis nudata coloribus.[1]

That this is the source of the fable in the Latin Aesop is obvious—
the very language is borrowed. But why does Horace quote the
fable? It is to warn his friend Celsus against plagiarism.

It seems all but certain that in his attack on the 'Crow beautified
with our feathers' Greene was thinking of the Latin Aesop and not
of Horace. But even the Latin Aesop makes a point of the 'stolen'
colours (*furtivis* coloribus). In what sense could an actor be said
to 'steal' fine words supplied him by the dramatist? The dramatist lent them or was paid for them. We may say that Greene was
too angry to reflect on this—that all he was thinking of was the
vanity of actors, whose very words are not their own. But, thus
applied, the fable loses a good deal of its point. One thing we
may say. He could hardly be serious in advising his fellow-
playwrights to have nothing more to do with the players, for
they needed the players rather more than the players them. And
now it looked as if they did not need Robert Greene at all, having
found Shakespeare. That quotation may have more in it than
appears at first. Here is part of the context:

[1] 'What, pray, is Celsus doing? He has been advised, and greatly needs the
advice, to ransack his own resources and not touch any of the books contained
in the library of the Palatine Apollo, lest, if some day the flock of birds should
happen to come to demand back their feathers, he should prove the poor old
crow that got laughed at when stripped of her stolen finery.'

O tiger's heart wrapt in a woman's hide! . . .
Woulds't have me weep? Why, now thou hast thy will . . .
There take the crown, and, with the crown, my curse;
And in thy need such comfort come to thee
As now I reap at thy too cruel hand! (3 *Henry VI.* i. iv)

There is no doubt that Greene's pamphlet created some sensation. Of this there are several indications. The earliest appears to be some verses published in 1594.

Greene gave the ground to all that wrote upon him.
Nay more, the men that so eclipsed his fame
Purloined his plumes, can they deny the same?

The author of these lines, a certain R.B., who is called or calls himself a 'gentleman', clearly thought of Shakespeare as a poet, who had eclipsed the fame of Greene, but had done so unfairly by picking his brains or in some way appropriating his work; he was not thinking of Shakespeare as a player. Of course he may have put a wrong interpretation upon the words of Greene. But that this misinterpretation should have been made so soon after the publication of the *Groatsworth*, among men too who had known the author and must have canvassed the meaning of every allusion in the pamphlet, is surely somewhat remarkable. For nobody is likely to deny that R.B. is here alluding to Greene's attack upon the upstart crow. In the interval the 'crow' had published *Venus and Adonis* and so eclipsed the fame of Greene. It is worth noting that 'purloined his plumes' shows that R.B. had *furtivis coloribus* in his mind and believed that Greene had it too. There are some expressions also in Chapman's poems which seem to point in the same direction, but they are too obscure to be used in evidence. The matter invites further consideration. And at the end of it all one may still be left wondering what was the point of Greene's attack. Was it an offence for an actor to write a play? Was that the sole ground on which Greene appealed to the public for sympathy? If so, one would have expected Shakespeare and his friends to remain untroubled by it. But apparently they felt it acutely enough. At any rate we find

Henry Chettle, who had edited the *Groatsworth*, apologizing to Shakespeare as early as 1592.

'I am as sorry as if the original fault had been my fault, because myself have seen his demeanour no less civil than excellent in the quality he professes: besides, divers of worship have reported his uprightness of dealing'—had this been called in question?—'which argues his honesty, and his facetious grace in writing, that approves his art.'

That is as much as to say, 'Shakespeare *is* a gentleman and writes like one, and, if he is an actor, is a very good one'. Observe that to Chettle at least, and this a year before the publication of *Venus and Adonis*, Shakespeare is an approved author as well as an actor. Since Chettle is using words very carefully here, it is possible that he meant the expression 'facetious grace' to recall the compliment, familiar then to all reading men, of Horace to the style of Virgil's *Eclogues*: *molle atque facetum*, of which 'facetious grace' is an admirable Elizabethan translation.[1] That is as it may be; what is certain is that Chettle meant to be apologetic and complimentary.

But Greene's was not the only criticism. We may listen next to Thomas Nashe:

'It is a common practice nowadays among a sort of shifting companions, that run through every art and thrive by none, to leave the trade of *noverint*, whereto they were born, and busy themselves with the endeavours of art, though they could scarcely Latinize their neck verse if they should have need.'[2]

Here Shakespeare is not named, and in what follows recent scholarship has made it seem probable that, if Nashe is referring to some particular poet, he is referring to Kyd. But Kyd was associated with Shakespeare in more ways than one, and especially in this respect, that neither was university bred, which is the point that Nashe is chiefly concerned to make. So his sneer may be taken as referring to Shakespeare almost as much as to Kyd. It is worth then considering what he says. To begin with, 'the shifting companions, that run through every art and thrive by none'

[1] *Sermones*, I. 10. 44.
[2] Preface (with modernized spelling) to Greene's *Menaphon*, 1589.

cannot but remind us of Greene's *Johannes factotum*. The type of *Johannes factotum* is exactly that of *Margites* in a Greek poem old enough to be attributed to Homer. Of Margites it is written that 'he knew many jobs and knew them all badly'.[1] Observe—what I do not find often observed—that the fatal weakness of Johannes is rather his incompetence than his readiness to turn his hand to anything. No one could say that the ancient Greeks or the men of the Renaissance had a poor opinion of versatility in itself. The Latin word *noverint* means 'let them know'—'let them know', that is to say, 'what they do know'—let the cobbler stick to his last. Nashe could evidently trust his readers—he could not to-day—to see the implications of his key-word. The 'art' with which these charlatans must not concern themselves is the art, based on a study of ancient models, worked out by the University Wits. Nashe goes on to speak of 'threadbare wits', who were induced 'to empty their invention of their apish', that is, imitative, 'devices and talk most superficially of policy, as those that never ware gown in the University; wherein they revive the old said adage, *Sus Minervam*, and cause the wiser to quip them with *Asinus ad Lyram*'. It must be allowed that this is altogether like the language aimed at Shakespeare by Greene. As for the adages, familiar to a generation that knew its Erasmus, they come to much the same thing. The pig proposed to teach Minerva, and the donkey undertook to play the lyre. To these we may add another, which was doubtless in Nashe's mind, as it may have been in Greene's, *Nihil cum fidibus graculo*, 'The jackdaw has nothing to do with stringed music'—with the lyre, with poetry.

Nashe, who loved a quarrel of words, does not seem to have entered into any controversy with Shakespeare, perhaps because he was working now for Shakespeare's company, perhaps because Shakespeare did not take up the challenge.[2] But, if Nashe recedes into the background, his place is taken by George Chapman.

---

[1] πόλλ' ἠπίστατο ἔργα, κακῶς δ' ἠπίστατο πάντα

[2] He did so later, if, as seems probable, Moth in *Love's Labour's Lost* is meant for Nashe.

On the relations between him and Shakespeare a good deal has been written by scholars who are more familiar with the literary history of the period than I am, so that I must restrict myself in the main to such remarks as occur to a student of the ancient classics. The reader is probably not ignorant that reasons—some of them, as I think, highly persuasive—have been adduced in favour of the view that the rival poet mentioned in the Sonnets is Chapman, and of the view that he is satirized in the person of Holofernes in *Love's Labour's Lost*. But I do not found my case on either of these opinions. I shall be content if I can satisfy reasonable people that Shakespeare met from Chapman, as from others, criticism which he regarded as pedantic, absurd, and, at last, intolerable. It is the criticism with which I am concerned, and the effect which it had on Shakespeare. Whether in his revolt against it he had Chapman particularly in mind, does not, from my point of view, seriously matter. It is however certain that some of the criticism came from Chapman, and that in a manner obliges me to say something about him and his point of view.

George Chapman was a disappointed man, and he was not able to keep his disappointment to himself. The world did not accord him that regard to which he conceived himself entitled, and this neglect he attributes to the jealousy, ignorance and self-seeking of unworthier men. This makes it difficult to sympathize with him. Yet he deserves a little sympathy. He was at once something less and something more than a scholar. His learning, which was almost wholly classical, was neither so extensive nor so accurate as he believed and wished others to believe. On the other hand he was a poet as well as a scholar. It would have been easier for him if he had been solely the one or solely the other. The Renaissance scholar was the victim of a cruel paradox. Nothing was so much admired as classical scholarship, and nothing was done for the scholar. If he was lucky, he found a patron; if he was not lucky, he went hungry.[1] Chapman had for the most part to go hungry.

[1] I may refer the reader, who wishes this topic developed, to that terrible sub-section in Burton on the miseries of scholars, *Anatomy of Melancholy*, Pt. 1, sec. 2. mem. 3. subs. 15—a passage which, as I believe, made an unforgettable impression on the mind of Samuel Johnson.

If his manners were as ungracious as his Prefaces, it would be difficult for him to win or keep a patron. Yet he had to find one, if he was to find the leisure needed by a scholar. We cannot do justice at all to Chapman, he will seem merely a disagreeable pedant, unless we allow for his moral dilemma. When we are disgusted with his querulous vanity—it is only fair to add that he has his moments of humility—let us remember his single-minded devotion to learning. He belonged to a type which had been common enough in France and Italy, though it was rarer in England, for the English have never idolized the scholar. In Chapman's eyes to have learning was to be superior to other men —to successful soldiers and statesmen, to the rich and the noble. Therefore, to achieve learning, he toiled, under serious disadvantages, with unwearied diligence. How hard then that his merits should not be recognized!

Like many others of his time he suffered from a misconception. When he read the Latin poets he found them commended for their *doctrina*, of which the obvious translation is 'learning'. To be a *doctus poeta* then—that, he conceived, was the great object of ambition. But Chapman failed to grasp the true meaning of the epithet, which in the best period of Latin literature meant no more than 'skilled in the art of poetry'. Since the subject-matter of this art was for the most part ancient mythology, no doubt a comprehensive knowledge of that mythology was a necessary part of the education of a poet. But if he knew the somewhat strict and elaborate rules of his art, and if he was familiar with the varied mythology of the Greeks, nothing more in the way of learning was expected of him. Chapman however did not perceive or would not accept this limitation. For one thing the poet's 'learning' involved him, he concluded, in the study of philosophy, which he goes so far as to call his 'mistress' in the sonnet-sequence entitled *A Coronet for his Mistress Philosophy*. Here again Chapman shows himself more in conformity with foreign than English scholarship. The interpretation of ancient poetry in terms of a not very well understood Platonism, made Christian so far as that was possible, had been eagerly prosecuted in Italy by the Florentine Academy and others. It was not without influence in England. More, without subscribing to his doctrines, had translated a *Life of Pico della Mirandola*, while Spenser's *Hymns* show the attraction exercised on him by Platonism as he understood it. But Spenser does not seek to track Plato in the ancient poets. The same prudence may be observed in his use of allegory. He had enough learning to be aware that there was a powerful school of thought which sought, and naturally believed that it found, all kinds of allegorical implications in the great poets of antiquity. But the allegory of the *Faerie Queene*, though it may not always be clear, is always straightforward allegory. I mean there is never any doubt as to whether it is allegory or not.

Chapman however convinced himself that all good poetry should be full of hidden meanings. In the Dedication of *Ovid's Banquet of Sense* to Matthew Royden he commits himself to this opinion: 'that Poesy should be as pervial as oratory, and plainness her special ornament, were the plain way of barbarism'.[1] A little afterwards he says: 'Obscurity in affection of words and indigested conceits is pedantical and childish; but where it shroudeth itself in the heart of his subject, uttered with fitness of figure and expressive epithets, with that darkness will I still labour to be shadowed'. That was the theory which led him to compose *The Shadow of Night*, *Ovid's Banquet of Sense*, *A Coronet for his Mistress Philosophy* and the rest of those strange productions which he wrote when he was not engaged in translation or working for the theatres. It would take too long to analyse these poems, nor, I am thankful to say, is that my business here. But Homer meant so much to Chapman that it is impossible to pass over in silence his views upon the poet he translated, the more so because one rarely finds any but the most superficial discussion of them. The reason for this omission is largely because Chapman's version of Homer is perfectly straightforward, at least as straightforward as Chapman's poetic diction permitted, for the translator is not always content with the Homeric simplicity and directness. Nevertheless, as one reads Chapman, one feels that he takes

---

[1] 'Barbarism' here means illiteracy. It was Aristotle who laid it down that 'plainness' was the 'special ornament', or rather the basic virtue, of 'oratory'.

Homer to be, what in fact Homer is, a poet whose meaning lies on the surface. But that was far from being the view of Chapman. Listen to what he says in his introductory epistle to *The Tears of Peace*.

> Where high Poesy's native habit shines,
> From whose reflections flow eternal lines,
> Philosophy retired to darkest caves
> She can discover: and the proud world's braves
> Answer in anything but impudence
> With circle of her general excellence.
> For ample instance Homer more than serveth,
> And what his grave and learned Muse deserveth . . .

His *learned* Muse! And we know what Chapman understood by learning. Here is a specimen of his exegesis. In the eighth book of the *Iliad*, towards the beginning of the book, Zeus, finding some of the gods inclined to dispute his authority, challenges them in a more or less sporting spirit to a trial of strength. One end of a golden chain is to be fastened to Zeus, and all the other Olympian gods and goddesses are to haul on the other, Zeus being confident that they will not be able to shift him. There may be some ancient myth behind this; but, if such existed, Homer does not know it. For him it is just a tug-of-war. Now listen to Chapman:

> The golden chain of Homer's high device
> Ambition is, or cursed avarice . . .

and so on. He has some lines in his *Eugenia* to the same effect, with a marginal note: 'Homeri Aurea Restis, afflatu divino Resurrectionis praefiguratio', 'Homer's golden chain, by divine inspiration a prophetic symbol of the Resurrection'—which of course is quite another interpretation. Such were the meanings that Chapman read into Homer. He had evidently given much thought to the subject, on which he had even projected a book. For in the verses *To the Reader* prefixed to his translation occur these lines.

> They fail'd to search his deep and treasurous heart;
> The cause was, since they wanted the fit key

Of Nature, in their downright strength of Art,
   With Poesy to open Poesy:
Which, in my poem of the mysteries
   Reveal'd in Homer, I will clearly prove.

The most poetical, and therefore the truest, interpretation he considered to be that which looked for a hidden meaning in all that the poet said. Chapman did not invent the method; the allegorists had got to work upon Homer quite early in classical antiquity itself. But he might have known that the allegorists had been repudiated by the Alexandrian scholars who first put the study of Homer on a critical footing. The truth is that Chapman was not so good a scholar as he imagined himself to be. I am far from saying this by way of disparagement. What he achieved was, considering his opportunities, highly creditable to him. But, since one observes a tendency, even after the researches of M. Schoell and Professor Douglas Bush, to think of Chapman as an eminent Grecian, it is as well to say that, compared with a truly eminent Grecian like Casaubon, he was an uncritical amateur. In view of his own asseverations we must accept it as a fact that he translated Homer directly from the Greek.[1] But when we look into the matter we find that he made out the sense of the Greek by the aid of the Latin translators, of Spondanus and Scapula's lexicon. No harm in that, but it does not justify the boast in his title. Besides, he makes a good many serious blunders of his own. That was inevitable, since he had to teach himself in the intervals of his other occupations and without money to buy books. In the Epilogue to his translation of the Homeric Hymns he exclaims:

Yet then, our learn'd men with their torrents come
Roaring from their forced hills, all crown'd with foam,
That one not taught like them, should learn to know
Their Greek roots, and from thence the groves that grow,
Casting such rich shades, from great Homer's wings,
That first, and last, command the Muses' springs.
Though he's best scholar that, through pains and vows

[1] The title of his complete version of the Iliad is: *The Iliads of Homer, Prince of Poets, never before in any language truly translated.*

Made his own master only, all things knows.
Nor pleads my poor skill form or learned place,
But dauntless labour, constant prayer, and grace . . .[1]

This means, as Dr. Phyllis Bartlett has pointed out, that Chapman, like Shakespeare, had not gone to a university. It is difficult to read the lines without a movement of sympathy and admiration, although Chapman does his best to damp these emotions by proceeding to argue that the trained scholars were no good, since they could not find those esoteric meanings which he himself read into the ancient poets. And it is another disappointment when one discovers that the learning which he is so fond of displaying is so often not his own but copied, sometimes *verbatim*, from others, in particular from the mythologist Natalis Comes.

As Chapman never mentions the name of Shakespeare, nor Shakespeare the name of Chapman, there can be no certainty in any discussion of their relations. Yet in reading the Poems and Prefaces one finds it hard to resist the conclusion that Chapman is often thinking of Shakespeare. For indeed how could it be otherwise? About 1594 Shakespeare was young, of good appearance and engaging manners, the author of a brilliantly successful poem on a classical theme, and all this without having laboured at Latin and Greek. To poor Chapman it must have seemed quite unfair. 'I could have painted pictures like that youth. . . .' The feeling was natural. One thing at least Chapman makes very clear. *Venus and Adonis* was not the kind of poem of which he for one could approve. It carried its meaning on its surface, and that meaning was immoral. If he himself had written a *Venus and Adonis*, it would have concealed an esoteric moral, making it (in spite of appearances to the contrary) highly edifying. That I am not misrepresenting him will be admitted by anyone who has read *Ovid's Banquet of Sense*. Shakespeare would, more or less politely, laugh at this; but it was no laughing matter to Chapman. Nor indeed altogether to Shakespeare. For Chapman had, at least in the early part of his career, some not uninfluential sympathizers. I have already said that I think he was the rival

[1] 33 f. modernized.

poet of the Sonnets. I have been led to this opinion partly by what other people have said, partly by some evidence which appears to have escaped their notice. This I will now state as concisely as I can.

In the *Inductio* to *The Tears of Peace* Chapman relates how—he does not say where—the spirit or ghost of Homer appeared to him and said, among other things, these:

> 'I am', said he, 'that spirit Elysian,
> That (in thy native air, and on the hill
> Next Hitchin's left hand) did thy bosom fill
> With such a flood of soul, that thou wert fain
> (With acclamations of her rapture then)
> To vent it to the echoes of the vale;
> When (meditating on me) a sweet gale
> Brought me upon thee, and thou didst inherit
> My true sense, for the time then, in my spirit;
> And I, invisibly, went prompting thee
> To those fair greens, where thou didst English me.'[1]

I cannot attach any other meaning to these words than this—that Chapman claims to have been directly inspired in his translation of Homer's poems by Homer himself or (what amounts to the same thing) Homer's *anima*, which came to him from Elysium. The classical words are appropriate because they indicate that the passage was suggested by some classical parallel, since, according to the Christian theology of Chapman's time, the soul of Homer would not be in Heaven but, at best, in some such tolerable region of Hell as we find him placed in by Dante. I do not forget that visions of the kind described in *The Teares* are almost wearisomely common in medieval and even Renaissance literature; and that in them a dead poet will often appear in order to console or instruct the dreamer, as for instance Virgil appears to Dante. But Dante does not claim to be inspired by Virgil, at least in any literal way. Again, from the earliest classical times poets have prayed for inspiration to Apollo or the Muses, and have sometimes felt or imagined that they received it. But in general that is only a convention; when it is more, the meaning will be that

[1] 74–85, modernized.

SHAKESPEARE AND THE CLASSICS

the poet is convinced that some power not himself has suggested thoughts or words beyond his unaided reach. Even Milton, even Blake does not seem to go much beyond that. But Chapman's language admits of no such interpretation. It either means nothing —which is incredible in so earnest a man—or it means that there was some mystic affinity between his soul and Homer's akin to that which subsisted between a Greek man and his *daemon*, between a Roman and his *genius*. This is the sense of the couplet (91–2):

> Who[1] told me, he brought stay to all my state;
> That he was Angel to me, Star and Fate.

Chapman was scholar enough to know what these words meant. As it will be necessary for me to touch upon the ancient conception of the daemon or genius in a later place, it will be enough to say here that it came to be thought of as a spiritual *alter ego* of the man whom it accompanied through life. In the philosophy of the Stoics it was made subservient to the over-ruling Providence in which they believed; and in this way, from being simply a man's guardian angel or just his 'luck', it became in a larger and more cosmic sense his 'star' or 'fate'. From this it will appear how extraordinary is the claim of Chapman that Homer is his genius. He may of course have felt that his claim was justified by some genuine psychic experience. But anyone who has read Chapman will feel certain that even so he would seek to fortify his claim by some classical precedent. He had no difficulty in finding that, and it is more than probable that it put the whole thing in Chapman's head.

The *Annales* of Ennius, the first great epic of Latin literature, had, like *The Tears of Peace*, an 'induction', in which the ghost of Homer appeared and spoke to the poet. It appeared to him in a dream as he slept. Cicero quotes some of the actual words of Ennius: *visus Homerus adesse poeta*, 'I saw in a dream the poet Homer.' This dream was very famous in antiquity, although the original is lost. Lucretius alludes to it (I. 124 f.):

> unde sibi exortam semper florentis Homeri

[1] Homer.

commemorat speciem lacrimas effundere salsas
coepisse et rerum naturam expandere dictis.[1]

What Homer expounded to Ennius was the Pythagorean philosophy. This he was able to do because his soul had been re-
incarnated in the body of Pythagoras. There is a reference to
that in Horace (*Ep.* II. 1. 50 f.):

Ennius et sapiens et fortis et alter Homerus,
ut critici dicunt, leviter curare videtur
quo promissa cadant et somnia Pythagorea.[2]

Persius, who so often echoes Horace, echoes him here. He says
(VI. 10, 11):

cor iubet hoc Enni, postquam destertuit esse
Maeonides Quintus pavone ex Pythagoreo.[3]

Quintus was the praenomen of Ennius, and Maeonides was the
patronymic of Homer; so that to say 'Maeonides Quintus' is as
much as to say 'Homer Ennius'. One of the ancient and well
informed *scholia* that have been transmitted with the text of
Persius tells us that the soul of Ennius had been (1) a peacock,
(2) Euphorbus, a Trojan warrior killed at the siege of Troy,
(3) Homer, (4) Pythagoras. A half-line is quoted from the lost
Annales: *memini me fiere pavom*, 'I remember becoming a peacock'.
Lastly Porphyrion, who lived in the first half of the second century, when the level of scholarship was still high, observes in his
commentary on Horace: 'in principio annalium suorum somnis
se scripsit admonitum, quod secundum Pythagorae dogma anima
Homeri in suum corpus venisset.' 'In the beginning of his
Annals he', Ennius, 'has written that he was instructed in his

---

[1] 'Whence'—that is, from the world of the dead—'he'—that is, Ennius—
'relates that the appearance of ever-living Homer arising for him began to shed
salt tears and to display in words the nature of things.'

[2] 'Ennius, whom the critics describe as accomplished, spirited, a second Homer,
need not, it appears, be over-anxious as to how his promises and Pythagorean
dreams are fulfilled.' The words have been variously explained, but the allusion
to the dream about Pythagoras does not admit of the least uncertainty.

[3] 'So says Ennius' brain, when he had been roused from dreaming himself
Maeonides Quintus developed out of Pythagoras' peacock.' Conington's
translation.

sleep, because the soul of Homer had passed, according to the teaching of Pythagoras, into his body'.

Anything that had reference to Homer was avidly read by Chapman; and this particular story is alluded to in books—Cicero's *de natura deorum*, Horace's *Epistles*, the *Satires* of Persius—which were familiar to every educated man in the sixteenth century. On the natural assumption that Chapman came to know about the vision of Ennius at a comparatively early period of his life, the vision in the *Tears* loses its singularity. If the spirit of Homer appeared to Ennius, it might appear to Chapman; if it claimed a special relation to Ennius, it might claim a special relation to Chapman. The relation could not be quite the same. Chapman could not venture—though one has a feeling that he would have liked, if it had not been heretical—to claim that he was a reincarnation of Homer. But he went as far as he could; he said that Homer was his 'angel'.

The *Tears*[1] was published in 1609; but this does not in any way help us to fix the date when Chapman first believed that he was writing under the immediate inspiration of Homer. The conviction seized him when he was living in the neighbourhood of Hitchin; presumably therefore before he settled in London. It cannot be dissociated from his resolve to devote himself to the study and translation of Homer, for the words of the spirit can have no other meaning than that he suggested to Chapman the true sense—alas, he did not always do so!—of his Greek, or even 'prompted', that is dictated, the words of the translation, the spirit evidently having acquired a mastery of English in the Elysian fields. The first part of Chapman's translation came out in 1598. But it must have been preceded by years of study, directed and inspired, he says, by the spirit of Homer. During these years his friends, and probably his enemies, must have heard a great deal about that. For he was not a man to consume his own smoke.

Have we not got now a very probable explanation of the famous couplet in Sonnet LXXXVI?

> He, nor that affable familiar ghost
> Which nightly gulls him with intelligence.

[1] The full title was *Euthymiae Raptus or The Teares of Peace.*

The ghost, I think, is Homer, the 'genius' of Chapman. Here is a perfectly apt comment from Burton (*A.M.*, Pt. I. sec. II. mem. I. subs. 2, forming part of the 'Digression of Spirits').

'Cardan . . . out of the doctrine of Stoics, will have some of these genii (for so he calls them) to be desirous of men's company, very affable and familiar with them.'

Burton need not have gone to Cardan and the Stoics for evidence in favour of so common a belief; and no doubt he knew this; but scholars must quote authority. The couplet however will not be fully understood until we remind ourselves that such an affable ghost would, according to Elizabethan notions, have very doubtful credentials. We may remember Hamlet's scruples:

> The spirit that I have seen
> May be the devil and the devil hath power
> T'assume a pleasing shape; yea, and perhaps
> Out of my weakness and my melancholy,
> As he is very potent with such spirits,
> Abuses me to damn me (II. ii. 628 f.)

What the couplet suggests then is that Chapman's visitant, so far from being his good 'angel', is a lying spirit, a devil, who 'gulls' his dupe. Shakespeare in fact does not believe Chapman's spirit is Homer at all; and he refers to it with an amused contempt.[1]

I do not however rest my case on what is no more than a probability, however high. What is beyond question is Chapman's bitterness against poetry which he regarded as both sensual and ignorant. To that double charge he reverts again and again. In Chapman's mind the sensuality and the ignorance are complementary, if not identical. He has reached this conclusion, I suppose, as a result of his conviction that the appeal of great poetry is through sensuous images to a hidden or 'dark' truth, which, since it is true, is therefore (as Plato would agree) good and even divine. The first sonnet of *A Coronet for his Mistress Philosophy*, the most

[1] I have not added the evidence of Professor Minto, who was the first to identify the rival poet with Chapman; what I have written is merely corroborative of his view, which (I may add) has not been helped by much that has been written since in his support. Nor do I even now accept it as an article of faith.

intricately designed and attractive of his original poems, may be quoted.

> Muses that sing love's sensual empery,
> And lovers, kindling your enragéd fires
> At *Cupid's* bonfires burning in the eye,
> Blown with the empty breath of vain desires:
> You that prefer the painted cabinet
> Before the wealthy jewels it doth store ye,
> That all your joys in dying figures set,
> And stain the living substance of your story,
> Abjure those joys, abhor their memory,
> And let my love the honoured subject be
> Of love, and honour's complete history.
> Your eyes were never yet let in to see
> The majesty and riches of the mind,
> But dwell in darkness; for your God is blind.

To exemplify his own teaching in this matter he wrote the incredible poem entitled—what a title!—*Ovid's Banquet of Sence.* It appeared in 1595, just after Shakespeare's two poems had taken the town by storm, and, directly or indirectly, it is a challenge to *Venus and Adonis.* Shakespeare had taken the subject of *Venus* from Ovid and had treated it with a superficial brilliance and lucidity, which Chapman was perfectly entitled to criticize adversely, if he wished; I mean, it is quite arguable that great poetry is not written in that way. But the line taken by Chapman is hardly that. His argument is that those who, like Shakespeare, considered Ovid to be a 'pervial' author were wrong. How far wrong, he sets out to show in the *Banquet.* It has to be read to be believed. Ovid surprises Julia bathing *al fresco*; and Chapman describes how the five senses of the poet were affected, which was by no means all at once, but in the following order, (1) hearing (*auditus*), (2) smell (*olfactus*), (3) sight (*visus*), (4) taste (*gustus*), (5) touch (*tactus*); though when it comes to *tactus*, he (in the words of the argument) 'is interrupted'. This pedantry was evidently suggested by Ficino, whose commentary on Plato's *Symposium* was familiar to Chapman.[1] It would seem that Chapman supposes

---

[1] There is now a convenient edition, with a (generally) accurate translation, of the commentary by Sears H. Jayne, 1944.

himself to be relating a tale of Platonic love. 'The doctrine'—I
quote Dr. Phyllis Bartlett[1]—'is that man must partake to the full
of sensual contentment in order that his mind may be excited to a
higher love'. What Plato would have thought of such a doctrine,
God knows, not I. Dr. Bartlett calls it 'Neoplatonic'. But it is
neither Platonic nor Neoplatonic; it is nonsense. Let no one
imagine that Chapman found it in Ficino. If he had looked there,
he would have found the exact opposite: 'amor ergo in tribus eis
(i.e. 'mente, visu, auditu') terminatur. Appetitio vero, quae
reliquos sequitur sensus, non amor sed libido rabiesque vocatur.
'Love therefore finds its end in these three (thought, sight, hearing). But the desire which accompanies the other senses is not
called love but lust and madness.'[2] This absurd attempt of Chapman to make out that Ovid and Julia were going through some
profound spiritual experience is infinitely more distasteful than
the behaviour of Venus in Shakespeare's poem, ill as that goddess
there behaves. But it never really mattered. For, apart from any
question of taste, the writing in the *Banquet* is so clumsy and per-
plexed that readers could not, then any more than now, be
troubled to make out the sense.

Chapman had already, in his *Hymnus ad Cynthiam*, which is the
second part of *The Shadow of Night* (1594), used these words:

> Presume not then, ye flesh-confounded souls,
> That cannot bear the full Castalian bowls,
> Which sever mounting spirits from the senses,
> To look in this deep fount for thy pretences.[3]

This has the appearance of an attack—look at the change to the
singular 'thy'—on Shakespeare, who had prefixed, or allowed to
be prefixed, to *Venus and Adonis* that motto:

> Vilia miretur vulgus; mihi flavus Apollo
> Pocula Castalia plena ministret aqua.

[1] *Poems of George Chapman*, Introduction, p. 5.
[2] Is it too late to protest against the growing habit of calling anyone—even
Cicero—with Platonic sympathies a Neoplatonist? It makes nonsense of the
history of philosophy. Ficino was a Platonist or hoped to be.
[3] 161–4, modernized.

We cannot be quite sure, because the Ovidian lines, which are beyond question alluded to, were well enough known before the publication of *Venus and Adonis*. On the other hand their quotation at the head of a poem which Chapman had read with outraged feelings would be very likely to rankle in his mind until they led to some such explosion as finds ungrammatical utterance in the four lines I have quoted from the *Hymnus ad Cynthiam*. It must be confessed too that it is altogether in Chapman's manner to attack indirectly and by way of allusion. Thus after a furious invective against what he calls 'a certain envious windsucker' he adds, 'I have stricken, single him as you can'. I do not mean that Chapman is solitary among Elizabethan authors in making such dark insinuations. On the contrary they are characteristic of the period. But they are rather specially characteristic of Chapman, whose resentful, unhappy mind seems on occasion to be touched by something like a persecution mania. On the whole there is only too much reason to think that his attitude to Shakespeare was pretty consistently that of open or veiled hostility.

Although Chapman was a person of great intelligence, his criticism of Shakespeare, so far as we can make it out, was coloured by a doctrine—the necessity in great poetry for an esoteric obscurity—which could never be popular with the reading public, even supposing they understood it.[1] In addition to this Chapman affected in these Poems and Prefaces of his to despise the vulgar, with the natural result that the vulgar with perfect satisfaction to itself merely ignored them. To a large extent then Shakespeare could afford to disregard his influence. He could not in the same way disregard the influence of Ben

---

[1] The association in some recent criticism of Chapman with Donne is, I think, a serious error. They seem to me totally different not merely in temperament but in the quality of their thought. Chapman is continually labouring with some idea or conception for which he cannot find exact or apt expression; Donne can always express what he has in his mind. It is the subtlety of thought that perplexes the reader in Donne; in Chapman it is the incoherence and involution of the language.

Jonson and his criticism, which we have now to consider. I am absolved from discussing the question in detail by Dover Wilson's paper on 'Ben Jonson and *Julius Caesar*';[1] so I confine myself to one or two observations. As the title of Professor Wilson's paper indicates, Jonson's criticism became explicit on the appearance of *Julius Caesar*, which was notably successful on the stage. There may have been some more or less subconscious jealousy on the part of Ben—indeed that is obvious—but he did not mean to be unfriendly. It was simply that the whole tendency of his criticism ran counter to the assumptions which underlie *Julius Caesar*. He believed that he had the ancients on his side; and that was enough for him, as it was enough for every academic critic then and for long afterwards. How could the ancients be wrong and Will Shakespeare right? That was what puzzled Ben, and we must not blame him too much. We may take it as certain that he attributed Shakespeare's faults or heresies in the main to his deficiency in scholarship, on which he was apt to dwell. As Rowe puts it in the anecdote already quoted which introduces Mr. Hales, what provoked the Etonian to his outburst was 'hearing Ben frequently reproaching him'—Shakespeare—'with the want of learning and ignorance of the ancients'. But probably Jonson was not so much 'reproaching' Shakespeare for his ignorance of the ancients as regretting it on the ground that a better knowledge of them would have taught his friend a more chastened style. Everybody remembers the phrase in *Discoveries*: 'aliquando sufflaminandus erat', 'There were times when he had to be checked.'[2] The context seems to imply that Jonson was thinking of Shakespeare's manner of writing rather than speech. Fluency or over-facility in composition was a literary misdemeanour in the eyes of Jonson because it had been such in the eyes of his idol Horace, who had censured it in

---

[1] In *Shakespeare Survey* 2, p. 36 f.

[2] *Sufflaminare* means 'to put the brake on a wheel', so as either to stop or retard it. We cannot be sure how Jonson took the word in its application to Shakespeare. In its original application—to the orator Haterius—it could have meant either that Haterius was too copious in his diction or that he was too torrential in his delivery.

Lucilius, his predecessor in Roman satire. To quote one passage, he says:

> at dixi fluere hunc lutulentum, saepe ferentem
> plura quidem tollenda reliquendis. (*Serm.*, I. 50, 51)[1]

And of course everyone knows that Horace constantly recommends the use of the file. This was the critical doctrine taken over from the Roman poet by Jonson and practised by him in his own poems, often (as in his lyrics) with the happiest effects. But when he condemned Shakespeare for not practising it he was condemning him less on his merits than on a theory borrowed from a Latin author. It does not follow that Jonson had no case at all, or that he was entirely wrong when, in answer to the players who boasted that Shakespeare had never blotted a line, he growled, 'Would he had blotted a thousand.'[2] I am not at all sure that Shakespeare would not have agreed on that point with Ben. But Jonson does not prove his case. He produces no evidence. He relies on a single citation which does not raise the question of style at all, unless it be true that to write without due reflection is to write badly. A very odd citation it is. Shakespeare, he writes, made Caesar say

> Caesar did never wrong, but with just cause.

This Jonson regards as a piece of nonsense, as perhaps it is.[3] Only it is not in Shakespeare. At least in *Julius Caesar*, as we now have it, there is no such line. What we read there is this:

> Know, Caesar doth not wrong, nor without cause
> Will he be satisfied (III. i. 47, 48)

And this, if not so epigrammatic, at least makes sense. It is scarcely credible that Jonson did not remember correctly a passage which had struck him as absurd and which he quotes for its absurdity.

---

[1] 'But I did say of Lucilius that he runs in a muddy stream, often carrying down more that ought to be removed than that ought to be left behind.'

[2] To 'blot' means of course to correct; Pope speaks of 'the last and greatest art, the art to blot'.

[3] It could be defended if 'wrong' were pronounced as if it were between quotation marks.

It is quite incredible that he deliberately misquoted it. It must have been what Shakespeare originally wrote. Later, the line was altered in deference to Jonson's criticism.

It is not improbable that it was the success of *Julius Caesar* with the public, and Ben's reflections on this, that led him to write *Sejanus* and *Catiline*, as if to show the world how a drama on a classical theme ought to be composed. There is no point now in examining these plays, because they were never more than estimable failures. Yet perhaps one may fairly deduce from them the lines on which Jonson must have criticized *Julius Caesar*. He must have scrutinized it not merely for literary but for historical and archaeological blunders; for he himself can, and does, quote chapter and verse from ancient authorities for every topical statement he makes in his two Roman dramas. We may, I think, be certain that he believed that only a classical scholar was equipped for writing a classical play. According to this view Shakespeare was disqualified from the outset for such a task.

I have given the gist of the criticism levelled against Shakespeare in his lifetime. It amounts to little more than the charge that his ignorance led him to write in ways for which there was no ancient authority. If we are to understand what the criticism meant to him, we must keep in mind what was said at the beginning of this book about the prestige of the classics in Shakespeare's world. He had to adjust his thoughts and feelings to that. Can we discover at all how he succeeded in adjusting them?

The first recorded criticism of Shakespeare was the outburst of Greene about the upstart crow. What lies behind it, it is impossible now to discover. The two men must at one time have known each other well, perhaps been friends. For my own part I confess that I cannot read the passage without a strong persuasion, amounting almost to conviction, that Greene's connexion with Shakespeare had been a good deal more than casual, so that the dying man's complaint of being 'deserted' found an echo in the hearts of some who knew more than we do, though less no doubt than the whole truth. This would explain the lines in *Greene's Funerals*, which have already been quoted in part:

> Greene is the pleasing object of an eye:
> Greene pleased the eyes of all that look'd upon him.
> Greene is the ground of every painter's dye:
> Greene gave the ground to all that wrote upon him.
> Nay more, the men that so eclips'd his fame
> Purloin'd his plumes. Can they deny the same?[1]

The last three of these punning lines reveal sympathy with Greene and dissatisfaction with Shakespeare. There was probably nothing in the charge or insinuation, all the evidence suggesting that Greene had only himself to blame for the distresses into which he had fallen. But he was, in addition to his qualities as a poet and dramatist, an accomplished journalist, or rather pamphleteer, who knew very well how to make literary capital out of his own sins and sufferings. His pamphlet had a success of the same kind as Burnet's account of Rochester's death-bed repentance, and for much the same reason. Rochester's repentance was evidently sincere, while Greene's as evidently was not. But the average English reader, then as now, would have the feeling that, whatever Greene's weaknesses may have been—even if he was a manifest humbug—at least his sufferings were real. On that ground he obtained, when his disreputable presence had been removed by death, a good deal of sympathy. People were inclined to say, 'Poor Greene after all! Could not Will Shakespeare at any rate have visited him when he was dying?' Nobody likes that kind of suggestion, and Shakespeare would feel it more than most. For a gentleman does not desert his friends, and he liked to think of himself as a gentleman. That is probably why he or his friends got Chettle, who had edited the *Groatsworth* after the death of Greene, to apologize in such a way as to make it clear that there was no stain on Shakespeare's reputation as a gentleman. His literary reputation could look after itself.

This was proved when, very shortly afterwards, he published *Venus and Adonis* (1593), followed a year later by *The Rape of*

---

[1] Sonnet IX, modernized.

Lucrece. These poems, as the Latin motto to *Venus* implies, do not make their appeal to the 'vulgar' but to readers of a kind that might regard Lord Southampton, to whom both are dedicated, as fairly representative of their own tastes. The author writes as one who himself belongs to this class, or at least has mingled with it and understands it. One gets the same impression from the early comedies, especially *Love's Labour's Lost,* and from the early tragedy *Romeo and Juliet.* Shakespeare knows all about young people of fashion, their manners, their 'notions', their special talk. These, and those who went along with them, formed the main body of the readers of *Venus* and *Lucrece;* and Shakespeare became their poet. It is not that he set out to be startling or original. Although he already possesses a recognizable style of his own, it is composed of elements found elsewhere though not mingled in the same proportions—in Sidney and Spenser and Lodge and Marlowe, whose *Hero and Leander* it is very likely that he read in manuscript. The subjects of *Venus and Adonis* and of *Lucrece* were among the most frequently treated in Renaissance poetry all over Europe, and this for at least a century and a half. Nor was what Shakespeare gave new wine in old bottles, for the spirit of both poems is characteristically of the Renaissance, far more so than the spirit of Spenser, which was touched by medievalism and puritanism. What gave pleasure to their readers was not so much the voluptuous quality of the verses as their intellectual brilliance —their ingenious antitheses and conceits. It is in truth their deficiency in real passion that injures them now. This is just as true of *Lucrece* as of *Venus.* I cannot accept the view that *Lucrece* is a sort of palinode after the *Venus;* it is rather its complement. The rôles are only reversed. In *Venus* it is the goddess who is lustful, in *Lucrece* it is the man. In neither was it the subject, in both it was the 'wit' and the sweetness of the versification that enchanted contemporary readers.

But we are less concerned with that than with something else which distinguishes the two poems from others of their kind. This is the absence, almost complete, of classical learning. Ovid's own poetry is loaded in every rift with mythological allusions, and his Renaissance imitators, both in Latin and in their mother tongues, had followed him in this. But anyone who reads the Poems of Shakespeare with an eye solely to their matter will be astonished to find how meagre and perfunctory is the element of classical allusion. We, who think little of such allusions and rarely find them in contemporary verse (unless when a writer wishes to make some symbolic or inverted use of them) do not notice this characteristic of *Venus* and *Lucrece*. But it was noticed in Shakespeare's own day. Chapman, who crams as much learning as he can into all his non-dramatic writing, is obviously enraged that such an ignoramus should write upon a classical subject at all. Others might not be enraged, they might even like the change from mythology to the description of English sights and sounds; but they were bound to notice it. For it was something that no one had quite ventured to do before. Certainly not Marlowe, whose *Hero and Leander*—although no doubt it is a kind of translation—is full of classical lore even where the original is not being followed. How far Shakespeare deliberately kept such lore out of his own Poems, is hard to say. It could not have been mere ignorance, because the *Metamorphoses* would give him an education in mythology. So he must have known, at least to some extent, that he was challenging the tradition, dating from Ovid and long before, of the need for mythological learning in this kind of poetry. I say in this kind, for much depends upon that. A poet writing a comedy or a satire or even a pastoral was not bound to show his learning. But if he was re-telling a myth, like Shakespeare in *Venus*, he was so bound. Even here Shakespeare was not entirely original. Even as early as Chaucer one detects an impulse to break loose from the tradition of the scholars, nor did the Renaissance succeed in checking this impulse altogether. Spenser had written *The Shepheard's Calender* in striking contrast with the pedantic commentary which accompanies it. But it was reserved for Shakespeare to make out of a classical myth what was practically an English poem.

Since both the *Venus* and the *Lucrece* were, in spite of the more academic type of critic, more than well received, it may be wondered why Shakespeare did not follow up this vein. A possible explanation is that he was too busy in other directions.

Perhaps he thought the vein was getting exhausted. Neither of these explanations is very convincing. It is much more probable that, if he did not write more such poems, it was because he did not want to. He may have felt, what every modern reader feels, the emotional shallowness of them, the lack of human sympathy with the characters which is so unlike the Shakespeare of the plays. Is it possible that the experience which has found its utterance in the sonnets will give us the clue? Certainly in writing the sonnets Shakespeare found a new style expressive of a new range of feeling, most passionate and sincere. There was no going back to prettiness and red-rose chains.

Of the Sonnets it is necessary for me to say something because of these moods they reflect. I would say as little as possible about the problems they involve, of which one is their dating. This cannot be fixed, except perhaps in the case of CVII, which Professor G. B. Harrison has assigned to 1596 for reasons that are all but convincing.[1] Sonnet CVII clearly looks back to a period of some length, during which Shakespeare's love had been clouded in some degree by sorrow and disappointment. Again, the style of the Sonnets reminds one less of his later style, as we trace its development in the plays, than of the style of the lyrical parts of *Love's Labour's Lost*. I am therefore drawn to the conclusion that many or even most of the Sonnets were composed very soon after the publication of the Poems; and this, I think, is the opinion of most students of the problem. It is also the opinion of most students that the Sonnets—apart from the 'Dark Lady' sequence—are addressed to a young man of a rank socially superior to the poet's. Beyond these two generally received positions I do not propose to go.

The poetry of a young man is usually touched with melancholy; it is often steeped in what to older people seems a somewhat causeless gloom. But Shakespeare was hardly a young man, at least for an Elizabethan, when he was writing the Sonnets,

---

[1] Sir Edmund Chambers's argument against Harrison has weight, like everything he writes, but does not seem to me conclusive. Dr. Leslie Hotson's theory that the sonnet alludes to the defeat of the Spanish Armada in 1588 is moonshine.

and he feels bitterly the disparity of age between himself and his friend. Also he was a practised writer; and, while it is easy to find parallels to his modes of expression and even of thought in the sonnets of other men, he does not take his tone from anyone else; he has his own personal experience, which he puts into his own words. What sensitive reader does not feel their poignancy? True, every lover for whom one can have any respect is filled at times with a profound sense of his own unworthiness. But this kind of humility, though there is a good deal of it in the Sonnets, is not the only kind to be found there. In poem after poem, after the first happy or not unhappy score or so, the reader is pained by the self-abasement, amounting at times to self-contempt, the sense of rejection, the deep unhappiness of the poet. This mood or these moods are not of course permanent, but they are prevalent. We cannot be sure what caused them. But on the whole it is pretty clear that Shakespeare was made to realize that the perfect intimacy which he had hoped to establish between himself and his friend could not be assured. It was not that the friend was unresponsive; but simply it would not do. An actor could not at that date and place in history be the *alter ego* of a young nobleman.

> Let me confess that we two must be twain,
> Although our undivided loves are one:
> So shall those blots that do with me remain,
> Without thy help, by me be borne alone.
> In our two loves there is but one respect,
> Though in our lives a separable spite,
> Which though it alter not love's sole effect,
> Yet doth it steal sweet hours from love's delight.
> I may not evermore acknowledge thee,
> Lest my bewailed guilt should do thee shame,
> Nor thou with public kindness honour me,
> Unless thou take that honour from thy name.
>   But do not so; I love thee in such sort,
>   As thou being mine, mine is thy good report   (XXXVI)

Although the meaning of these lines is clear enough, the intensity of the feeling involved may surprise an age in which social distinctions are being ignored or lost. Why should the poet be so painfully conscious of his rank in society? We may wonder, we may be sorry for it; but the fact remains. He hates having to make his living on the boards.

> Alas, 'tis true I have gone here and there,
> And made myself a motley to the view (CX)

Again, in even more famous words:

> O for my sake do you with Fortune chide,
> The guilty goddess of my harmful deeds,
> That did not better for my life provide
> Than public means that public manners breeds.
> Thence comes it that my name receives a brand,
> And almost thence my nature is subdued
> To what it works in, like the dyer's hand (CXI)

Shakespeare believed, apparently with justice, that he was of gentle birth; and he could not but feel that, with ordinary luck, he would have had a gentleman's education at one of the universities. Let us not think, because this matters less than nothing to us, it did not matter to him. His feeling about it seems to have come to a head during the reign, apparently very brief, of the 'rival poet'. It is one of the arguments in favour of identifying this poet with Chapman that he was 'learned'. Whoever he was, his superiority to Shakespeare was held to consist in his greater learning.

> Thine eyes, that taught the dumb on high to sing
> And heavy ignorance aloft to fly,
> Have added feathers to the learned's wing (LXXVIII)

It is of course Shakespeare who is represented here as dumb and ignorant compared with the other. It is the old argument. Shakespeare was not academically learned, he did not really know Latin or Greek; therefore he could not be a poet of any mark or estimation. The young friend for a time probably believed this, for all his teachers seemed to believe it; and, as a patron then expected to be rewarded for his patronage by the immortality of fame conferred upon him by his poet's verses, he may have dallied with the thought of patronizing the more learned rival. If so, he quickly changed his mind, but not before inflicting another, though apparently not a deep or lasting, wound upon the feelings of his friend.

If we disregard such oblique depreciation as we find in the University Wits and Chapman, we are left to conjecture what the adverse criticism of the Poems was like. But it need not be baseless conjecture, for *Love's Labour's Lost*, which is an attack on pedantry in letters as well as in love, shows us at least the kind of criticism to which Shakespeare objected. It has already been noted that there is a tendency among Shakespearian scholars to think that Holofernes is a caricature of Chapman. That of course would suit me very well. But I hesitate to make the complete identification on grounds which I have already stated. I prefer to regard Holofernes for the moment as a typical pedant (as Shakespeare conceived such a being) with mannerisms suggested by pedants of his acquaintance, such as George Chapman. So much, I imagine, will be allowed me; and I ask for no more.

> HOLOFERNES. What, my soul, verses?
> NATHANIEL. Ay, sir, and very learned.
> HOL. Let me hear a staff, a stanza, a verse; lege, domine.

Nathaniel then reads a 'sonnet', much in the style of the young Shakespeare himself.

> If love make me forsworn, how shall I swear to love?
>   Ah, never faith could hold, if not to beauty vow'd!
> Though to myself forsworn, to thee I'll faithful prove;
>   Those thoughts to me were oaks, to thee like osiers bow'd.
> Study his bias leaves and makes his book thine eyes,
>   Where all those pleasures live that art would comprehend:
> If knowledge be the mark, to know thee shall suffice;
>   Well learned is that tongue that well can thee commend,
> All ignorant that soul that sees thee without wonder;
>   Which is to me some praise that I thy parts admire:
> Thy eye Jove's lightning bears, thy voice his dreadful thunder,
>   Which, not to anger bent, is music and sweet fire.
> Celestial as thou art, O, pardon love this wrong,
> That sings heaven's praise with such an earthly tongue.
>   (*Love's Labour's Lost*, IV. ii. 108 f.)

That is the poem, which, it will be observed, expresses a sentiment about learning not likely to please a schoolmaster. Here is Holofernes' criticism:

'Here are only numbers ratified; but, for the elegancy, facility and golden cadence of poesy, caret. Ovidius Naso was the man: and why, indeed, Naso, but for smelling out the odoriferous flowers of fancy, the jerks of invention? Imitari is nothing: so doth the hound his master, the ape his keeper, the tired horse his rider. . . . I will prove those verses to be very unlearned, neither savouring of poetry, wit nor invention.'

Now the verses which Holofernes regards as 'unlearned' are really very much in Shakespeare's earlier manner, though the metre is one which he does not greatly affect. They have a good deal of 'the elegancy, facility and golden cadence of poesy'. They also contain some 'jerks of invention'. They are in fact distinctly Ovidian—or let us say Neo-Ovidian, Renaissance-Ovidian. Holofernes is such an ass that he does not recognize the Ovidian qualities when he meets them. He simply parrots the critical chatter of the day without understanding in the least what it means. His own notion of the poetical may be inferred from the verses composed by him when he was presenting the youthful-looking Moth in the character of Hercules.

> Great Hercules is presented by this imp,
>> Whose club kill'd Cerberus, that three-headed canis;
> And when he was a babe, a child, a shrimp,
>> Thus did he strangle serpents in his manus.
> Quoniam he seemeth in minority,
> Ergo I come with this apology (v. ii. 592 f.)

There is learning for you! Of course it is mere burlesque, but it is burlesque of something actual; for in Elizabethan times literary criticism, so far as it existed at all, was very much in the hands of the schoolmasters, not of course so stupid as Holofernes, but tending like Holofernes to judge poetry from the point of view of the grammarian and the rhetorician. His conversation shows the quality of his mind.

HOL. The deer was, as you know, sanguis, in blood; ripe as the pomewater, who now hangeth like a jewel in the ear of caelo, the sky, the welkin, the heaven; and anon falleth like a crab on the face of terra, the soil, the land, the earth.

NATH. Truly, Master Holofernes, the epithets are sweetly varied, like a scholar at the least: but, sir, I assure ye, it was a buck of the first head.

HOL. Sir Nathaniel, haud credo.

DULL. 'Twas not a haud credo; 'twas a pricket.

HOL. Most barbarous intimation! yet a kind of insinuation, as it were, in via, in way, of explication; facere, as it were, replication, or rather, ostentare, to show, as it were, his inclination, after his undressed, unpolished, uneducated, unpruned, untrained, or rather, unlettered, or ratherest, unconfirmed fashion, to insert again my haud credo for a deer.

DULL. I said the deer was not a haud credo; 'twas a pricket.

HOL. Twice-sod simplicity, bis coctus! O thou monster Ignorance, how deformed dost thou look! (IV. ii. *ad init.*)

Would anyone at any time talk like this? Why, yes; schoolmasters, some schoolmasters, did. They learned the habit of it from their Latin grammars and dictionaries, which gave two or three English equivalents for a Latin word. Shakespeare is simply remembering his schooldays, with a spice of humorous malice. Then Holofernes, like most pedants, loves to use words, derived from the Latin, in their original, or what he supposes to be their original, significance. All that grandiloquent balderdash beginning 'Most barbarous intimation!' amounts to nothing more than this, that Holofernes considers that he has been interrupted by an ignoramus.[1] And, you know, it reads almost like a parody of Chapman's prose. Here are the first two sentences in the Dedication of *The Shadow of Night*.

'It is an exceeding rapture of delight in the deep search of knowledge (none knoweth better than thyself, sweet Matthew) that maketh men manfully endure the extremes incident to that Herculean labour: from flints must the Gorgonean fount be smitten. Men must be shod by Mercury, girt with Saturn's adamantine sword, take the shield from Pallas, the helm from Pluto, and have the eyes of Graea (as Hesiodus

[1] See p. 67 f.

arms Perseus against Medusa) before they can cut off the head of benumbing ignorance, or subdue their monstrous affections to most beautiful judgement.'

Those who have read Chapman's prose will agree that this is far from an unfavourable specimen of it, for in general it can only be described as execrable. But the passage I have given is sufficiently pedantic. I have chosen it because it seems impossible to doubt that Shakespeare had read that Dedication, unless one is prepared to alter (as some do) the reading of our authorities for the text. In Act IV. scene iii. 254, 255 the King says

> Black is the badge of hell,
> The hue of dungeons and the School of Night.

Recourse was had to emendation,[1] chiefly no doubt because the allusion in the King's words was not taken. But now it seems generally supposed that there is an allusion to *The Shadow of Night*, which embodies the doctrine of some 'school' or society which held, among other opinions, that

> No pen can anything eternal write,
> That is not steeped in humour of the Night.
>
> (*Hymnus in Noctem*, 376, 377)

That some reference is intended is next to certain, although it is very possible to go beyond the evidence when one attempts to recover the names of members, not to mention the principles, of the 'school', which after all may have existed only or mainly in the imagination of ill-wishers. The tone of the King's allusion suggests amusement on his part rather than hostility. At any rate it gives us a date, for *The Shadow of Night* was published in 1594. The date of *Love's Labour's Lost* cannot be much later, for such allusions lose their point if they are delayed. Since then we can believe that the play was acted in 1594, or 1595 at latest, we can fairly draw the inference that as early as that the quarrel between Shakespeare and the schoolmasters was on. It was much more than a personal quarrel with Chapman, although Chapman may have so regarded it, for he was too ready to look on a difference of opinion as a personal affront. At any rate he habitually

---

[1] E.g., 'suit of night'.

speaks of the 'ignorant' as being not only sensual and avaricious but consumed with 'envy' of himself. He complains that 'Homer no patron found nor Chapman friend'. How could he expect to keep friends if he was so self-righteous and censorious? For a time he was friendly with Ben Jonson, perhaps because of a common disgust at the ignorance of the public. But there was a violent quarrel, and there survives from Chapman's hand an unfinished diatribe against Ben, incoherent with outraged dignity. Shakespeare, having none of this touchiness himself, would be half irritated, half amused by it in other people. Holofernes is rather ridiculous than odious, but it is impossible to respect him. His very 'learning' is a sham. He imposes upon Nathaniel, who is a mere hedge-schoolmaster and almost a half-wit, but he ought not to impose upon us. Certainly, if Chapman had reason to believe that he had been caricatured in Holofernes, nothing would gall him so much as the suggestion that his learning was a pretence. That suggestion would not have been fair, although the suggestion of pedantry would have been fair enough. But comedy is comedy, and the author must be allowed his fling.

To be sure Chapman was particularly sensitive about his reputation for scholarship. That comes out very clearly in the various introductions, in verse and prose, to his translations. It is more than likely that it was some animadversion by Jonson upon his scholarship that bred the rupture between the two men, for the tenor of Chapman's invective is that Ben has too high an opinion of Ben's learning. There is no doubt that, if Jonson looked for deficiencies in Chapman's scholarship, he would easily find them. Even judged by the standards of his own day, Chapman was singularly uncritical. He is a medieval rather than a Renaissance type of scholar. He believes what the Middle Ages believed about Homer and Musaeus. It was enough for him as for them that a statement—any statement—appeared in some ancient authority. The new critical methods devised by Joseph Scaliger and the great Dutch savants, who were Chapman's contemporaries, were not understood, perhaps were hardly known, by him. In a word his scholarship was obsolescent. Then he has the medieval innocence in borrowing. He borrows freely, without much and sometimes without any acknowledgment, so that he appears to have more original knowledge than he actually possessed. His Latin, though printers have mangled it, is sometimes incorrect. Jonson, who did not, I think, profess to be a Grecian, was the better latinist, and (as he was never the man to hold his tongue about a friend's mistake) he may have been critical. Shakespeare would know that all learned men did not accept without qualification Chapman's claim to a special place in their company, and he would feel entitled to use this knowledge in a comedy. I do not say that he did; I am stating a possibility. The reader may put any value on it he likes.

Shakespeare did not follow up the Senecan *Titus Andronicus* and the Plautine *Comedy of Errors* by other plays on classical subjects. It may be asked why. No certain answer is possible, because we do not know what special calls may have been made upon him in his function of working dramatist in a company of actors. It is certain that in the early and perhaps middle part of his career he could not have been entirely his own master. It would therefore be an unwarranted assumption to maintain that he was 'put off' classical plays by some revulsion of feeling. It may have been something of an accident that had drawn him to *Titus* or *Errors* at all. But we may feel that he was pretty certain to give up the writing of such plays as soon as he had the opportunity. For the characters in these are types, and the characters in Shakespeare are not. No doubt it is possible to give a type individualizing touches, as it is possible to treat an individual so that he becomes typical. Clytemnestra in the *Agamemnon* of Aeschylus is as much an individual as Lady Macbeth. But Seneca was not Aeschylus, still less were Seneca's imitators; and Shakespeare could never have been content to go on following such models. He felt that he could do something else and something better. How could a man who had it in him to write *Romeo and Juliet* and *A Midsummer Night's Dream* go on writing more *Tituses* and more *Errors*? Yet the fact that he had written (or rewritten) *Errors* and prepared *Titus* for the stage makes it impossible to argue that his attitude to Roman drama was the result of ignorance. Far from that, he had thus early mastered the construction of a Roman tragedy and a Roman comedy. He was thus in a better position to judge of them than the student in his library. If then he turned his back on Seneca and Plautus, it was largely an instinctive gesture; at any rate he never reverted to the style of either.

What he now writes are plays like *Love's Labour's Lost*, *A Midsummer Night's Dream*, *The Merchant of Venice*, with an excursion into what might be called romantic tragedy in *Romeo and Juliet*; at the same time he continues the production of historical or chronicle dramas, at which he had first tried his hand in *Henry VI*. Then accident or design led him to a closer study of North's *Plutarch*. The result was *Julius Caesar*, written probably in 1599. Here was a new play by Shakespeare on a classical subject. But there was next to nothing of Seneca about it. It was not only a new play but a new kind of play. Its importance in Shakespeare's development has always been recognized, but not always, I venture to think, fully measured or understood.

There was nothing new about the subject, which had been dramatized before, in Latin by Muretus in 1544, in French by Grévin and by Garnier. Garnier's play, the title of which is not, like Grévin's, *César* but *Cornélie*, was translated by Kyd in 1595. This translation Shakespeare had evidently read; but the debt, if it exists at all, is highly negligible. Muret's drama, which influenced the rest, is, as we might expect from the author, composed in elegant and sometimes eloquent Latin. But the hero is a mere stage tyrant, alternately boasting and blustering, and the whole piece is carefully constructed on Senecan lines. The tradition has not been entirely without effect on Shakespeare's tragedy, where Caesar boasts and blusters not a little. The play is Senecan in another respect, in that it is fundamentally a Revenge play. But these characteristics, while they must not be neglected, are altogether vestigial. They do not make *Julius Caesar* a Senecan play; on the contrary they lose their Senecan character in it.

The proof that Shakespeare himself attached importance to *Julius Caesar* is derived from the unusual care with which it is constructed and written. Of the writing it has been observed that it is succinct, plain, studious of a certain noble directness or simplicity in a degree which one does not elsewhere find in Shakespeare's maturer manner. It is particularly interesting to see how different it is from the style of *Antony and Cleopatra*, in which, though the theme is drawn from Roman history, Shakespeare is dealing in the main with Egypt and Egyptians. It is clear that he had formed for himself the notion of a style corresponding to the Renaissance conception of the Roman character, which in turn was influenced by the Greek conception of the Spartan character, with its martial virility and laconic speech. This is the style he uses in *Julius Caesar*. It is remarkably effective, and one does somehow feel, when Brutus or Cassius or Casca is speaking, that this is rather how a Roman would speak. But Shakespeare's care in that respect can be shown even more convincingly by concrete instances. Here I may be allowed to quote from myself.

Shakespeare 'read in Plutarch that Antony was a distinguished orator in the Asiatic, and Brutus in the Attic, style. These remarks are made quite by the way, except that Plutarch does dwell a little upon the style of Brutus and makes a few quotations from his letters which exhibit his bare, thin, excessively antithetic manner.[1] Now in *Julius Caesar* we have the great funeral oration of Antony, entirely the work of Shakespeare, for it is not in Plutarch:[2] and if it is hardly so florid as a speech in the Asiatic style might be expected to be, it sufficiently develops all the resources of rhetoric. Contrast the speech of Brutus, which is also entirely the work of Shakespeare. It is in prose, and the imitation of the Attic style as Roman orators practised it is so perfect that unless we knew it was Shakespeare's, we might suppose it was a translation.'[3]

In face of this one cannot maintain that Shakespeare had no views upon style at all. That is a mistake, begotten of his prodigious versatility in expression, and nourished by the boast of his player-colleagues that he 'never blotted a line.' Jonson knew better, and bestows generous, and not merely conventional, praise on his great

---

[1] The Latin name for this style was *exilis oratio*.

[2] This statement requires a little modification, but not much.

[3] *The Classical Background of English Literature*, p. 185.

rival's 'art'. The fact is that Shakespeare, when he was not writing in too great a hurry—which no doubt often happened—kept experimenting with style to the very end. This is why we cannot speak of a Shakespearian style as we speak of the style of Spenser or Marlowe or Milton. The style of *Julius Caesar* he did not care to continue, for it cannot be said to appear in *Coriolanus*, an equally Roman play.

As for the structure of *Julius Caesar*, although it may seem to break in the middle—the first half of the play culminating in the assassination, the second dealing with its consequences—it is really formed with great art. It might be compared with the structure of the *Ajax* of Sophocles, where the latter part of the play exhibits the consequences of the hero's death. In both dramas these consequences are regarded as vital to the theme. Why that should be so for Sophocles, may be left to classical scholars to explain. But Shakespeare's reason was this, that the sequel to Caesar's death was the only thing that made the play in the full sense a tragedy. Philippi was the inevitable consequence of the death-blows at Pompey's theatre. It was Shakespeare's design to show that it was inevitable, and it is this design that makes an organic connexion between the two halves of *Julius Caesar*. No one who has gone into the matter can doubt that Shakespeare took unusual pains to find or fashion connecting links in the plot. He has studied Plutarch's *Life of Caesar* with great attention, and not only that but the *Life of Brutus*, the *Life of Antony*, the *Life of Pompey*, perhaps the *Life of Cicero*. Incidents of one Life are interwoven with incidents of another, and that with such skill that the joinings do not show.[1] The pains that Shakespeare took to get the structure and the style of *Julius Caesar* exactly to his mind are proof of a serious artistic purpose.

It has been suggested that the originality of the play extends no further than this, that Shakespeare now applied to Roman history the method he had already applied to English. There is some truth in this, but not, I think, any important truth. *Julius Caesar* is a tragedy, the scenes bound together not by their chronological

[1] For details the reader may consult the *New Shakespeare* edition of *Julius Caesar*.

succession but by an artistic unity to which the historical plays make no pretension. That is the new and important element. In what then does this artistic unity consist? The answer I shall give to this question will appear at first indirect or even irrelevant. Yet I hope its relevance will gradually become apparent.

Yet I ought not to say that it is *my* answer. It is in Plutarch, only people do not read Plutarch carefully enough. Towards the end of his *Life of Julius Caesar* there occurs the passage which gives the clue to Shakespeare's play. It is for obvious reasons advisable here to give the passage in the form in which Shakespeare read it, that is of course in North's translation.

'So he'—Caesar—'reaped no other frute of all his raigne and dominion, which he had so vehemently desired all his life and pursued with such extreame daunger: but a vaine name only and a superficiall glory, that procured him the envy and hatred of his contrie. But his great prosperitie and good fortune that favored him all his lifetime, did continue afterwards in the revenge of his death, pursuing the murtherers both by sea and land, till they had not left a man more to be executed, of al them that were actors or counsillors in the conspiracy of his death.'[1]

There is here a misunderstanding of the Greek. In a more exact version the second sentence would run like this.

'Howbeit the great daemon, which companied him all his life, did even after his death go in pursuit seeking vengeance for his murder over every land and sea, chasing and tracking them down, until he left not one of those who slew him, etc.'[2]

What then does Plutarch mean by the 'great daemon' of Caesar? To explain this fully would be a business of immense scope and detail, which cannot be attempted here. I shall be as brief as I can, referring to authorities whom I cannot quote in full.

The belief in daemons was a part of Greek popular religion and of immemorial antiquity. In its original form it is not much alluded to in Greek literature, which reveals little, in classical

[1] I quote from the Shakespeare Head Press edition (1928), vol. v, p. 348.
[2] ὁ μέντοι μέγας δαίμων ᾧ παρὰ τὸν βίον ἐχρήσατο, καὶ τελευτήσαντος ἐπηκολούθησεν τιμωρὸς τοῦ φόνου διά τε γῆς πάσης καὶ θαλάσσης ἐλαύνων καὶ ἀνιχνεύων ἄχρι τοῦ μηδένα λιπεῖν τῶν ἀπεκτονότων κ.τ.λ.

times, of the modern interest in the primitive and irrational
except as something to be overcome. Yet there is clear evidence
of the persistence of the belief all through Greek and Greco-
Roman times, and Plutarch is vividly alive to it. It is this. Men
live surrounded by a vast number of invisible, or normally invisible, superhuman and long-lived (though apparently not immortal) beings, who exert a determining influence upon their
lives. These are the daemons (δαίμονες). They must not be
thought of as possessing moral qualities in any strict sense. But
they are more powerful (κρείττονες) than men; and so can, and
do, hurt or help them as they please.

How does the daemon get control of the man? This is never
quite clearly explained, perhaps because it was never quite clearly
envisaged, perhaps because people did not like to talk about it, the
subject being uncanny. But normally, it would seem, it happened
at birth. A daemon entered into the new-born child, and thereafter continued with it (or in it) throughout the mortal life. As
Menander (fourth century before Christ) has put it, 'A daemon
becomes the companion of every man at the moment he is
born'.[1] This explains why the Romans had no difficulty in
identifying such a being with the Latin genius, which is etymo-
logically connected with the words for birth and generation. The
passage in Menander goes on to protest against the popular notion
that a man's daemon may be 'bad', Menander being a person of
humane and civilized temper. The popular notion persisted.
Menander's criticism was in fact founded on a misconception, for
he thought (as we do) of the soul as a non-corporeal substance capable of moral good and evil. But all that simple people meant by a
'good' daemon was one that treated them well, by a 'bad', one that
treated them ill. The ethical question was raised by the philosophers.

The majority of daemons, like the majority of people, would be
moderately kind or moderately unkind, and these would have no
great interest except to their possessors. It was the markedly
beneficent or maleficent daemon that attracted attention. A man
—and of course a woman—whose daemon was conspicuously
favourable was described as eudaimon, 'happy'; when the daemon

[1] ἅπαντι δαίμων ἀνδρὶ συμπαρίσταται | εὐθὺς γενομένῳ fr. 550, Waddell.

196

was strikingly hostile, the man was called *dusdaimon* or *kakodai-mon*, 'unhappy' or 'unfortunate'. The Greek moralists found it very difficult to argue plain people out of the notion that happiness was dependent on some non-human agent, who showed them favour or disfavour. When after his defeat by Caesar Pompey was reunited to his wife Cornelia in the island of Lesbos, she said to him: 'Why did you come to see me instead of leaving me to my grievous daemon?'[1] Pompey had been supremely fortunate—he was even given the by-name of Felix—until he married her. Consequently she assumed that it was her bad fortune that had ruined them both—her bad fortune embodied in a malignant spirit, daemon or genius. It would be easy to multiply illustrations of this frame of mind in ancient literature, but it can be understood without them.

The daemon, being the *cause* of good or evil fortune, was readily confused in the popular mind with the fortune itself. This may be illogical, but it is infinitely natural, at any rate for people who were incapable of giving an abstract or generalized meaning to a word like 'fortune' or 'luck'. Your 'good' or 'bad' daemon *was* your good or bad luck—its source and its embodiment. There was even a growing tendency, at least from the time of Alexander the Great when the old Greek faith in reason had some difficulty in maintaining itself against Oriental mysticism, to think more of the external manifestation of the daemon, in the 'fortune' ($\tau \acute{\upsilon} \chi \eta$) of a state or individual, than of its power within the soul, although that was far from forgotten. Throughout the whole of Plutarch's voluminous writing we find a deep impression of the power of Fortune in human affairs. In this he is the child of his time (about A.D. 50 to 120): the sentiment is constantly recurring both in Greek and Latin literature.

But the daemon may not only be 'good' or 'bad' or neutral. He may also be strong or weak or something between. No doubt all daemons had some degree of power, but this was not always exerted, at least to the full. On the other hand in the case of some exceptional men the daemon was obviously powerful and masterful to an extraordinary degree. It was so in the case of

[1] Plutarch, *Pompey*, LXXIV (659).

Alexander, who was on that account called 'the Great' (ὁ μέγας).
It was so in the case of Julius Caesar. So now we understand in
part what Plutarch meant by 'the great daemon of Caesar'.

It is interesting to note some indications of the daemon's
presence in him. We have already touched on the story of Caesar's
attempt to cross the Adriatic in a storm. When the master of the
ship wished to turn back, Caesar told him who he was. I will now
quote what Shakespeare read in North. '*Caesar* then taking him
by the hand sayd unto him, good fellow, be of good cheere,
and forwardes hardily, feare not, for thou has *Caesar* and his
fortune with thee.'[1] Plutarch might just as well have said
'daemon' as 'fortune', the words, as we have seen, having become
in this connotation practically synonymous. The effect on the
sailors was that they 'forgot the storm'. The daemon of Caesar,
they felt, was mightier than any storm. Perhaps the best commentary is another story, told of Octavius, who afterwards
became the emperor Augustus. Octavius was only the grand-
nephew of Julius Caesar, but he was his son by adoption, and that
circumstance was quite likely to create in many minds the presumption that he had inherited his 'father's' daemon, much as
Orestes was supposed to inherit the spirit of his father Agamemnon. At any rate the daemon of Octavius was also 'great'. It
appeared whenever he came into competition with Antony in
any game of chance—where his 'fortune' could operate—when
Antony always lost. The reason was explained by 'a kind of
soothsayer', who told Antony that his 'fortune' (τύχην), though
very brilliant and great, was 'dimmed' (ἀμαυροῦσθαι) by that of
Caesar, that is Octavius. 'For your daemon is afraid of his, and
though haughty and lofty when it is by itself, becomes humbler and
weaker under the influence of his, when it comes near '[2] Shakespeare remembered this when he made Macbeth say:

> 'under him[3]
> My Genius is rebuked; as, it is said,
> Mark Antony's was by Caesar' (*Macbeth*, II. i. 55 f.)

---

[1] Καίσαρα φέρεις καὶ τὴν Καίσαρος τύχην συμπλέουσαν. *Caesar*, XXXVIII(726).
[2] *Antony*, XXXIII (930).
[3] Banquo.

At this point we may dispel a confusion which has obscured the minds of many readers, and even some commentators, of *Julius Caesar*. It is no doubt partly the fault of Shakespeare himself, whose own mind was confused on the subject, as with his lights it could not fail to be. For he was dependent on North, and North had already fallen into the error, as may be illustrated from the passage to which we have just referred, where, when he speaks of Antony's daemon, he adds the explanation (not in Plutarch)— ('that is to say, the good angel and spirit that keepeth thee'). Now it cannot be too clearly stated that the belief I have been trying to explain is quite different from, even contradictory of, the doctrine that every man is attended through life by a morally good *and* a morally bad daemon or 'angel'. That doctrine was invented by ancient philosophers, and from them inherited by Christian theologians. The word 'angel' came to be used in this way. There had always been a disposition to regard the daemons as in some way intermediaries between gods and men. It was easy then to think of them as messengers of God, as Hermes and Iris were messengers of Zeus. The Greek word for 'messenger' is ἄγγελος, 'angel', and in this way we arrive at the conception of the daemons as angels. It was the word chosen by the translators of the Septuagint to designate the celestial beings who go on Jehovah's business in the Old Testament. Ultimately the whole demonology and angelology of the East—a system not originally Greek at all—gets involved.

For the student of Shakespeare it is the views of Plutarch on daemons that are important. They need careful consideration. In particular we must distinguish between the popular conception of a daemon and certain theological speculations about the daemonic nature which he has derived mainly from Plato, and discusses in some essays or dialogues intended for a public with some training in philosophy. I do not propose to enter into these speculations, because they do not appear in the *Lives*. There the popular belief is accepted. It is however so far moralized that it is natural for Plutarch to think of a daemon as ethically good or bad, instead of merely beneficent or mischievous. But the point that really concerns us is this. The theory of the good and bad angel is not in Plutarch, and the notion that it is there must be dismissed from our minds if we are to understand what he says.

The crucial instance, no doubt, is that of the apparition which showed itself (twice) to Brutus before the battle of Philippi. Its first appearance is described by North in these words, which I transcribe with some omissions which do not affect the point at issue. 'One night . . . he thought he heard one come in to him, and casting his eye towards the door of his tent, that he saw a wonderful strange and monstruous shape of a body coming towards him, and said never a word. So Brutus boldly asked him what he was, a god or a man, and what cause brought him thither. The spirit answered him, "I am thy evil spirit, Brutus: and thou shalt see me by the city of Philippes". Brutus, being no otherwise afraid, replied again unto it: "Well, then I shall see thee again". The spirit presently vanished away: and Brutus called his men unto him, who told him that they heard no noise, nor saw anything at all.'

This translation comes reasonably near the original, and yet one may doubt if North really understood what Plutarch meant. He pretty certainly fancied that the point of the anecdote lay in this, that the good angel of Brutus had at last deserted him, leaving him entirely to his bad angel. But the truth is that Brutus had only one daemon or angel, and that was malignant. We know, mainly from Plutarch himself and Cicero, that Brutus—the Brutus of history—had embraced the Stoic creed or philosophy in one of its more rigorous forms. The central tenet of Stoicism in its ethical aspect was expressed in the epigram 'Nothing is good but goodness'. It follows that the good man is invulnerable. Brutus understood perfectly what the threats of his daemon meant, knew that they would be fulfilled.[1] He would be defeated and no doubt slain at Philippi. But the daemon could only destroy the body, he could not touch the soul, of the good man. Accordingly Brutus merely answers in one contemptuous word, 'I shall see thee'.[2] It is sublime. Shakespeare makes the most of it.

[1] 'I know my hour is come', v. v. 19.
[2] ὄψομαι, one word in Greek.

> 'Well; then I shall see thee again?'
> 'Ay, at Philippi.'
> 'Why, I will see thee at Philippi, then.'

And at this *Exit Ghost*.[1]

Critics are apt to call this banal. Shakespeare knew better. Or if the answer of Brutus is banal, it is intentionally so. Nothing could better express his quiet contempt for such spiritual terrors, and it is to be remembered that, to an Elizabethan audience, such terrors were very real. Elsewhere Plutarch repeats a story that, when all was over on Philippi field, Brutus quoted a striking couplet from a lost Greek tragedy: 'Poor Virtue, I find you now a fable, yet I practised you as if you were real.' That was a cry of despair, but it is also evidence that Brutus *had* been convinced that virtue could be practised in spite of any daemon.

Let us now go back to Caesar. Plutarch's charge against Caesar is that he did not show this virtue. He did not effectively resist his daemon, which had an insatiable thirst for power. This is what Plutarch means by his 'ambition' (φιλοτιμία). The theory on which the ancient city-state was erected implied that all its citizens had equal rights and privileges. Therefore for one citizen to usurp the rights and privileges of the others was the crime of crimes. It was putting oneself above the law, and putting oneself above the law was the very definition of tyranny. The will of Caesar had become the law of Rome; therefore no Roman could have liberty. Now the best men of antiquity all believed that without political and civic liberty you could not be a free agent, and unless you were a free agent, you could not be as good a man as was possible for you if you were a free agent. It was this conviction that made Cato fall upon his sword, and Cato's son-in-law Brutus kill 'his best friend'. The clue to the behaviour of the historical Brutus—who in some respects was a harsh and disagreeable character—is that he was a genuine, if mistaken, idealist. Part of this idealism was the duty of tyrannicide. But where a Greek said 'tyrant' a Roman said *rex*, which in English is translated 'king'. No Elizabethan could be expected to understand fully the Roman horror at the very name of 'king';

---

[1] IV. iii. 285 f.

and one may doubt if Shakespeare did. Hence perhaps the embarrassed argument of the soliloquy in which Brutus makes up his mind to join the conspirators (II. i). But that Brutus was an idealist, as compared for example with Cassius, Shakespeare understood very well.

Julius is killed. What happens to 'the great daemon of Caesar' then? It is liberated from the body in a state of furious rage against the assassins. It becomes a vengeful ghost. We are back in the world of folk-belief. In moving there we may find an instructive parallel in the Orestes trilogy of Aeschylus. Agamemnon, returning from conquered and ruined Troy, seems of all men most fortunate (*eudaimon*). But in fact what really inspires him, as we soon discover from his words, is not so much a 'good' as a 'great' daemon. He is murdered, and then his vengeful ghost comes into action. It is not finally appeased until his wife and her paramour have been killed by his son. One must not look for great consistency in these primitive notions. They never had it. No clear distinction was drawn between a soul, a ghost, a daemon. The popular mind found no difficulty in accepting the view that the daemon of a living man might become a ghost after his death.

It may be asked, how much of this did Plutarch accept as true? Did he seriously believe that Brutus was visited by his daemon? Did he suppose that it was an adequate explanation of Caesar's character and career to say that he had 'a great daemon'? But questions of that kind do not take us very far, because there is no more agreement now than there was in Plutarch's time about the limits of the supernatural. In one of his essays Macaulay can hardly find words strong enough in which to express his contempt for Laud because the archbishop used to note down his dreams. In another he treats Doctor Johnson's interest in the Cock Lane ghost as proof positive that he was full of degrading superstitions. It is now Macaulay who seems to be narrow-minded on these points. A great deal hangs upon terminology. Plutarch used the traditional religious or mythological terms in which to describe the mystery of human personality. Goethe, whom no one will accuse of ignoring science, appears to have had much the same opinion as Plutarch that the genius of great men, like Napoleon or Byron, could be explained only on the assumption that there was something 'daemonic' (*dämonisch*) about it. As for ghosts, it would be absurd to suppose that Plutarch believed in them in the same way as a savage. His attitude was probably not far from Johnson's; that is, he had an open mind on the subject and was always willing to look at the evidence. In the same way it is useless to ask if the author of *Hamlet* and *Macbeth* believed in ghosts; it is enough that he could sympathize with those who did. Certainly his audiences for the most part did. The demonology of Plutarch—to give it that somewhat invidious name—would not leave them in any way puzzled or incredulous.

In particular they were familiar with the avenging ghost. Their disposition to believe in such a creature was confirmed by a series of 'Senecan' plays, where such ghosts continually appear, above all by *The Spanish Tragedy*. This matter is very familiar to students of Elizabethan drama, and is mentioned here only to remind us how easy it would have been for Shakespeare, with the evidence supplied by Plutarch, to make of *Julius Caesar* a conventional Revenge play. It is not that in the least, yet it would be fair to describe it as a Revenge play of a new kind. To some extent, though not in any vital way, he may have been influenced by the older play *Caesar's Revenge*, which is conventional enough. What is certain is that he has made Plutarch's sentence about the great daemon of Caesar cardinal for his own drama. The daemon becomes Caesar's ghost, which is all the more terrible because it retains its mightiness.

> Woe to the hand that shed this costly blood!
> Over thy wounds now do I prophesy . . .
> A curse shall light upon the limbs of men;[1]
> Domestic fury and fierce civil strife
> Shall cumber all the parts of Italy;
> Blood and destruction shall be so in use
> And dreadful objects so familiar
> That mothers shall but smile when they behold

[1] For 'limbs' Johnson would read 'lives'; but this is to forget the *physical* effect of a curse, for which the evidence is in all the anthropological books. Cf. also Aeschylus, *Choephori*, 277 f.

Their infants quartered with the hands of war;
All pity choked with custom of fell deeds:
And Caesar's spirit, ranging for revenge,
With Ate by his side come hot from hell,
Shall in these confines with a monarch's voice
Cry 'Havoc', and let slip the dogs of war;
That this foul deed shall smell above the earth
With carrion men, groaning for burial

(III. i. 258 f., Antony speaks)

From this point onward it may be said that *Julius Caesar* becomes a Revenge play, with Antony and Octavius as the avengers. This is explicitly stated by Octavius (v. i. 50 f.):

Look;
I draw a sword against conspirators;
When think you that the sword goes up again?
Never, till Caesar's three and thirty wounds
Be well avenged.

Brutus recognizes in the end that the avenging ghost has conquered (v. iii. 94 f.):

O Julius Caesar, thou art mighty yet!
Thy spirit walks abroad, and turns our swords
In our own proper entrails.

'Mighty yet'—the mighty spirit of Caesar, his great daemon. It is true that Shakespeare confused Caesar's daemon with that of Brutus. Yet the error (which was not originally Shakespeare's and was almost inevitable in the state of Greek scholarship in England at that time) has great dramatic advantages. It impresses on the reader, and still more on the spectator, the truth that Caesar being dead yet liveth.

Julius Caesar then is not an ordinary Revenge drama; indeed it is half over before the revenge begins to operate, and when it does operate it is as much in the hearts as in the fortunes of the conspirators. One sees this as early as the quarrel scene, and Brutus at Philippi is without hope. His tragedy is a spiritual tragedy, so far as it is not a spiritual triumph, since he vindicates his cause by suffering for it. Nevertheless in conception it is a Revenge tragedy. Only if we accept this view of it can we altogether defend its artistic unity, the uniting factor being the daemon of Caesar. It does not follow that all the artistic problems implicated have been solved with equal success. As it appears to me, Shakespeare did not—how could he?—understand all the motives of the Plutarchan Brutus. In fact they are not easy to understand. That a man should kill his friend *in case* he prove a tyrant, is a proposition that shocks the moral sense. Shakespeare gets over this difficulty by making us accept Brutus as a man whose motive we can respect, even if we cannot understand it. In the language of the stage Brutus is 'sympathetic'. But, in order to keep him so, it was necessary to make Caesar 'unsympathetic'. And so he is. He prates, he keeps changing his mind, he is a lath painted to look like iron. The result is that we do not greatly care whether he lives or dies. But in this way Shakespeare has created a new problem for himself. There is now a danger that it will be felt that the spirit of such a man, even when released by death from a rather sickly body, cannot be overwhelmingly powerful or formidable. So in the funeral oration Antony builds him up again as a great man, and the dictator who has manifestly lost his grip is forgotten in the memory of the conqueror as he was that day he overcame the Nervii. Then the omens that precede the death of Caesar—and Shakespeare makes a great deal of them—with the special prodigy of the blood spouting from Pompey's statue, deepen the impression that Caesar was a being of almost superhuman qualities, whose death was certain to be fearfully avenged.

The character of Cicero is another problem of *Julius Caesar*.

CASSIUS. Did Cicero say anything?
CASCA. Ay, he spoke Greek.
CASSIUS. To what effect?
CASCA. Nay, an I tell you that, I'll ne'er look you i' th' face again: but those that understood him smiled at one another and shook their heads; but for mine own part, it was Greek to me. (I. ii. 281 f.)

We have seen how carefully Shakespeare studied his North for *Julius Caesar*. It is obvious that he must have read with particular attention all the circumstances of Caesar's assassination, which was the core of the matter for his play. Yet it is one of these circumstances that Casca, when Caesar turned upon him after receiving the first wound, cried out 'Brother help me!' in *Greek*. Casca then did know Greek, and knew it so well that in a moment of intense excitement Greek words came naturally to his lips.

If this were all, we might suppose that Shakespeare, who was admittedly careless in such matters, had merely forgotten the incident or decided to ignore it. But this will not cover the case of Cicero. For the circumstance of Cicero's speaking in Greek is not in Plutarch (or North) at all. It is deliberately invented and inserted in the play by Shakespeare himself. He must have had a reason for this. Was it only to raise a laugh? Even if we accept that as an adequate explanation, we have still to ask ourselves why he should wish to raise a laugh at the expense of Cicero. Of course Shakespeare would not be aware of the fact that to most educated Romans in Caesar's time Greek was a second language, like French to Frederick the Great or the Russian aristocracy of last century. He might perhaps have inferred it from the circumstance that it came natural to Casca and to Caesar, who spent his last breath in three Greek words,[1] although this piece of information is not in Plutarch but comes from Suetonius, an author much read in Shakespeare's time, though possibly not by Shakespeare. Yet, since he did read North, it is not likely that he omitted to read North's version of the *Life of Cicero*, seeing that he proposed to make Cicero one of the characters in his play. In that Life he would find ample warrant for thinking that Cicero was likely to speak Greek. For Plutarch says that when Cicero came first to Rome 'he was not greatly esteemed; for they commonly called him the *Graecian* and scholar, which are the two words in which the artificers (and such base mechanical people at Rome) have ever ready at their tongues' end'.

'Grecian and scholar.' Shakespeare had heard these words before, though never applied to himself. But to Cicero, yes; to him they applied exactly. If the representation of Cicero in *Julius Caesar* appears somewhat unusual, even odd, to us, it cannot

[1] καὶ σύ, τέκνον.

be the result of ignorance on the part of Shakespeare, who had
been hearing about him all his life. For Cicero was, with Ovid,
the idol of Renaissance scholars. He was their master and model
in the composition of what they regarded as artistic prose. There
were historical reasons for this into which we need not go. One
perhaps should be mentioned. Cicero had been recommended as
the unapproachable master of prose style by Quintilian, whose
authority with the schoolmasters was final. Whatever Latin
Shakespeare read at school, it is not unlikely that part of it was
some portion of Cicero. It is not likely to have been one of the
speeches (which were rather too political for schoolboys), but
might have been some of the *Letters* or a book of the *De Officiis*
or the *De Amicitia* or the *De Senectute*. At any rate he could not
have avoided hearing a great deal about Tully. Perhaps he heard
too much.

It is not that the delineation of Cicero in *Julius Caesar* is mali-
cious. But it is slightly satirical. And this must be intentional,
because (apart from the jibe about his Greek) the record has been
altered. For example, when the conspirators decide not to make
Cicero privy to their plot, the only reason given is that

> he will never follow anything
> That other men begin (II. i. 151)

But the true reason was quite different, and is clearly stated by
Plutarch. It was that the conspirators feared his timidity. So far
is Shakespeare's reason from the truth that the usual complaint of
historians against Cicero is just that he failed so often to make up
his own mind on a policy and then stick to it. He was always
looking for somebody to give him a lead, although when the lead
was given it is true enough that he did not like to play second
fiddle. If he had a consistent policy it was to get the 'governing
classes' to agree among themselves (*concordia ordinum*). So far was
he from disagreeing with everybody. At the same time the
charge of 'timidity' needs some explanation. The ancients were
no good (or very little) at psychological analysis. They could
create character but not dissect it. (It is apt to be the other way
with us.) For one thing they had not the requisite terminology.

Thus they did not draw much distinction, in words, between physical and moral courage. They knew, but they could not dissect, the temperament which oscillates between daring and panic. That was the kind of temperament that Cicero had. He showed real courage in facing Catiline and in facing Antony—after, it must be said, Brutus and Cassius had run away. But he was not a 'strong' man; he had the nerves of the orator and the artist. At the time of the conspiracy he was old, anxious-minded, shrinking instinctively from deeds of blood and violence. He would have been a very bad conspirator, and the conspirators could see that.

The most tiresome thing about him was his vanity, and it might be argued—though the context hardly supports the argument—that it was this weakness that Brutus had in his mind when he said that Cicero would not follow anything that other men began. Certainly he was inordinately sensitive to praise and blame, and when touched on the raw would express his feelings in very bitter language. His sarcastic wit was notorious. It is therefore a good touch of Shakespeare's when he makes Brutus say (I. ii. 185 f.)

Cicero
Looks with such ferret and such fiery eyes
As we have seen him in the Capitol,
Being cross'd in conference by some senator.

But, though this might very well be true of Cicero on a particular occasion, it is not true of the man in general, for by nature he was kindly and placable. So the reader is left with at least a partially false impression of the man as he really was.

The only scene in which Cicero speaks is the third of the first act, and even there he does not say much or remain long upon the stage. It is midnight, and there is a violent storm, during which a number of alarming portents occur. Casca and Cicero encounter in a street. It is not explained why they are out at such an hour —a most unusual time for a Roman or Elizabethan gentleman— especially in such a tempest. But of course Shakespeare's audience would not trouble their heads about that. What has been noted as remarkable is an apparent change in the character of Casca.

From being a somewhat cynical humorist, disguising a good deal of penetration under an affectation of rusticity, he has now become a creature of superstitious terrors, speaking rather high-flown verse instead of the colloquial prose he used before. The inconsistency may be only apparent, but there must be some reason for bringing it out; and the choice of Cicero as the foil that throws it into relief is not at once obvious. It may be said that the rationalizing tone in which Cicero speaks of the prodigies is not unlike the tone he adopts when he is discussing dreams and oracles in the *De Divinatione*. But it is most unlikely that Shake-speare is thinking of the *De Divinatione*. I should rather suppose that Shakespeare, knowing that scholars had a tendency to pooh-pooh most of the supposed evidence in favour of the super-natural, attributed that tendency to Cicero. It would then be part of the portrait of him as 'Grecian and scholar'.

In this scene Cicero is treated by Casca with deference and respect. Elsewhere too he is spoken of with respect, as by Metellus:

> O, let us have him, for his silver hairs
> Will purchase us a good opinion
> And buy men's voices to commend our deeds:
> It shall be said, his judgement ruled our hands;
> Our youths and wildness shall no whit appear,
> But all be buried in his gravity. (II. i. 144 f.)

The picture is of a highly respectable personage, a little rationalistic in his opinions, silver-haired, with fiery, ferret eyes, learned enough to know Greek and to speak it. The portrait is distinct enough to give the impression that some actual scholar may have sat for it. But that is hardly Shakespeare's way. It is much more likely that what we have is a sketch from his hand of a typical scholar of the best kind. Of the best kind, but a scholar; and, since Cicero was that, Shakespeare could not refrain from having a dig at him.

I shall seem to have dwelt at disproportionate length upon this play of *Julius Caesar*. But its importance in the development of Shakespeare as a tragic dramatist has, I think, hardly been sufficiently recognized; and, for the student of the classical element in him, it naturally has a special significance.

In 1598, that is a year before *Julius Caesar*, Chapman published the first instalment of his Homeric translations under the title of *Seven Books of the Iliad*.[1] It was dedicated to the Earl of Essex, who is described as 'the most honoured instance of the Achilleian virtues'. Shakespeare surely read this, and then read the seven books. It is worth noting what they were. They were I, II, VII, VIII, IX, X, XII, to which was added *The Shield of Achilles*, Book XVIII. Now when one has read the *Iliad* through, it is possible to feel sympathy and admiration for Achilles; but it is not possible unless one has read the last books, in which the young hero atones for his pride and implacability. Until he so redeems himself he is as Horace describes him: 'impiger, iracundus, inexorabilis, acer', 'headlong, passionate, implacable, fierce'; he is worse, he drags the body of Hector at his chariot wheels, and takes young Trojans alive, that he may offer up a human sacrifice to the *manes* of Patroclus. Perhaps Chapman never felt this objection. We may imagine him arguing as follows. Homer is 'the prince of poets', the *Iliad* is his chief poem, the hero of the *Iliad* is Achilles: therefore Achilles must be a model of all the virtues. Chapman does in fact write in that strain. The theory that the hero of an epic poem must be perfectly virtuous was maintained as late as Dryden's time by Rymer. No doubt it was suggested by the character of Aeneas in Virgil. Mischievous and absurd as it is, it was the prevailing academic theory for a long time. Chapman has the great merit of seeing the supremacy of Homer and maintaining that against the general preference for Virgil which had been asserted by the elder Scaliger. But in his eagerness to peg out Homer's claim he claims everything— including a kind of hero that Homer never thought of delineating. It is indeed arguable that the *Iliad* has not got a hero at all, though the *Odyssey* has.

[1] The original title is *Seaven Bookes of the Iliades*. Chapman no doubt had some precedent for saying *Iliads* instead of *Iliad*, but it is wrong, as he might have known.

That Shakespeare read the *Seaven Bookes* appears to be almost proved by the circumstance that it is in these books that so much happens that comes into *Troilus and Cressida*. It has been argued, and it is doubtless true, that this material could have been derived from other sources; but here is the obvious source. The Dedication, as we saw, was to the famous Earl of Essex, who is compared to Achilles. 'Most true Achilles (whom by sacred prophecy Homer did but prefigure in his admirable object) and in whose unmatched virtues shine the dignities of the soul, and the whole excellence of royal humanity; let not the peasant-common politics of the world, that count all things servile and simple, that pamper not their sensualities, burying quick in their filthy sepulchres of the earth, the whole bodies and souls of honour, virtue and piety, stir your temper from perseverance in godlike pursuit of Eternity.' Well, Shakespeare was of Essex's party in the sense that he was intimate with Southampton, who was devoted to Essex. So he could not fail to be struck by Chapman's comparison of Essex to Achilles. For the tradition, inherited from the Middle Ages and still prevalent, was dead *against* Achilles, the slayer of the noble Hector, the great enemy of the Trojans our ancestors. And when Shakespeare read the *Seaven Bookes*, what did he find? A young man who quarrels with his chief about a girl whom neither of them proposes to marry, thereafter sulks in his tent when his comrades are fighting for their lives, and when the amplest apologies and restitution are offered him loudly declares that nothing will induce him to accept them. What sort of compliment was it to compare him to this young savage?

Certainly Essex would not have liked to be compared to the detestable Achilles of *Troilus and Cressida*. It is a play that presents a number of serious problems, with which I am not qualified to deal. I gather that in all probability it was written after *Julius Caesar*, but not long after; and that it may not have been publicly acted at all. Professor Alexander has suggested, and he may very likely be right, that *Troilus* was intended to be performed at one of the Inns of Court. If this be so, we must consider the audience. For if the play was composed for representation before a select audience of this kind, we should expect it to contain many allusions to contemporary events and persons. One is confirmed in this suspicion by the *Epistle to the Reader*, which was printed at the head of the play on its second issue.[1] In this *Epistle*—a rather silly performance—the strange view is taken that *Troilus* is a comedy; nay of all Shakespeare's comedies 'there is none more witty than this'. Of course it is not a comedy; it is a 'history' or even a 'tragedy'. Where then does the fun come in? With Pandarus and Thersites? But these characters are secondary and not a great deal on the stage; when they are, their cynical humour does not much dispose us to laughter, though no doubt an Elizabethan audience would be less squeamish. So it looks as if there were some hidden vein of humour or irony concealed in the play, which rendered it the more suitable for 'private theatricals'. I have not the special knowledge requisite for exploring this, but I suspect it is there. At least I find myself not prone to accept the view that *Troilus and Cressida* is the conventional treatment of a traditional point of view. That there is a large traditional element in it is very obvious, and Chapman has nothing to do with this; it is medieval. The Middle Ages had steadily denounced the Homeric Greeks as cruel and treacherous and sympathized with the Trojans, admiring Hector above all, considering him a model of chivalry. Again, the story of Troilus and Cressida was itself a medieval invention, and one in which Britain had a special interest because of its magnificent development in the hands of Chaucer and of Henryson. It cannot be denied that Shakespeare takes all this up in *Troilus and Cressida*. He has evidently not read Henryson, nor perhaps Chaucer's *Troilus and Criseyde*. But he had at his disposal the *Recuyell of the Historyes of Troye*, translated by Caxton out of the French, and there was Lydgate's *Troy Book*. Yet in the arrangement of his materials, the relative importance assigned to his characters, above all in the spirit which runs through most of the play, we find a difference amounting to a contrast. What for instance is the plot? The story of Troilus is not told consecutively, but into it is thrust a long debate among the Greek captains on the best way of reducing Troy, another long debate among the Trojans on the advisability

[1] In a quarto, 1609.

of giving up Helen, the 'sulking' of Achilles in the company of his friend Patroclus, and other matters which have hardly the slightest relevance to the story of the two lovers. This intrusive matter evidently comes in the main from Chapman, but is given a new bias. It is this new reading of the evidence that is significant. Consider for instance the case of Ulysses, who plays so important a part in *Troilus*. The Middle Ages had a low opinion of Ulysses, derived in part from Virgil and Ovid, but chiefly from the matter of Troy as presented by Dares, Dictys and their successors. He is never painted so black as Sinon, who was considered a kind of Judas; but he is not very far below him in 'falseness', and is a kind of Greek Achitophel. In Shakespeare however he is the wisest of statesmen. His wisdom indeed is of the worldly or 'politic' sort, but even in this respect he is rather superior to the prelates at the beginning of *Henry V*. His kindness to the distracted Troilus is a beautiful piece of courtesy to an enemy. This is quite a different Ulysses from the astute rascal of the medieval tradition. The treatment of Ajax in the play is equally surprising. The medieval, and for the matter of that the Renaissance, judgment of Ajax was in the main derived from the thirteenth book of the *Metamorphoses* of Ovid. This book opens with two long speeches, one by Ajax, the other by Ulysses, each claiming to have the arms of the dead Achilles awarded to himself. Ulysses makes the cleverer speech, but Ajax has, or is supposed to have, the stronger case. The arms are adjudged to Ulysses, whereupon Ajax, cut to the heart, becomes demented and kills himself. It is the brave, ineloquent Ajax who wins the sympathy of the reader. But in *Troilus and Cressida* the man is a lout, sick of self-love and without a single good quality except brute courage. So in these two characters, not to mention other points, Shakespeare is at variance not only with medieval sentiment but even with the prevailing sentiment of his own time. Who would care to argue that this reassessment of values is without significance, whatever that significance may be? Then, in long stretches of the play, especially when Pandarus or Thersites is on the stage, there is a tone of what can only be described as savage cynicism. The author, through the mouths of these two degraded (though by no means stupid) creatures seems to take a pleasure in showing up the weak points of a romantic or chivalrous view of life. But it is not a genuine pleasure. It sounds like the mockery of a man who, like Troilus, has been deceived and disenchanted. A play of this temper could not be 'traditional', in whatever age it was written.

One thing is very clear. In *Troilus and Cressida* Chapman's idolatry of Achilles is treated with complete disrespect. That hero is portrayed as a treacherous bully, above all as completely unchivalrous. To say that this is in the medieval tradition is not really true. The medieval Achilles is cruel, dreadful, ready to take any advantage; but he is not a cowardly assassin. It was left to Shakespeare to represent him so. But with such a picture in his mind, what would he think of Chapman's comparison of Achilles to Essex? He would think it an outrage. Yet I do not suggest that *Troilus and Cressida* was inspired merely by resentment at Chapman's Dedication. It is much more probable that the Dedication was the last straw in an accumulation of small annoyances. The only certain thing about the play is the state of mind it reveals. In that state of mind Shakespeare tramples with scornful feet on the carpets of Chapman's dreams. It is unfortunate of course that he did not know his Homer better. But it was entirely natural that he should be enraged at Chapman's insinuation that Achilles—the Achilles of the *Seaven Bookes*—was the perfect knight and the ideal gentleman, and at that other insinuation that he himself was taught by Homer's ghost to make a verbally inspired translation. To all that Shakespeare was entitled to say, 'I flatly disbelieve it'; and, if he said this with excessive emphasis, a dramatist is not bound by what his characters say. Plutarch had taught Shakespeare something that Chapman shows no sign of having learnt: that the ancients were no better and no worse than the moderns.

If, as seems a fair inference from the statement of the 1609 Quarto that it was 'never stal'd with the Stage, never clapperclaw'd with the palms of the vulgar', *Troilus* was not written for performance in one of the public theatres, but for an audience at court or at one of the Inns of Court, it is all the better evidence of his personal feelings. For he would have an audience which would take his points in a way that the mixed audiences at the Globe could not be expected to do. The young noblemen or young lawyers whom he was addressing were not likely to be so medievally-minded as the majority of the Bankside theatre-goers with their simple traditional education. To the former the question, 'Were the ancients such paragons as the scholars make out?' would be, I suggest, a topical issue. One has only to think of Francis Bacon to see that. But consider what the feelings of Chapman must have been. Certainly the war between Shakespeare and the schoolmasters was still on when he wrote *Troilus and Cressida.*

Some time after, perhaps in 1607, he returned to Plutarch and wrote *Antony and Cleopatra* according to the method, though hardly the style, of *Julius Caesar.* He had not been in any way convinced by Jonson's arguments or Jonson's effort in *Sejanus* to show him a better way. It is easy to say that Shakespeare could not have followed this way, if he had desired; that he did not have the necessary reading and scholarship, nor, perhaps, the necessary patience. As to that, it may be admitted that his rebellion against the schoolmasters was rather instinctive than the result of study or reflection upon the principles of dramatic art. Yet it is surely an unwarranted assumption to suppose that he never reflected upon them at all. (There are in fact some indications that he did.) No doubt the truth is that he both felt and thought that the dramatic theory of the schoolmasters was narrow and pedantic. We now all agree with him. But in Shakespeare's own time it called for real courage to defy the majority vote of the critics and the universities. It is of course barely possible—and one occasionally sees the view expressed—that Shakespeare did not mind the critics, so long as he pleased his audience. But surely few will find it ultimately credible that a mind so sensitive and subtle was not in any way touched by the strictures of those who were supposed to be the authorities on dramatic art. I for one believe that he was making fun of them when he made Polonius say:

'The best actors in the world, either for tragedy, comedy, history, pastoral, pastoral-comical, historical-pastoral, tragical-historical, tragical-comical-historical-pastoral, scene individable, or poem un-limited. Seneca cannot be too heavy nor Plautus too light for the law of writ and the liberty.'

The words are obscure, but they are obviously jargon—the jargon of the academic critic. Shakespeare is deriding it.

In *Antony and Cleopatra* he goes his own way. As when he wrote *Julius Caesar,* so here he is content with what Plutarch gives him. His source is the *Life of Antony,* perhaps the most brilliant and fascinating of all the Plutarchan biographies. Critics have often expressed surprise at the readiness of Shakespeare to follow North with such fidelity, sometimes doing little more than versify his prose original. But what this shows is Shakespeare's recognition of the fact that Plutarch was supplying him with matter that was already half-dramatized. At the beginning of the *Life of Alexander* the author described his method. He explains that he is not a historian, that he makes no attempt to treat in detail all the events in which the subject of a biography was involved, even when their historical importance was highest, but that he selects significant actions and speeches which throw light on the char-acter of his hero; and he compares himself to a portrait-painter. It was just these traits of character that enabled Shakespeare to 'see' the people in his classical dramas, so that his Antony and his Cleopatra are as real to us—that is an understatement—as Richard II or Henry V. But there is more to it than that. A large propor-tion of the stories in Plutarch had, before he repeats them, passed through the popular imagination. The popular imagination is an unconscious dramatist, working on simple traditional lines, turning fact not necessarily into fiction but into something that often resembles a heroic legend. It is interested in persons rather than events, or only in events so far as they happen to persons. This altogether suited the genius of Plutarch, who himself is interested in events as they happen to persons. He believes in the moral governance of the world, as a corollary of which he believes that every man must fulfil his destiny, a creed which aptly lends itself to a dramatic representation of human affairs. Thus it came about that Shakespeare had often little more to do than disengage the dramatic elements from the connecting narrative in Plutarch.

It would be doing an injustice however both to Shakespeare and Plutarch to disregard the proofs of Shakespeare's interest in the political and local setting of the scenes in which he concentrated the action of his play. One of the unsatisfactory things about the classical drama in modern times is that the persons seem to act in a kind of vacuum, or at best against a kind of conventional back-cloth. Think of *Merope* or *Atalanta in Calydon*. Part of that in-the-round livingness of Shakespeare's characters derives from the way in which they fit into their surroundings. Consider the vividness which he gives to the background of Juliet or Falstaff. It was for him a necessity of the imagination, when he was thinking of Julius Caesar or Cleopatra, to place them in their setting; and for this, Plutarch, who loved such details, gave him all he needed. The use which Shakespeare made of them is known by all to be very marvellous; perhaps nowhere so marvellous as in *Antony and Cleopatra*.

> The barge she sat in like a burnish'd throne
> Burn'd on the water . . .

Many have essayed to recreate the ancient world in the imagination of the modern reader; none, that I know of, has had more than a partial success. I am not sure if people continue to read *Hypatia*. The principal scene of that romance is Alexandria—an Alexandria differing very little, except in its religion, from that of Cleopatra. Yet, quite apart from the fact that none of the characters in *Hypatia* carries much conviction, the reader never gets from the elaborate descriptions of Kingsley so piercing a sensation of the Egyptian city as Shakespeare conveys with hardly a word of direct description at all. Or take a more accomplished story, the *Thaïs* of Anatole France, which is largely concerned with Alexandria at no great distance of time from *Hypatia*. The picture it gives of the Alexandrine world is vivid, and sharp with ironic observation. But this very irony in a manner destroys the truth of the representation. We are made to see everything through the eyes of Anatole France, and the reader is conscious of this and feels that he must make allowance for it. Then there is Flaubert's *Tentation de S. Antoine*, which is set in much the same period and places as *Thaïs*. That strange book is a panoramic vision of ancient Egypt, a phantasmagoria, a dream; it is wonderful, but it is not Egypt, or only a part of Egypt. But the Alexandria of Shakespeare is the Alexandria of history, or at least of Plutarch, a *Greek* town dissolved in luxury. As for Shakespeare's Cleopatra, she is so real that many critics have persuaded themselves that she is drawn from the life. But Shakespeare was quite capable of giving us Cleopatra without a model he happened to know in London. Historians may tell us that he has not done justice to the political sagacity or even to the moral character of the Egyptian queen. Yet he, following Plutarch, has done something the historians have failed to do. For after all the great historical fact about Cleopatra is that she almost shook the ancient world to pieces by the force of her personality. And Shakespeare alone has created a woman capable of doing that. It illustrates the truth of Aristotle's remark that poetry is more philosophical— that is to say, goes deeper—than history.

In Shakespeare's best work then—and he hardly ever wrote a better play than *Antony and Cleopatra*—a perfect harmony is achieved between the characters and the circumstances in which they act their parts. In this way the truth of presentment becomes absolute. In Shaw's *Caesar and Cleopatra*, which to some extent was written in rivalry with *Antony and Cleopatra*, the characters are out of harmony with their environment. That is part of the fun. But, while we laugh at a character like Britannus, speaking like a Shavian Englishman at the court of Cleopatra, we must not let Shaw impose this on us for history; while his negroid tigress-kitten Cleopatra is absurdly unlike that accomplished Macedonian princess. In the best dramatic art the persons fit naturally and as it were imperceptibly into their surroundings. But this happens only when the scene in which a character appears is realized with the same intensity of imagination as the character himself. To get the circumstances archaeologically right is not enough. This is the mistake into which Jonson fell. He quoted authority for every detail in *Sejanus* and *Catiline* evidently under the impression that, when he had done that, he had done all that could be expected of him. But what the audience desired was not information but illumination. Shakespeare saw, as if he lived there, the Rome of Caesar, the Alexandria of Cleopatra; and he communicated his vision to his auditors. Jonson's imagination does not permeate his knowledge in that way, and so he cannot give us his vision of Rome. In him it is just the capital of Italy.

Shakespeare was always experimenting in his art; and we have to note that the structure of *Antony and Cleopatra* is novel, at least compared with *Julius Caesar*, where almost all the action is concentrated in two places, Rome and Philippi. In *Antony* the scenes change and shift continually. I suppose this is mainly due to the fact that, while everything in *Julius Caesar* leads up to and away from a single act—the assassination of Julius—there is no central act in *Antony*, the theme of the drama being the relations between the hero and the heroine. These are most clearly brought out when the situation of the characters is being constantly changed. It is true that in this Shakespeare is only following Plutarch, but the rapid changes of scene in Plutarch are forced upon him by the story and are not dictated by any conscious artistic purpose. It was the drama of Antony and Cleopatra which interested Shakespeare, and he perceived that it was played out on a wider stage than Alexandria. The destinies of Egypt and the Roman empire were involved. This was no private love-affair (like Juliet's) but a political event of transcendent importance. As Dryden put it later, it was a case of All for Love and the World well lost; so the world that was lost had to be shown. In general the political sense revealed in these classical plays by Shakespeare is remarkable. If some reader doubts this, let him look at anything that passed for a representation of the ancient world on the English stage before *Julius Caesar*. It will be found like nothing on earth, then or at any time; and this is true even when the author had a good knowledge of ancient literature. The appreciation of political issues, the sense of political realities, in *Julius Caesar*, in *Antony and Cleopatra*, in *Coriolanus* is, under the circumstances, astonishing. No doubt there is a good deal of misunderstanding; that was inevitable, and some of it comes from Plutarch. But Shakespeare's insight into political human nature has hardly received the attention it deserves, because critics are so much impressed by his knowledge of men as men. To discuss the point in detail would take me too far from our subject. But it must be considered even an artistic virtue of the Shakespearian classical drama, as compared with the Senecan or the romantic-idyllic type, of which *Campaspe* may be taken as an example, that it is so much more true to ancient life. It is only fair to say that Jonson—though later than *Julius Caesar*—gave an accurate enough presentation of Roman politics at the time of Catiline and at the time of Sejanus. But the result is not the same, for Jonson largely fails to revivify the political issues for us, and Shakespeare succeeds.

Plutarch fully realized the dramatic quality of the story he had to tell of Antony and Cleopatra, and a great deal that he says about them is fine and moving. But he is not, nor did he imagine himself to be, a great literary artist. So there was a good deal for Shakespeare to do before the material which he found in Plutarch could be worked up to the level of *Caesar* or *Antony*. Much could be done by selection, by leaving out comparatively uninteresting details which a biographer, if he was to perform his function faithfully, could not omit. But selection alone would not be enough, for what was selected would not always explain itself. Some kind of commentary was needed. This is very interesting to the student of drama. It is known to everybody that Greek tragedy had a Chorus, which from time to time comments on the action of the play or the behaviour of the characters. The Chorus has met with much criticism from the moderns, chiefly on the ground that it prevented the drama from moving in the direction of greater realism, the critics taking it for granted that such a movement was desirable or at least inevitable. But the Chorus was not a mere anachronism; and the proof of this is that in all great drama it may be detected under a change of form. In *Antony and Cleopatra* the Chorus is Enobarbus, whom Shakespeare 'builds up' for that very purpose, for there is very little about Enobarbus[1] in Plutarch. It is the comments of Enobarbus that keep alive our common sense and our moral sense in that Alexandrine enchantment; and his suicide is the tragic preparation for that of the two chief actors; for in tragedy it is necessary to create

[1] Domitius Ahenobarbus.

a tragic atmosphere, if the conclusion is not to seem a mere fatality.

But the chief instrument in the poet's hand when he was creating the tragedy of *Antony and Cleopatra* was the magic of style. Of that something will have to be said. In the meantime a few words must be devoted to *Coriolanus* and *Timon of Athens*.

Coriolanus was probably written soon after *Antony and Cleopatra*, perhaps the very next year. It proves Shakespeare's continued interest in Plutarch and in the kind of play he had invented in *Julius Caesar*. It is far from clear what induced him to choose Coriolanus for the hero of his next classical drama. As a character he cannot compete in interest with Julius Caesar or Mark Antony, and the difficulty of finding a great dramatic situation in his story is a little felt even in Shakespeare's treatment of it. And Coriolanus himself is so unreasonable that we do not feel his tragedy so fully as his flashes of nobility would otherwise deserve. Yet *Coriolanus* is a fine play—Granville Barker, an excellent judge, thought one of the finest. It gives the impression of having been written under some pressure—of time or temper or both. Whole passages of North are flung down with the minimum of change necessary to make metre and poetry. And there is a vast amount of invective, eloquent and no doubt in character, but so abundant, compared with what is given or suggested by Plutarch, as to make one wonder if it was not, in part at least, a safety valve for some temporary mood of Shakespeare himself. The image of the 'gentle Shakespeare' is no doubt too present with most of us. There is every indication that normally he was gentle; contemporary evidence (including Jonson's) makes that certain. It is clear that he had what people now call 'charm' in a notable degree. But a man cannot write with the intensity that burns through *Lear* or *Othello* without a reaction; it would be strange if Shakespeare was never depressed or ill or even (like Swift or Carlyle) angry with the world. It is hardly possible to explain *Troilus* or *Timon* unless one allows for that. If he felt an impulse to express himself on the subject of the 'vulgar' and their political guides, he could not have chosen a better subject than the fate of Coriolanus. Otherwise one would have thought almost any other of Plutarch's Romans would have provided him with more strikingly dramatic material—Marius, perhaps, in particular. For whatever reason, Shakespeare chose Coriolanus.

Coriolanus is the most political of all his plays. It has been suggested that Shakespeare meant his audience to find there a parallel to, or a parable of, the state of politics in contemporary England or London. There may be some truth in the suggestion, but it is one that cannot be proved. What requires no proof is the vividness of the political scenes in the play. There is little profit in asking how far they are true to history. The whole story of Coriolanus, if it has any foundation in history at all, is clouded by legend. But, however fabulous in itself, it was set in a period which was not fabulous—the period of the early Roman Republic when the plebeians were struggling to obtain more recognition of their rights from the patricians. This struggle is represented by Shakespeare too much in terms of Jacobean life, but essentially as it was, because he understood political human nature, which in all ages is much the same. It is even possible that he comes nearer the truth than Livy or even Plutarch. For Livy had no political insight, and though he had much pictorial, had little historical, imagination, while Plutarch, though more sympathetic than Livy with the commons, was a Greek, and saw in republican Rome what he would expect to see in a Greek city-state. But Shakespeare, though taking all his information from Plutarch, sees deeper. One consequence is that *Coriolanus* is still a political force and awakens political passions.

Shakespeare had one other play to make out of Plutarch, *Timon of Athens*. The subject was not Roman but Greek, and it may be said at once that he had no such clear notion of the Greeks as he had of the Romans. Plutarch is not the only source, for much comes, ultimately, from Lucian. But Shakespeare must have known about Timon before. His story is told in Painter's *Palace of Pleasure* (1566), and he had long been the type of 'misanthropy'

in Renaissance literature. There is said to have been no English
translation of Lucian's *Timon* available to Shakespeare, but few
will suppose that he read Lucian in Greek. Whatever his sources
it is certain that they were ultimately classical. The mood
in which the play is written is so strange that there are sober
critics who have considered it proof that the author was 'on the
verge of a nervous breakdown'—one is familiar with the euphem-
ism—when he composed it. Perhaps he was. At any rate *Timon*
is full of rage, unhappiness and misanthropy. To say that this was
inevitable because the hero himself is full of these emotions leaves
unanswered the question why Shakespeare made choice of such
a hero. It will probably never be answered.

Except for one or two speeches from Timon of a stormy
magnificence, and a lovely elegiac touch at the close, the play is,
for the reader unattuned to its temper, comparatively uninteresting. It has a truncated, unfinished appearance, and is very ill
organized. The style in the more elaborate speeches is in Shakespeare's late manner, highly figurative and elliptical. There is no
attempt to reproduce a 'classical' fashion of speech, such as we
find in *Julius Caesar* and even in *Troilus and Cressida*, where the
diction is often studiously latinized, as in Ulysses' great oration
upon Order or in the Prologue, where come the lines about the
gates of Troy which incurred the censure of Matthew Arnold—
the gates which

> with massy staples
> And corresponsive and fulfilling bolts
> Sperr up the sons of Troy.

It is not however the Latin word 'corresponsive' of which he dis-
approves, but 'sperr', which he describes as both quaint and
antiquated. But surely a word may be both quaint and antiquated
and yet, in the right setting, poetically justified. Besides, Arnold
should have known (as he evidently did not) that 'sperr' is a
mere conjecture for 'stir'. Critics should make sure of their
ground. As for 'corresponsive', it is held to be a new formation
from the Latin. Certainly it is admirably descriptive of the
arrangements for bolting and barring the ancient city-gate. But
there is no evidence in *Timon* of any attempt to suit the style to

the subject such as we find in *Julius Caesar* and even in great part of *Troilus*.

There is however a certain affinity with *Troilus* in mood or temper. It is always dangerous to infer from the spirit of a work of art, especially when it is dramatic, the spirit of its creator. Sophocles wrote the gloomiest of tragedies, yet the cheerful serenity of his temper was almost proverbial. We had better confine ourselves then to the mood of the plays themselves. Now of *Timon* there is one thing we may freely assert. It shows as little respect as *Troilus* for the schoolmasters' worship of antiquity.

Hitherto what has been under discussion is Shakespeare's treatment of his classical material. We have now to consider the style which raised it into the Shakespearian poetry. This is not an irrelevant or unnecessary inquiry, nor is it enough to say that we should be content with the fact. And for this reason. The Shakespearian poetic is intrinsically different from that of classical drama and of the styles that follow the classical. Indeed it is in the application of the Shakespearian style to classical dramatic themes that the revolution begun by *Julius Caesar* mainly consists.

Greek tragedy is a unique form of art. It has come to be so by retaining and developing certain traditional features which in their combination have made it what it is. Consequently Greek tragic style cannot be understood in isolation from the other elements of Greek tragedy. The most striking and characteristic of these elements is the Chorus. Indeed it may be said that Greek tragedy grew out of the Chorus by increasing the importance of the speaking, as distinct from the singing, parts. Originally, one must suppose, the Chorus 'imitated'—it is the Greek word—the actions and passions of the god Dionysus. Later they also re-enacted the sufferings of some hero who need have no direct connexion with Dionysus. The hero was not anybody, historical or fictitious, who had suffered and whose story seemed to the poet a good one to dramatize. The tragedians of the fifth century before Christ were not allowed, or did not allow themselves, any such choice. Their heroes were in practice limited to a comparatively small number. They were the heroes—or heroines —of certain 'myths', as we call them, traditional stories about the 'heroic' age of Greece. Thus a Greek tragedy never deals with the present or the recent past, but with a distant past, which was always—whatever the ordinary Greek may have thought— almost wholly 'a past that never was a present'. In other words it was an *ideal* past.

To express this ideal past it was found artistically necessary to have an ideal language. It could not be ordinary speech because it was not speaking of ordinary matters. The Greek artistic conscience was extraordinarily sensitive to this consideration. In the *Frogs* of Aristophanes, Aeschylus, 'the creator of Greek tragedy',[1] is criticized by Euripides for writing in a style that was too grandiose and remote from ordinary usage. Aeschylus replies that such a style is natural on the lips of demi-gods because their thoughts are loftier than ours and 'their dress is grander'. The second reason is ridiculous and is meant by Aristophanes to seem ridiculous, but he knows in his heart that Aeschylus is essentially right. It would not do for legendary kings to speak as if they were characters in a domestic drama—not unless they were meant to be funny. The style of Euripides himself, though less remote from that of everyday life than the style of Aeschylus, is still far removed from it. It is 'the language of the gods', apt to the gods and to those legendary beings who were the sons or grandsons of gods. Now and again, when a speaker of humble origin makes a report, a word or phrase of a colloquial sort may be given him, but, in Virgil's phrase, *pudenter et raro*, and with a special care that the general tone of a remote, yet strangely impressive, dignity is not seriously affected. This is only the exception that proves the rule.

Now a style of this kind must deal in general rather than particular sentiments and descriptions, and this for several reasons. In a traditional tale, such as are these myths which form the subject of the ancient tragedies, the characters have traditional qualities; alter these qualities, and the myth no longer makes sense. Achilles must not be represented as like Ulysses, nor Medea as

[1] Gilbert Murray.

like Alcestis. We may go so far as to say that the myth in each case is the story of how such and such a legendary hero acted according to the character assigned to him by tradition. He becomes a type or at any rate a person with fixed characteristics. As Horace puts it, Medea must always be a creature of ungoverned passions, Ino a thing of tears, Ixion treacherous, Io a wanderer, Orestes darkly brooding.[1] The poet therefore must refrain from giving his characters such individualizing traits as may obscure the type. Again, it is often complained that the Chorus in a Greek tragedy too often deals in sententious generalities. The reason is that the Chorus is the vehicle of traditional morality, which loves the sententious generality. A witty or ironical Chorus would ruin the artistic harmony of the drama. Thirdly, the religious aura which hovers about Greek tragedy is best preserved by a certain vague sublimity, and is apt to be dispelled by definite statements and 'points'. It may be added that there is no room within the brief compass of an ancient tragedy for the lavish use of particularizing details.

All this is preserved in Roman tragedy, which means Seneca. But whereas the characters in the great Greek masters, though typical, are entirely human, in Seneca they have become almost abstractions. On the other hand he really had a genius for brilliant generalization; and this, powerfully affecting his style, powerfully affected also the style of his Renaissance imitators. But the generalizing tendency is not confined to Seneca and his followers in the vernacular literatures. It is found in all the serious *genres* of classical poetry; and this not merely in the form of maxims and reflections or in their modes of thinking, but in narrative and set description. 'The business of the poet', says Imlac in *Rasselas*, giving the classical theory as he understood it, 'is to examine, not the individual, but the species; to remark general properties and large appearances. He does not number the streaks of the tulip, or describe the different shades in the verdure of the forest: he is to exhibit in his portraits of nature such prominent and striking features, as recall the original to every mind;

---

[1] 'Sit Medea ferox invictaque, flebilis Ino, perfidus Ixion, Io vaga, tristis Orestes. (*Ars. P.*, 123, 124.)

and must neglect the minuter discriminations, which one may have remarked, and another neglected, for those characteristics which are alike obvious to vigilance and carelessness.' That sums up the teaching of critics, from Scaliger and earlier through Boileau and Bossu to Pope and later, as the result of their meditation upon the practice of Virgil and the Latin poets in general. It has become so unfamiliar to us now, that some illustration of its meaning may not be impertinent. It is worth while trying to discover what it means, for it had great influence at one time on our own poetry.

Let the reader look at the description of the storm which falls upon the fleet of Aeneas in the first book of the *Aeneid*, 81 f. It may be called the type of a storm—the essence of all tempests. There is in ancient poetry something like a formula for a storm at sea. In this it often happens that all the winds blow at once with equal violence, which in nature would result in a dead calm. The poets thought only of making their storm as stormy as possible. If you examine the details in Virgil's tempest, you will find that they do not come from observation. The winds do not blow 'all together' (*una*, 85), nor will the north wind blow in the teeth of the south, at least on the same level, which is what Virgil is thinking of. It is not inconceivable that in the shallows of the Syrtes it may have been possible to catch at intervals a glimpse of the sandy bottom. But it is improbable that Virgil knew that. What he did know was that in a poetical storm the waves go up to heaven and down to hell. You get the same thing in Ovid, in a passage evidently familiar to Shakespeare, *Metamorphoses*, XI. 498 f.:

> fluctibus erigitur caelumque aequare videtur
> pontus, et inductas aspergine tangere nubes . . .
> ipsa quoque his agitur vicibus Trachinia puppis:
> et nunc sublimis veluti de vertice montis
> despicere in valles imumque Acheronta videtur:
> nunc, ubi demissam curvum circumstetit aequor,
> suspicere inferno summum de gurgite caelum.[1]

[1] 'The sea rises with its waves and seems to reach the sky and to touch with its spray the lowering clouds. . . . The Trachinian ship herself is driven thus up and down, and, now aloft, seems to look as from the top of a mountain into the valley of lowest Acheron, now, when she is down and girdled by the curving water, to look on highest heaven from the infernal gulf.'

Shakespeare is capable of saying:

> And in the visitation of the winds,
> Who take the ruffian billows by the top,
> Curling their monstrous heads and hanging them,
> With deafening clamour in the slippery clouds . . .[1]

Here is a more normal example from Dryden:

> Scarce the third glass of measured hours was run,
> When like a fiery meteor sunk the sun,
> The promise of a storm; the shifting gales
> Forsake by fits, and fill the flagging sails;
> Hoarse murmurs of the main from far were heard,
> And night came on, not by degrees prepared,
> But all at once; at once the winds arise,
> The thunders roll, the forky lightning flies.
> In vain the master issues out commands,
> In vain the trembling sailors ply their hands,
> The tempest unforeseen prevents their care,
> And from the first they labour in despair.
> The giddy ship betwixt the winds and tides,
> Forced back, and forwards, in a circle rides
> Stunned with the different blows; then shoots amain;
> Till counterbuffed, she stops, and sleeps again.[2]

This is a literary storm, full of classical memories. It describes not what Dryden had seen, but what he supposed would be the behaviour of a ship in a storm. Contrast the storm in the first scene of *The Tempest* or that in the second canto of *Don Juan*. The shipwreck in *Don Juan* is a unique event.

The modern taste for realism predisposes us against the classical method. Yet it may be defended. It helps understanding if we reflect on the history of painting. Think how the Virgin and Child are painted in Italian art. How traditional, repetitive, conventional it all is; yet how beautiful! In the same way, in certain kinds of literature the generalized type may be more suitable than the distinguishing particular. That at least was the view of the ancients. The realism which is often supposed to be a modern

---

[1] *Henry IV*, Part Two, III. i. 21-3.
[2] *Cymon and Iphigenia*, 327-42.

discovery was familiar to them. You get it often even in Homer.[1] It was the chief characteristic of the Mime. But it was not characteristic of Tragedy, which was of all the ancient poetic forms the most ideal.

This brings us back to Seneca and his influence. He carries the generalizing mode of expression far beyond what we find in the Greek tragic poets, who never, as he constantly does, lose touch with reality. He lacked the poetical genius which is needed to justify his method. So in him the faults of the style become apparent. From him they passed into the style of those who sought to naturalize the Senecan drama in English. But, as the English dramatists learned their business, they began to supply the poetical genius in which Seneca, for all his brilliance and effectiveness, was comparatively deficient. The result is often striking and impressive. On the whole this is what we get from Jonson's classical plays. The writing is good of its kind and comparatively free from the Senecan bombast. But the rhetorical generalities tire us. I will give an illustration, not from him but from Congreve, whose *Mourning Bride* shows the 'classical' style as it had come to be under the influence of the doctrine of 'correctness' and good taste. I quote it because that doctrine permeates eighteenth-century poetry, and because the passage seemed to Johnson the finest single passage in English poetry.

> How reverend is the face of this tall pile,
> Whose ancient pillars rear their marble heads
> To bear aloft its arch'd and ponderous roof,
> By its own weight made stedfast and immovable,
> Looking tranquillity! It strikes an awe
> And terror on my aching sight; the tombs
> And monumental caves of death look cold,
> And shoot a chillness to my aching heart.
> Give me thy hand, and let me hear thy voice;
> Nay, quickly speak to me, and let me hear
> Thy voice—my own affrights me with its echoes.

That is very good indeed in its own way; but the way is no longer

[1] The description of the Cyclops and his behaviour in the *Odyssey* is as good realism as Flaubert's.

ours. It does not satisfy our imaginations. It might be any temple
that Congreve is describing, and therefore we do not quite believe
in it; for any temple is no temple. Now listen to Shakespeare
describing another 'lofty pile'.

> This guest of summer,
> The temple-haunting martlet, does approve,
> By his loved mansionry, that the heaven's breath
> Smells wooingly here: no jutty, frieze,
> Buttress, nor coign of vantage, but this bird
> Hath made his pendent bed and procreant cradle:
> Where they most breed and haunt, I have observed,
> The air is delicate.[1]

What delights the imagination in this castle is that which distinguishes it from other castles—the martlets that nest and fly
about it.

Such generalized descriptions as that which I have quoted from
Congreve are the rule in serious Latin poetry. They may be
brilliant, detailed and picturesque, as they often are, for example, in
Ovid's *Metamorphoses*—that 'Bible' of the Renaissance[2]—but the
picture built up is that of a typical landscape, a typical storm, a
typical battle, a typical hunter or shepherd or shepherdess. Other
favourite poets in the post-Virgilian age proceed in the same way,
so far as that is compatible with their subject. Lucan for example
had to describe Caesar as an individual in order to distinguish him
from Pompey. But when, in a passage already alluded to, he
describes the storm when Caesar tries to cross the Adriatic in a
small ship, what we get is a typical storm, and that exaggerated
beyond the bounds of credibility and common sense. I have come
to believe that the influence of Lucan on Elizabethan style is
seriously underestimated. It is very evident (to me) in the blank
verse of Marlowe, who translated into that metre the first book of
the *Pharsalia*. The translation was made on the mechanical and
ill-considered principle—suggested no doubt by current Latin
versions—that each line of the translation should match each line of
the original. This gave no scope to the translator. But Marlowe

---

[1] *Macbeth*, I. vi. 3 f.
[2] La bible des poetes.

was not bound by it in his own dramatic verse. He has far more poetry in him than Lucan, but, if you leave out the poetry, the Marlovian style in drama, which looks so original, reads like Lucan in English. As I am not writing about Marlowe, I must leave this suggestion to scholars who know both poets. But I think it certain that much in Elizabethan poetry that is credited to Seneca should be credited to Lucan. It would be easy for this to happen because the faults of Seneca are also the faults of Lucan, who however has a larger sweep and movement, a longer roll of metre, as befits an epic poet. But if I am not to quote Marlowe, I may quote Shakespeare. The Pyrrhus speech in *Hamlet* has every quality of Lucan.

> The rugged Pyrrhus, he whose sable arms,
> Black as his purpose, did the night resemble
> When he lay couched in the ominous horse,
> Hath now this dread and black complexion smear'd
> With heraldry more dismal; head to foot
> Now is he total gules; horridly trick'd
> With blood of fathers, mothers, daughters, sons,
> Baked and impasted with the parching streets,
> That lend a tyrannous and damned light
> To their lord's murder: roasted in wrath and fire,
> And thus o'er-sized with coagulate gore,
> With eyes like carbuncles, the hellish Pyrrhus
> Old grandsire Priam seeks . . . (*Hamlet*, II. ii. 473 f.)

That seems to me pure Lucan, and not Lucan at his best. However the Player also gives us Lucan at his best:

> But, as we often see, against some storm,
> A silence in the heavens, the rack stand still,
> The bold winds speechless, and the orb below
> As hush as death, anon the dreadful thunder
> Doth rend the region . . .

The contrast between this speech and the normal style of the play in which it occurs is felt by every reader. Why does such a diction fit the account of Pyrrhus? Because he is a type; he is an embodiment of the cruelty of war. But in general Shakespeare does not deal in types, and so the diction appropriate to a type is

231

not characteristic of him. Here in the same play is another description.

> There, on the pendent boughs her coronet weeds
> Clambering to hang, an envious sliver broke;
> When down her weedy trophies and herself
> Fell in the weeping brook. Her clothes spread wide;
> And, mermaid-like, awhile they bore her up:
> Which time she chanted snatches of old tunes;
> As one incapable of her own distress,
> Or like a creature native and indued
> Unto that element... (IV. vii. 173 f.)

Ophelia is not a type but a person, the circumstances of her death unique.

It is the easiest thing in the world to find examples of the classical or generalized style in Shakespeare. In the Poems it is normal.

> By this, poor Wat, far off upon a hill,
> Stands on his hinder legs with listening ear,
> To hearken if his foes pursue him still:
> Anon their loud alarums he doth hear;
> And now his grief may be compared well
> To one sore sick that hears the passing-bell.
>
> Then shalt thou see the dew-bedabbled wretch
> Turn, and return, indenting with the way;
> Each envious brier his weary legs doth scratch,
> Each shadow makes him stop, each murmur stay.[1]

Wat is not a particular hare, he is a typical hare.

It would be interesting to pursue this subject by showing how the intense individualizing imagination of Shakespeare came more and more firmly to reject this way of writing, and to present persons and places as they were in themselves. But this can be done by anyone who will take the trouble and has a feeling for the distinction involved. One may, I think, venture to say that the process was complete when Shakespeare came to write the Plutarchan plays. For in them we find him applying the realistic

---

[1] *Venus and Adonis*, 697 f.

manner which he had used to such effect in *Romeo and Juliet* and *Henry IV*.[1]

Before *Julius Caesar* plays with a classical subject had taken, in English, two main forms, the Senecan and what, for want of a better description, we may call the Romantic. This was the result of applying to a classical story the style and technique which had been worked out for themselves by the University Wits and other dramatists contemporary with them. The effect is often strangely unclassical. Think for instance of Lyly's *Campaspe* and Peele's *Arraignment of Paris*. It is perhaps not an unfair criticism even of *Dido Queene of Carthage* in spite of the fact that Nashe and Marlowe had Virgil to keep them right. The characters of the play have no substance, their sentiments are the romantic commonplaces of their situation, the language is often, though not always, rather emptily decorative.

But in Shakespeare this vagueness and generality is all swept away. We are dealing with real men in such a world as this is. No English writer before Shakespeare tried, or at any rate was able, to make a play about Romans that was truly historical. He alone achieved the imaginative feat of seeing them, not as they were supposed to be, but as they were. He could not have done it without Plutarch, but with Plutarch he could.

> Let me have men about me that are fat;
> Sleek-headed men, and such as sleep o' nights:
> Yond Cassius has a lean and hungry look;
> He thinks too much: such men are dangerous.[2]

That is not 'Cassius an assassin'; it is Cassius himself, at least as Plutarch and Shakespeare saw him.

> I saw her once
> Hop forty paces through the public street;
> And, having lost her breath, she spoke, and panted . . .
> Age cannot wither her, nor custom stale
> Her infinite variety: other women cloy

---

[1] I am aware of everything that can be objected to the word 'realistic'; but, as I have now explained what I mean at some length, I may be excused for using the word in the interests of brevity.

[2] *Julius Caesar*, I. ii. 192 f.

The appetites they feed; but she makes hungry
Where most she satisfies: for vilest things
Become themselves in her; that the holy priests
Bless her when she is riggish.[1]

That is not 'Cleopatra a queen'; that is Cleopatra.

It is not however merely a question of Shakespeare's appropriating what suited his purpose in North. He made it into poetry. Sometimes not very much change was necessary. The passage I shall now quote is perhaps too well known, but it is so illustrative that perhaps no other will serve the purpose so well. This is what Plutarch says according to North.

'She disdained to set forward otherwise, but to take her barge in the river of Cydnus; the poop whereof was of gold, the sails of purple, and the oars of silver, which kept stroke in rowing after the sound of the music of flutes, howboys, cithernes, viols and such other instruments as they played upon in the barge. And now for the person of her self, she was laid under a pavilion of cloth of gold of tissue, apparelled and attired like the goddess Venus, commonly drawn in picture: and hard by her, on either hand of her, pretty fair boys apparelled as painters do set forth god Cupid, with little fans in their hands, with the which they fanned wind upon her. Her ladies and gentlewomen also, the fairest of them, were apparelled like the nymphs Nereids (which are the mermaids of the waters) and like the Graces; some steering the helm, others tending the tackle and ropes of the barge, out of the which there came a wonderful passing sweet savour of perfumes, that perfumed the wharf's side, pestered with innumerable multitudes of people. Some of them followed the barge all along the river-side: others also ran out of the city[2] to see her coming in. So that in the end, there ran such multitudes of people[3] one after another to see her, that Antonius was left post alone in the market-place, in his imperial seat, to give audience: and there went a rumour in the people's mouths, that the goddess Venus was come to play with the god Bacchus, for the general good of all Asia.[4] When Cleopatra landed, Antonius sent to invite her to supper to him. But she sent him word again, he should do better rather to come and sup with her. Antonius therefore, to shew

[1] *Antony and Cleopatra*, II. ii. 233 f.
[2] Tarsus.
[3] The father of St. Paul among them?
[4] i.e., Asia Minor.

himself courteous unto her at her arrival, was contented to obey her, and went to supper to her: where he found such passing sumptuous fare, that no tongue can express it.'

That is fine prose, but it remains prose, and even shows a certain helplessness in the repetition of words ('apparelled', 'people'). It is fascinating to observe how Shakespeare makes it into magnificent poetry. It is done largely by metre, by extremely subtle and elaborate effects of alliteration and vowel-modulation, and small heightening touches, rather too 'conceited' for Greek and perhaps our taste but beautiful of their kind.[1]

> The barge she sat in, like a burnish'd throne,
> Burn'd on the water: the poop was beaten gold;
> Purple the sails, and so perfumed that
> The winds were love-sick with them; the oars were silver,
> Which to the tune of flutes kept stroke, and made
> The water which they beat to follow faster,
> As amorous of their strokes. For her own person,
> It beggar'd all description: she did lie
> In her pavilion—cloth-of-gold of tissue—
> O'er-picturing that Venus where we see
> The fancy outwork nature: on each side her
> Stood pretty dimpled boys, like smiling Cupids,
> With divers-colour'd fans whose wind did seem
> To glow the delicate cheeks which they did cool,
> And what they undid did . . .
> Her gentlewomen, like the Nereides,
> So many mermaids, tended her i' th' eyes,
> And made their bends adornings: at the helm
> A seeming mermaid steers: the silken tackle
> Swell with the touches of those flower-soft hands,
> That yarely frame the office. From the barge
> A strange invisible perfume hits the sense
> Of the adjacent wharfs. The city cast
> Her people out upon her; and Antony,
> Enthroned i' the market-place, did sit alone,
> Whistling to the air; which, but for vacancy,
> Had gone to gaze on Cleopatra too

[1] The passage has been analysed in a well-known essay by Stevenson.

And made a gap in Nature. . . .
Upon her landing, Antony sent to her,
Invited her to supper: she replied,
It should be better he became her guest;
Which she entreated: our courteous Antony,
Whom ne'er the word of 'No' woman heard speak,
Being barber'd ten times o'er, goes to the feast,
And for his ordinary pays his heart
For what his eyes eat only.[1]

But it is not merely in such passages of set description that
Shakespeare reveals the marvel of the new style. He knew as well
as any that verbal magic alone will not make a play. He must
contrive to give the characters naturalness, the incidents vividness,
the plot concentration and unity. To achieve these effects he takes
considerable, though for an artist allowable, liberties with the
text of Plutarch. A short excerpt will make this clear. It is taken
from the beginning of the second scene of *Julius Caesar*, act one.
A procession enters, the central figure in it Caesar.

CAESAR. Calpurnia!

CASCA.   Peace, ho! Caesar speaks.

CAESAR.   Calpurnia!

CALPURNIA. Here, my lord. . . .

CAESAR. Forget not, in your speed, Antonius,
          To touch Calpurnia; for our elders say,
          The barren, touched in this holy chase,
          Shake off their sterile curse.

ANTONY.   I shall remember:
          When Caesar says 'do this', it is perform'd.

CAESAR. Set on; and leave no ceremony out.

SOOTHSAYER. Caesar!

CAESAR. Ha! who calls?

CASCA. Bid every noise be still: peace yet again!

CAESAR.   Who is it in the press that calls on me?
          I hear a tongue, shriller than all the music,
          Cry 'Caesar!'. Speak; Caesar is turn'd to hear.

SOOTHSAYER. Beware the ides of March.

CAESAR. What man is that?

[1] *Antony and Cleopatra*, II. ii. 195 f.

236

BRUTUS. A soothsayer bids you beware the ides of March.

CAESAR. Set him before me; let me see his face.

CASSIUS. Fellow, come from the throng; look upon Caesar.

CAESAR. What say'st thou to me now? speak once again.

SOOTHSAYER. Beware the ides of March.

CAESAR. He is a dreamer; let us leave him: pass.

Is not all that wonderful 'theatre'? Yet to produce it Shakespeare makes very free with Plutarch. It was not in a procession that Caesar watched the Lupercalia, in which Antony, with others, ran naked according to the ancient ritual, striking with a thong any barren woman who chose to stand in his way. Caesar watched it from the tribunal. 'Caesar sat to behold that sport upon the pulpit for orations, in a chair of gold, apparelled in triumphing manner' (North). Nor does Plutarch make any mention here of Calpurnia; Shakespeare brings her in to make the scene more vivid in personality, to indicate that Caesar has no heir, and to unify the plot. Again, the soothsayer, in Plutarch's account, had warned Caesar against the ides of March many days before the Lupercalia. 'A certain soothsayer . . . had given Caesar warning long time afore to take heed of the Ides of March'. Shakespeare boldly transfers it to a moment when its dramatic force is immensely increased. How greatly increased the reader will feel if he imagines the emotions of the conspirators when Caesar hears the warning cry and insists on seeing the man face to face—then, after a long look into the mad eyes of the prophet, dismisses him.

Very often, again, Shakespeare contrives a wonderful effect by making one part of Plutarch's narrative illuminate another. Here also one brief quotation must suffice. At the end of *Coriolanus* Aufidius calls the young hero 'boy'—an epithet which wounds him to the quick.

CORIOLANUS.   Boy! false hound!
                If you have writ your annals true, 'tis there,
                That, like an eagle in a dove-cote, I
                Flutter'd your Volscians in Corioli:
                Alone I did it. Boy!

So, admitting that Shakespeare was not a scholar, let us consider in brief what use he made of such classical reading as he had, meaning by this not only what he had read in Latin but what he had read in translation, or had gathered from reading in English books or plays, or from conversation or sight-seeing. I am willing to agree that he had read more Latin—Greek is out of the question —than appears in the Poems and Plays, although, if he had read much more, it must have come out somewhere in works so voluminous. But there is in him no feeling for Latin as Latin; he is not thrilled by Latin poetic style as Jonson was, or Campion, or Milton. Had he really been a Latin *scholar*, he would, with his divine susceptibility to the beauty of words, have experienced this thrill. It is true that the Latin element in Shakespeare's style is surprisingly large, and words derived from the Latin are often used by him with what looks like an exquisite sense of their original meaning.

> The extravagant and erring spirit hies
> To his confines.

There 'extravagant', 'erring' and 'confines' are employed with a scholarly precision which Milton himself could not better. But we must not forget that in Shakespeare's day these words still retained most if not all of their original sense, and that it is later generations that have diverted them to other meanings. It was also a time when nearly every author, including self-educated people like the Water Poet, latinized heavily, and when new words, mostly formed from the Latin, were being coined every day. Shakespeare then was only doing what other poets were busily engaged upon, and he could have picked up a great many new words in this fashion. Many however do seem to be of his own coinage, and they do imply a certain knowledge of Latin. But it is hardly the same thing as appreciating the literary quality of Latin poetry.

If we pass from the form to the matter of what he read, we find that the mythology, which is interwoven through nearly all Latin poetry and is the staple of a very great portion of the best in it, is deeply loved by him, so far as he knew it, and his knowledge was not inconsiderable. Here again we must remember that this love and this knowledge were characteristic of the age, indeed of the whole Renaissance, of which the Elizabethan age was but an English episode. The poetry of Sidney and Spenser, of Lyly and Peele, of Lodge and Greene and Chapman and Marlowe, is full of mythological lore. But it is manifest that Shakespeare loved it of his own accord and for its own sake. He knows the *Metamorphoses* from end to end and clearly delights in its innumerable stories. (The evidence of that is displayed in the first half of this book.) What else than delight in the stories could have supported him through perhaps fifteen thousand of Golding's verses? It was from classical mythology—for the story of Lucrece belongs rather to mythology than to history—that he drew the matter of his two youthful poems. But here we encounter a paradox. If, at the time when he wrote these poems and his sonnets, Shakespeare already had this love and knowledge of classical mythology, why is it that in these there is so little evidence of that knowledge? That seems to require some explanation. I can only suggest, and it is with diffidence, that Shakespeare had not yet discovered how to use the ancient myths except in the way of incidental decoration. I suggest again that the man who taught him better was Marlowe.

Here is a decorative (and very beautiful) stanza from the *Faerie Queene* (I. vii. 32):

> Upon the top of all his loftie crest,
> A bounch of heares discolourd diversly,
> With sprincled pearle and gold full richly drest,
> Did shake, and seemd to daunce for jollity,
> Like to an almond tree ymounted hye
> On top of greene Selinis all alone,
> With blossoms brave bedecked daintily;
> Whose tender locks do tremble every one
> At everie little breath that under heaven is blowne.

Here now is Marlowe, boldly pillaging Spenser:

> And in my helm a triple plume shall spring,
> Spangled with diamonds, dancing in the air,

To note me emperor of the three-fold world;
Like to an almond tree ymounted high
Upon the lofty and celestial mount
Of ever-green Selinus, quaintly deck'd
With blooms more white than Erycina's brows,
Whose tender blossoms tremble every one
At every little breath that thorough heaven is blown.
Then in my coach, like Saturn's royal son
Mounted his shining chariot gilt with fire
And drawn with princely eagles through the path
Pav'd with bright crystal and encas'd with stars,
When all the gods stand gazing at his pomp,
So will I ride through Samarcanda streets.

(*Tamburlaine*, II. iv. 3)

Observe the greater excitement of the Marlowe passage. This
poet's imagination is not merely, like Spenser's, attracted by the
mythology; it is possessed by it. Inevitably one quotes the words
of Faustus to the phantasm of Helen.

Was this the face that launch'd a thousand ships
And burnt the topless towers of Ilium? . . .
O, thou art fairer than the evening air
Clad in the beauty of a thousand stars;
Brighter art thou than flaming Jupiter
When he appear'd to hapless Semele;
More lovely than the monarch of the sky
In wanton Arethusa's azur'd arms;
And none but thou shalt be my paramour!

That is not decorative verse, like so much of Spenser and like
Venus and Adonis; it is the fusion of the old imagination with the
new; it is the remaking of the myths. The effect is quite enchanting. It is likely that Shakespeare, who sooner or later discovered all poetic effects, would have, unaided, discovered this
also. But who can doubt that lines like these set his imagination
on fire? At any rate he is Marlowe's successor in this transmuta-
tion of the old mythology. And so we get:

Sing, siren, for thyself, and I will dote:
Spread o'er the silver waves thy golden hair

and

> Subtle as Sphinx; as sweet and musical
> As bright Apollo's lute, strung with his hair

and

> For valour, is not Love a Hercules,
> Still climbing trees in the Hesperides?

and

> In such a night
> Troilus methinks mounted the Troyan walls
> And sigh'd his soul toward the Grecian tents,
> Where Cressid lay that night. In such a night
> Did Thisbe fearfully o'ertrip the dew
> And saw the lion's shadow ere himself
> And ran dismay'd away. In such a night
> Stood Dido with a willow in her hand
> Upon the wild sea-banks and waft her love
> To come again to Carthage. In such a night
> Medea gather'd her enchanted herbs
> That did renew old Aeson.

Who will deny that, however little Greek or Latin Shakespeare may have known, he made the most wonderful use of what he did know? So that, in a perfectly real and genuine sense, the classics actually meant more to Shakespeare than to those who had only a book-knowledge of them. One thinks of Keats, and the parallel is very instructive. But even Keats did not attain the loveliness of

> O Proserpina,
> For the flowers now, that frighted thou let'st fall
> From Dis's wagon! ...
> violets dim,
> But sweeter than the lids of Juno's eyes
> Or Cytherea's breath,

or of this:

> stay for me,
> Where souls do couch on flowers, we'll hand in hand,
> And with our sprightly port make the ghosts gaze:
> Dido, and her Aeneas shall want troops,
> And all the haunt be ours.

The only later English poet who comes very close to Shakespeare in this imaginative handling of the ancient mythology is
Milton, and the handling of Milton is more studied and conventional or literary—adjectives which have now fallen into
disrepute but are not used here in any disparaging sense—but is
hardly less beautiful.

> That fair field
> Of Enna where Proserpine gathering flowers,
> Herself a fairer flower, by gloomy Dis
> Was gather'd, which cost Ceres all that pain
> To seek her through the world.

Indeed Milton is almost always at his best when reviving the
mythology of Greece.

> What could the Muse herself that Orpheus bore,
> The Muse herself, for her enchanting son,
> Whom universal nature did lament,
> When, by the rout that made the hideous roar,
> His gory visage down the stream was sent,
> Down the swift Hebrus to the Lesbian shore?

Shelley and Keats, Tennyson and Arnold have got in varying
measure the same magical touch in this matter, and it is undeniably
the source of some of the finest poetry in the language. Shakespeare is in the stream of this current. It is therefore just to say
that in one very important respect he was profoundly influenced
by the classics.

Profoundly influenced by the classics; that is to say, in this
matter of style, by Ovid and the Ovidian stories. But the influence of Plutarch has also to be measured. I will venture on a
statement that may surprise some of my readers. I believe that
it was from Plutarch that Shakespeare learned how to make a
tragedy of the kind exemplified in *Hamlet* and *Othello*, *Macbeth*
and *Lear*. It was, I think, in the course of writing *Julius Caesar*
that he learned it. *Julius Caesar* appears in the Folios among the
tragedies, and the description is true. It is not a chronicle play,

although the subject is historical, for Shakespeare has made no attempt to dramatize the life of Caesar. He has selected one incident—the incident of his death—and made that the centre of a number of episodes organically connected in the manner I have tried to explain; that is to say, there is a series of scenes progressively leading up to the death-scene, then another series naturally or necessarily consequent upon that. The construction is different from that of *Richard III* or *King John*, where the method is in the main annalistic, though the scenes may be tragic, or at any rate bloody, enough. This I suppose every reasonable critic would concede. But what of *Titus Andronicus* and *Romeo and Juliet*? Well, *Titus* is a tragedy, but it is a tragedy of the Senecan, not the Shakespearian, type and so falls out of our consideration here. In *Romeo and Juliet* the catastrophe is brought about by a piece of bad luck, and this has led many to hold that *Romeo* is only a romantic drama with an unhappy ending, which might (according to them) have just as well been a happy one. But no; that passion of love had to end in death; it was the only way of keeping the lovers for ever mortal and for ever young. Hence, although their death seems a mere caprice of fate, it is an imaginative necessity. On the other hand this is the only necessity that it has, and, although that may be enough for an elegy, it is not enough for a completely organized tragedy.

Now *Julius Caesar* is such a tragedy. It is pervaded by the tragic sense, and nothing in it happens, we feel, that could have happened otherwise. It will be remembered what Plutarch made of 'the great daemon of Caesar'; how he felt that Caesar's whole life and, after his death, the lives of his enemies had been dominated by that evil spirit. It will be remembered also how Shakespeare fastened upon this, recognizing the dramatic and artistic value of such a concrete embodiment of the tragic sense. This helped him, this made it possible for him to create a true tragic drama. Surely that is a very considerable debt which he owed to Plutarch. But Plutarch himself—and here lies the extreme interest and importance of the matter—was only the channel or medium of the Greek tragic spirit. This, as we all know, received its highest expression in the great Attic poets Aeschylus, Sophocles and

Euripides; of whom Euripides for many centuries after his death was by far the most influential. All through the fourth century before Christ, the third, the second and so on until at least the third century after Christ the serious mind of antiquity was steeped in Homer and Euripides; and the tragic spirit is only less pervading in Homer than in the other. But it is in no way peculiar to the poets. It is instinctive in the Greek mind. It permeates the history of Herodotus and the history of Thucydides. To the classical Greek mind, to the pre-classical popular mind, human history appeared as a tragedy, exalting as much as it saddens, or rather exalting more than it saddens, the actor and spectator. Nobody can read Plutarch without feeling that he has by nature a strong dramatic sense. But the chief reason why he sees history as drama is that he has been taught to see it so—taught by Homer and Euripides and Thucydides. It is not merely that he is perpetually quoting them; they have formed his mind. He is not pessimistic; he cherishes a gentle philosophy. But he sees the life of Caesar, the life of Antony, as a tragedy—as what the Greeks understood by a tragedy.

Not so long ago it was a widely accepted view among literary critics that the characters in Greek tragedy were the helpless victims of destiny, and it was quite usual to contrast Shakespearian tragedy with it on that ground. The fact that no one is perceptibly the wiser from drawing this contrast may suggest that it is superficial. Probably Aristotle is the unwitting cause. Aristotle, out of the many hundreds of Greek tragedies known to him, selected as the best-constructed the *Oedipus Rex* of Sophocles. Now in that play it is undeniable that Oedipus is the victim of destiny. So later critics, regarding the *Oedipus* on Aristotle's authority as the typical Greek tragedy, drew the inference that the typical hero of Greek tragedy was the helpless victim of destiny. But suppose that Aristotle, dealing with some other quality than construction, had chosen the *Prometheus Bound* of Aeschylus or the *Antigone* of Sophocles or the *Alcestis* of Euripides —I mention three of the best-known Greek dramas—he would have had to say that Prometheus defies the doom assigned to him, that Antigone chooses her fate by the exercise of her free will, that

Alcestis is rescued by Heracles from the death from which there was no appeal. The truth is that, the strictness of the form considered, the variety of the content in Greek tragedy is very remarkable. Even tragedies dealing with the same legend are found to differ strikingly from one another. To generalize from the *Oedipus Rex* therefore is not a logical procedure.

It is however true to say that the inevitability of fate is insisted upon in the Greek far more than in the Elizabethan tragedies, unless when these are strongly influenced by Seneca. For all that the characters in Greek drama never look like pawns in a game; they have in general pretty strong wills or at least passions. Above all, even when they are conquered by fate, it is always for some human reason. To put it somewhat differently, they suffer not from the caprice of destiny but from some flaw in their own nature which destiny uses to their destruction. If Oedipus had been less irascible and headstrong, he would not have killed his father for a word and a blow. If he had had a different temperament, he would have had a different fate. In the same way (as Plutarch sees it, and Shakespeare, following Plutarch) if Antony had been a different kind of man, if Cleopatra had been a different kind of woman, the history of the world would have been different.

There is however another reason why in some of the finest Greek tragedies the irresistible power of destiny is a good deal harped upon. The reason is that the poet wishes to obtain the effect of tragic irony. This is possible only when the audience knows the doom that awaits the speaker. For example, the power of *Oedipus Rex* is not due to the exciting way in which the solution of the mystery is contrived—for it is no mystery to the audience or the reader—so much as to the irony that runs through almost everything that is said. This is perhaps too well known to require illustration, but a very simple and obvious one will be forgiven. In his determination to find and punish the murderer of the old king, Oedipus invokes against the criminal an elaborate and fearful curse, which the audience know will be fulfilled to the letter upon Oedipus himself. Since the modern dramatist in general prefers to keep his audience in ignorance of the *dénouement* until it comes, he is precluded from using such effects, at least to any great extent. But their use is characteristic of Greek tragedy and even of the Greek mind, which had a poor opinion of the mere shock of surprise as an artistic effect, except in comedy.[1] It was perhaps Voltaire, in the Preface to his *Mérope*, who first plainly formulated the rule that the aim of a drama shall be to keep the audience in suspense as to what the *dénouement* will be. Observance of it has almost destroyed the poetic drama.

There is a great deal of tragic irony, no doubt often of the unconscious sort, in many of Plutarch's Lives, and the *Life of Julius Caesar* is one of them. The irony is, as we should expect, most apparent in the scenes which precede the death of Caesar and in those which precede the death of Brutus. Shakespeare observes this and makes the most of it. The words of Caesar and of Brutus in these scenes take an added significance from our knowledge of the stroke that is imminent upon them. Then he makes a great deal of the prodigies that give warning of Caesar's death. No doubt prodigies were very much to the taste of Elizabethan audiences, and any other Elizabethan dramatist might have dwelt upon them too. But not in the same way or with the same skill. The accumulation of omens is intended to load our spirits with apprehension, like the omens that gather about the end of the *Odyssey*. Unless we knew that they would be fulfilled, they would seem childish and irrelevant. In *Julius Caesar*—and of course elsewhere—Shakespeare works in the Greek way upon the knowledge of his audience in order to produce the effect of tragic irony. Consider, again, the manner in which Caesar is lured to his destruction by the conspirators. It is like the luring of Agamemnon by Clytemnestra to walk on the red tapestry to his death. Then there is the warning of the soothsayer, twice repeated, and most carefully timed by Shakespeare to create the maximum impression. The boastful language of Caesar is very like those hubristic utterances which proceed from great persons

---

[1] It is true that in Euripides the plot occasionally takes a surprising turn, or characters meet unforeseen *contretemps*; but these situations are always incidental to the plot or complications of it; they do not form the plot, which in its broad outlines the audience knew already.

in Greek tragedy on the verge of their downfall. In the same way, in the second half of the drama, the words of Brutus are increasingly suffused with tragic irony as he approaches his end, the prodigy of 'Caesar's ghost' much aiding the effect. These elements are all in Plutarch, but they have been noted, developed and emphasized by Shakespeare as they would have been by a Greek tragic poet. It cannot be accident; it is conscious and deliberate art. He could never have learned this from Seneca, who has no sense of irony; still less could he have learned it from the English followers of Seneca, whose chief concern is to be sensational or sententious. But it is in Plutarch, and he found it there.

Julius Caesar was followed, it would seem proximately, by *Hamlet*, and in that play we find him clearly applying the lessons he had learned in the former. That Shakespeare had Julius Caesar in his mind when he wrote *Hamlet* is clear from at least one reference there. But the decisive evidence is revealed on an examination of the play itself. From the very beginning of *Hamlet* Shakespeare sets himself to create a climate of apprehension, of impending fatality, because he has learned that you must take or present a tragic view of life itself, or of the life whose story you are making into a play, if that story is to appear more than an unfortunate experience, involving perhaps what people call a fatal accident. Hamlet is a tragic figure, a man foredoomed, from the outset. We feel this, and he himself dimly, but with growing conviction, feels it. That is the atmosphere which permeates the drama. It renders false and meaningless the theory that the 'delays' of Hamlet are undramatic. Did any spectator ever *feel* that? On the contrary their effect is to enhance and protract the dramatic tension. Of the old *Hamlet*, which existed before Shakespeare's, we know nothing; he may or may not have been an unhesitating avenger of the Senecan type; the cry of the ghost 'Hamlet, revenge!' does not solve that problem for us. It is commonly believed that the hesitating hero of Shakespeare's *Hamlet* owes something to Hieronimo in *The Spanish Tragedy*. But the 'delays' of our Hamlet are explained and elaborated in a manner which goes far beyond these precedents. Does anyone suppose that Shakespeare had not considered whether or not they would clog the action and diminish the tension of his play? They are also of course essential to his conception of Hamlet's character, which in some important respects resembles that of Brutus. Shakespeare understood that a tragedy, as distinct say from a melodrama or a chronicle-play, is the tragedy of a character, not merely a sequence of disastrous happenings. He had seen that at least as early as *Richard II*, which might be described as a chronicle-play on the way to becoming a tragedy. In *Julius Caesar* the final step has been taken. And *Hamlet* followed. For the rest, I attach little importance to the fact that both plays are at heart dramas of Revenge, each with a vengeful ghost in it, for that is largely a coincidence imposed by the traditional plot of the Hamlet story in the one case and by Plutarch's reading of the facts in the case of Caesar. Also it would be altogether an exaggeration to say that *Julius Caesar* imposed its pattern on *Hamlet*. The argument is merely this, that in conception and in treatment *Hamlet* follows the lines of *Julius Caesar*. And the point I wish to make is that this conception is Greek, and that Shakespeare in this way got nearer to the spirit of Greek tragedy than did Jonson and the schoolmasters.

The *Macbeth* with which we are familiar is perhaps abridged from an older version of uncertain date, but later than *Hamlet*, which perhaps it immediately followed. At any rate we may say that at some indefinite, but not distant, time after *Hamlet* Shakespeare wrote another tragedy more in the Greek manner than even *Julius Caesar*. The most strikingly Greek feature of *Macbeth* is the murder, which is done off the stage. It would be hard to prove, and it seems to me improbable, that Shakespeare borrowed it from the practice of Greek tragedy, although it would be familiar to him from Seneca. If Duncan had been murdered in view of the audience, it could only have been in dumb show, like the murder of the 'Player King' in *Hamlet*. Shakespeare never, I think, uses dumb show except as an accessory to the principal action, and the killing of Duncan is the action upon which the whole drama revolves. To have that done in dumb show by a Macbeth whose mind had not been revealed to us, as it is in those terrible dialogues with Lady Macbeth, would have appeared so atrocious that perhaps even an Elizabethan audience would have been shocked. It may have been some such consideration that impelled Shakespeare to use the method of narration. At any rate that is what is used. The death of Duncan is reported, not enacted, and produces the same effect—in this case overwhelmingly impressive—as the reported deaths in Greek tragedy. More significant and less doubtful is the tragic preparation, the sense of impending disaster, the irony which suffuses *Macbeth*. In a Greek tragedy the audience knows what is to come, and Euripides often reminds them of it in a Prologue. Observe what Shakespeare does. Not expecting his audience to know the obscure story of Macbeth, he brings in at once the Weird Sisters, who prophesy all that is to happen. The interest after that is exactly the same kind of interest that we get in *Oedipus Rex*, which is also a drama of the fulfilment of prophecy.

I do not know of any Greek tragedy in which the atmosphere is more heavily charged with doom. As if the Sisters were not enough, the poet adds omens and portents. It cannot be said that Macbeth is less the helpless victim of destiny than any character of the Greek stage. It cannot rightly be argued that his killing of Duncan was an act of deliberate choice; it was the only way he had of fulfilling the predictions of the prophetesses, and these *had* to be fulfilled. He was bound to kill Duncan in exactly the same way that Oedipus was bound to kill his father. There is, I think, a great deal to be said for Quiller-Couch's view that Macbeth is in a manner hypnotized by the Sisters. It is certain that on his meeting with them he is 'rapt' and ever after seems to behave almost in an automatic way, as if he were half-awake and half-asleep. 'The curse is come upon' him, as it comes upon Clytemnestra after the murder of Agamemnon, when she feels that the 'evil daemon' of the race has entered into her. He walks in an evil dream. Shakespeare feels that this would be the effect of committing a murder on a man of Macbeth's temperament. He was not consciously following any Greek. But it happens that Aeschylus had also a profound insight into the working of the human imagination under the burden of a crime, and so he depicts it in much the same way as Shakespeare. I am of course aware that Aeschylus took over the theory of daemonic possession from popular religion and superstition. But he understands it in his own way. His sympathetic imagination enables him to enter into Clytemnestra's point of view, so that he even sympathizes with *her*, while he condemns her. In the same way the reader cannot help feeling that Shakespeare, consciously or not, sympathizes with Macbeth.

It would be superfluous to labour the point. I am content with throwing out the suggestion that, through the medium of North's Plutarch, Shakespeare divined the true spirit of Greek tragedy. The possibility of this will not seem remote to anyone who has given serious attention to the nature and the development of ancient biography. From the first it had a dramatic tendency imposed upon it by the popular imagination, which had already made 'heroes' or 'villains' of at any rate the most famous of those who were likely to have biographies at all. Some, like Alexander the Great or Cyrus the Great, had created a myth about themselves in their own life-time. The general form of ancient biography has been exposed and delineated by modern investigators.[1] First there is an accumulation of details about the birth and genealogy of the hero (often involving some miraculous incident); then there is a full account of what was considered the crowning achievement of his career; lastly his death is related in all its circumstances. These are the three high-lights, as it were, of the ancient biography, and there is little in between them except a number of characteristic sayings and anecdotes.[2] The method is selective rather than exhaustive, and the interest concentrated on the personality rather than the environment of the subject. It will be seen that in the hands of an artist a biography of this kind will assume a dramatic character. And, since the end is always death, it will be touched with tragedy.

The tragic spirit, as it is expressed in its fullest or finest form in Aeschylus, Sophocles and Euripides, and in a less artistic or intense form in Plutarch, is somewhat unfamiliar to the modern mind.

[1] The most important perhaps, Norden.
[2] The Synoptic Gospels follow the general lines of ancient biography.

It is quite unchristian. For the Christian, death is the change to a happier existence, if only he obtain the grace of God, which he obtains not through his own merits but by a humble appeal to the divine mercy. The tragic spirit is therefore in a manner impossible to one who has that hope or confidence. It was not impossible to the Greek, because death to him really was an end. Life was a battle in which he knew beforehand that he would be killed. What then was a brave man to do? Why, make a good fight of it while the fight lasted. That is the tragic spirit, which is quite different from what people usually mean by 'pessimism'. The essence of every Greek drama is an *agon*, 'a struggle'. It is a contest in which the loser may win the spiritual victory. The interest lies in the contest. The ancient Greeks understood this very well; I am not putting a modern interpretation on the fact. The thought even penetrates their philosophy. Thus the Stoics were fond of illustrating their ethical system by a metaphor or simile drawn from the theatre. Every man has a rôle assigned to him by God. It may be very splendid or very humble—that of a prince or that of a slave. But in the eyes of God the only thing that matters is how you play your part; the only kind of success that counts with Him is the successful—that is, the brave and honourable—performance of your part. Such a view of life is not in the least the view expressed by the cynical and pessimistic Jaques in that famous soliloquy of 'All the world's a stage....' It is something much finer which, when reduced to artistic form by a great poet, gives us what Aristotle calls 'the pleasure appropriate to tragedy'. Nor does Aristotle think of this pleasure as merely aesthetic; it accompanies an exaltation of the human spirit.

Consider now how well this applies to the *Brutus* of Plutarch. The historical Brutus, though not a professional philosopher, had at an early age become a Stoic of a somewhat rigid type, probably under the influence of his father-in-law Cato. Plutarch, himself a philosopher, never forgets this, and you can see that he admires Brutus, who, perhaps mistaken and certainly unfortunate, nevertheless played his part in a manner worthy, on the whole, of his principles, and died rather than surrender. His career therefore is the very stuff of tragedy. This is also the view of Shakespeare, because, although the play is described in the Folio as the tragedy of Julius Caesar (because Caesar is killed), it is in reality the tragedy of Marcus Brutus, who 'slew his best friend'. The most illuminating commentary on the whole matter, as it appeared to Plutarch, is the fine ode to Brutus by Cowley, who is not influenced by Shakespeare's play but, like the good scholar he was, has read and understood the original. As the ode is perhaps not very well known, and is so much to the point, I dare say I shall be excused for quoting at some length from it; the whole deserves to be quoted.

> Excellent Brutus, of all human race
> The best till nature was improved by grace,
> Till men above themselves faith raiséd more
>   Than reason above beasts before;
> Virtue was thy life's centre, and from thence
> Did silently and constantly dispense
>   The gentle vigorous influence
> To all the wide and fair circumference. . . .
>
> From thy strict rule some think that thou dids't swerve
> (Mistaken honest men) in Caesar's blood;
> What mercy could the tyrant's life deserve,
> From him who kill'd himself rather than serve? . . .
>
>   Can we stand by and see
> Our mother robb'd, and bound, and ravish'd be,
>   Yet not to her assistance stir,
> Pleas'd with the strength and beauty of the ravisher?
> Or shall we fear to kill him, if before
>   The cancell'd name of friend he bore?
>   Ungrateful Brutus do they call?
> Ungrateful Caesar who could Rome enthrall!
>
> Ill fate assumed a body thee t'affright,
> And wrapp'd itself i' th' terrors of the night,
> I'll meet thee at Philippi, said the sprite;
>   I'll meet thee there, said'st thou,
>   With such a voice and such a brow,
> As put the trembling ghost to sudden flight.

What joy can human things to us afford,
When we see perish thus by odd events,
Ill men, and wretched accidents,
The best cause and best men that ever drew a sword?
When we see
The false Octavius and wild Antony,
Godlike Brutus, conquer thee,
What can we say but thine own tragic word,
That virtue, which had worshipped been by thee
As the most solid good, and greatest deity,
By this fatal proof became
An idol only, and a name? . . .

Shakespeare understood human nature, and Plutarch knew the facts, too well to believe that Brutus was the paragon of virtue that he seems to Cowley. Yet substantially they are in agreement. They understand the tragedy of Brutus.

It will be observed that Cowley knows that he is dealing with a pagan conception, for he thinks it necessary to excuse Brutus on the ground that he lived before the coming of Christ. There are indications, in *Cymbeline* and elsewhere, that Shakespeare was not unaware of the paganism of some of the sentiments appropriate to his characters. But he was not theologically minded and we need not suppose that he gave much thought to the matter. He simply did what was dramatically appropriate.[1] But every candid reader now admits that the great Shakespearian tragedies have little or nothing of the Christian spirit. The famous words of Gloucester in *Lear*,

As flies to wanton boys, are we to the gods,
They kill us for their sport,

are of course dramatically appropriate, and should not be quoted out of their context. Yet no classical student can read them without feeling that they are only a somewhat extreme expression of that belief in 'the jealousy of the gods' which underlies so many of the stories dramatized by the Greek poets. The special Christian virtues of humility and pious resignation are not the virtues which

---

[1] Even *Samson Agonistes* is far from a Christian work, although the author was theologically minded in all conscience.

SHAKESPEARE AND THE CLASSICS

the dramatist seeks in the tragic hero, who must be first and foremost a good fighter. All Shakespeare's tragic heroes, including Hamlet, are good fighters. If we must say that the pervading mood of his tragedies is hopelessness, it is hopelessness made splendid by courage.

Thus did Shakespeare penetrate through the Latin to the Greek influence, and the poet of *Venus and Adonis* becomes the poet of *Macbeth*. The spirit of great poetry transcends not merely the form but the language in which it finds expression. What I have written is a little chapter in the history of European literature.

GEORGE ALLEN & UNWIN LTD
LONDON: 40 MUSEUM STREET, W.C.1
CAPE TOWN: 58–60 LONG STREET
SYDNEY, N.S.W.: 55 YORK STREET
TORONTO: 91 WELLINGTON STREET WEST
CALCUTTA: 17 CENTRAL AVE., P.O. DHARAMTALA
BOMBAY: 15 GRAHAM ROAD, BALLARD ESTATE
WELLINGTON, N.Z.: 8 KINGS CRESCENT, LOWER HUTT

by J. A. K. THOMSON

THE CLASSICAL BACKGROUND OF ENGLISH LITERATURE

a. Cr. 8vo.   *2nd impression*   12s. 6d. *net.*

Serious students of English literature have long felt the want of a book which should define the extent and character of the influence which has been exerted upon it throughout its history by the ancient classics. To supply this want is the main purpose of *The Classical Background of English Literature.*

It is not expected of the reader that he should himself be able to read Latin or Greek. But, as the writer deals with the relations between ancient and modern literature, it is hoped that the book may have some interest and value for classical as well as English Students. Neither is there anything in it to deter the general reader who is fond of literature for its own sake.

THE CLASSICAL INFLUENCE ON ENGLISH POETRY

La. Cr. 8vo.   15s. *net.*

In his previous book *The Classical Background of English Literature* Professor Thomson made an estimate of the influence exerted upon our literature by the ancient classics. He found it impossible, within the limits of a single book, to illustrate by actual quotation the points made. In *Classical Influence on English Poetry* he sets out to remedy this deficiency, so far as the poets are concerned.

By a careful selection of typical passages the author gives a reasonably complete idea of what the classics have meant to a number of the most eminent English writers. The passages have been translated where necessary and a sufficiently full commentary added. The student and the lover of poetry will find here the materials they need for studying the literary influences of the classics on English Poetry.

GEORGE ALLEN AND UNWIN LTD